KILLER TWINS

". . . She invited me into her apartment. We sat on her couch in the living room area and smoked the crack. I had about ten bags and it took us a couple of hours to get through it.

"After we smoked it up we went into her bedroom and had sex. After we had finished she started in on me about giving her money for the sex. I told her that we had just smoked up about a hundred dollars worth of my dope and I wasn't about to give her money.

"She started getting really loud. She told me I couldn't leave until I had paid her the money. I started to get up and she slapped me across the face saying I wasn't going nowhere.

"I grabbed her, threw her on the bed, and started choking her with my hands. I grabbled an iron with a long dark cord attached to it and I wrapped it around her neck . . . she was struggling with me the whole time. It took me a couple of minutes to strangle her . . ."

KILLER TWINS

MICHAEL BENSON

PINNACLE BOOKS
Kensington Publishing Corp.
http://www.kensingtonbooks.com

PINNACLE BOOKS are published by

Kensington Publishing Corp.
119 West 40th Street
New York, NY 10018

All Kensington Titles, Imprints, and Distributed Lines are available at special quantity discounts for bulk purchases for sales promotions, premiums, fund-raising, and educational or institutional use. Special book excerpts or customized printings can also be created to fit specific needs. For details, write or phone the office of the Kensington special sales manager: Kensington Publishing Corp., 119 West 40th Street, New York, NY 10018, attn: Special Sales Department, Phone: 1-800-221-2647.

Pinnacle and the P logo Reg. U.S. Pat. & TM Off.

ISBN-13: 978-0-7860-2205-2
ISBN-10: 0-7860-2205-1

First Printing: February 2010

10 9 8 7 6 5 4 3 2 1

Printed in the United States of America

To Jerry Warren, who can cram more people into a windmill than anyone I know.

Acknowledgments

The author wishes to thank the many people and organizations that have cooperated with this effort. Without your assistance, this book would be a slender volume. Special thanks, as always, to my agent, Jake Elwell, of Harold Ober and Associates; my editor at Kensington Books, Gary Goldstein; former head of the FBI Behavioral Science Unit in Quantico, Virginia, Dr. Stephen Band; retired Monroe County second assistant district attorney Larry Bernstein; retired Rochester homicide investigator Tony Campione; Investigator Thomas Cassidy, of the Rochester Police Department; intrepid reporter Amy Cavalier; Paul Chappius Jr., the deputy superintendent of security at the Attica Correctional Facility; Elmira Heights acting chief of police Rick Churches; New York State Department of Corrections public information officer Linda Foglia; Georganna D'Angelo, records clerk, City of Elmira; director of transportation for this project, Anne Darrigan; Damita Gibson's mother and stepfather, Ethel and Mason Dix; Kelly Gangemi, Vicki Jobson's sister; deputy chief of the Elmira Police Department, David C. Gardner; Rosary Grande, Charles Grande's sister; Carol Greene and Sandra Prusak, inmate record coordinators for, respectively, the Great Meadow and Attica Correctional Facilities; retired Monroe County assistant district attorney Kenneth C. Hyland; librarian and archivist at the Rochester Museum & Science Center, Leatrice M. Kemp; Karen LaPolt, deputy superintendent of programs at the Great Meadow Correctional Facility; Elmira Heights Village attorney John McGlenn; New York State Supreme Court justice Stephen K. Lindley; retired Rochester Police investigator Mark Mariano; Elmira Heights deputy clerk Donetta D. Morey; former Chemung County sheriff and FBI special agent Pat Patterson; Chief Gerald Pickering and Lieutenant Joseph

Rieger, of the Webster Police Department; the many longtime residents of Elmira who, though remaining anonymous, were so generous with their memories of the Spahalski twins; the children of Ronald Ripley, David, Priscilla, and Ronjay; my Rochester historians, Rita Benson, Kathleen Schlaffer, and Muriel Dech; Phyllis Rogan, reference librarian at the Steele Memorial Library in West Elmira, and her volunteer assistant who, after getting married many years ago, bought her pots and pans from victim Ronald Ripley; Andy Schmitz, graphic designer; the Honorable Stephen Sirkin; Captain Laurie M. Wagner and Sergeant Kern Swoboda, of the New York State Police, Public Information Office; retired Elmira police chief Dick Wandell; the Transportation Security Administration; my old social studies teacher and photographer extraordinaire, Jerry Warren—and his eagle-eyed assistant, Erin Fenton; Chemung County district attorney Weeden A. Wetmore and his investigator, Jay Williams; and from the *Star-Gazette*, managing editor Lois Wilson, "Neighbors" columnist Jennifer Kingsley, and associate editor David W. Kubissa.

During the spring of 2009, Robert Bruce Spahalski and the author exchanged a series of letters. Spahalski answered almost every question he was asked. His twin, Stephen J. Spahalski, did not respond to the author's requests for an interview.

Author's Note

It occurs when a single egg in a mother's womb is fertilized to form a zygote, which, in turn, divides, forming two embryos. It is an anomaly that occurs about three times in every one thousand pregnancies. The result: identical twins.

Many twins experience delays in speech and language development, due perhaps to twin talk, in which twins communicate with one another by using a language unknown to all but the two of them.

During development identical twins prefer to stay together, and if separated, they will have unusually strong urges to share all consumables and experiences. Alone, they can feel inadequate, like only half of the whole.

It is not uncommon for twins to report clairvoyance, an uncanny ability to tell what the other is doing and thinking, even when separated. Less individualistic than other siblings, twins will tend to react the same to a variety of stimuli.

From the perspective of crime investigation, twins present a series of problems. In court eyewitnesses to a crime performed by a twin will find it impossible to tell which twin they witnessed committing the illegal act.

And although identical twins will have variant fingerprints, their DNA will be identical, a factor that can be construed by juries as reasonable doubt when one is accused of a crime.

We all know of persons who entered the world physically imperfect, the tragic victims of birth defects. Because of a damaged chromosome, birthing difficulties, or a contaminated prenatal environment, these babies are born with something wrong, something extra, something missing, something out of whack.

And all of us know of people born with faulty brains.

who lack normal cognitive abilities. We call them mentally handicapped, and though perhaps they do not think and learn as fast as the rest of us, they *feel* things the same. They can feel happy, sad, silly, serious, prideful, and guilty.

Then there are those—thankfully rare—who are born with brains of normal or sometimes even superior intellect, but who lack a portion of a normal psyche. Rather than missing a toe or a finger, they are born bereft of what Freud would have called a superego—more commonly known as a conscience.

These rare individuals are called sociopaths or psychopaths. They not only consciously disobey society's rules, they lack a three-dimensional understanding of why those rules exist in the first place.

If sociopaths were to be raised in the proper atmosphere, they could be developed—either intentionally or not—into psychos, human monsters, killing machines. They could take a human life, and never lose a wink of sleep.

Indeed, sociopaths could kill for fun—as an obsession, or just a casual hobby. Just as one person might collect baseball memorabilia, a serial killer might collect small souvenirs from his victims.

It didn't have to be a hobby. Sociopaths don't have to be killing enthusiasts in order to kill. They could kill as a matter of convenience, too—if killing clears an obstruction on the shortest path between them and their goal.

This brings us to Robert Bruce Spahalski and Stephen "Steve" Joseph Spahalski, who are an example of the very rarest (perhaps unique) birth defect. These supercompetitive twins didn't care who it was that they hurt. Or killed.

The Spahalskis were killer twins—yet they didn't work as a team. They were not partners in crime. Reality was more perverse. The Spahalski twins went out to do crimes individually, as part of a competition between them. *Biggest crime wins, bro.*

Even the sickest of competitions are played by their own rules, and have winners and losers. As we look back,

Robert won. Stephen killed only one man. There are some who call Robert a serial killer, not that he likes that name. Point is, Robert had the larger kill count. He won.

Although this is a true story, some names will be changed to protect the privacy of the innocent. Pseudonyms will be noted upon their first usage. In a couple of instances, to further protect my sources, characters are composites.

When possible, the spoken word has been quoted verbatim. However, when that is not possible, conversations have been reconstructed as closely as possible to reality based on the recollections of those that spoke and heard the words. In places there has been slight editing of spoken words, but only to improve readability. The denotations and connotations of the words remain unaltered. In some cases, witnesses are credited with verbal quotes that, in reality, only occurred in written form.

The Victims

November 24, 1971: **Ronald Jay Ripley,** forty-eight, found bludgeoned and stabbed to death in the basement of his store in Elmira Heights, New York.

December 31, 1990: **Moraine Armstrong,** twenty-four, found dead of ligature strangulation in her apartment in Rochester, New York. At the time, Robert Bruce Spahalski lived directly across the street.

January 24, 1991: **Damita Jo "D.J." Bunkley Gibson,** twenty-one, disappeared while walking home. She was found five days later alongside railroad tracks behind a building on Jay Street, Rochester, New York, having been strangled and stabbed.

July 21, 1991: **Adrian Berger,** thirty-five, found dead in her apartment in Rochester, New York. Cause of death initially undetermined.

October 2, 1991: **Charles Grande,** forty, was bludgeoned to death in his house in Webster, New York. His body was discovered on October 4.

October 1992: **Victoria "Vicki" Jobson,** thirty-one, disappeared from her apartment in Rochester, New York, the same building in which Robert Bruce Spahalski lived at the time, directly across the street from Moraine Armstrong's apartment. Her body was found December 7, near railroad tracks at the corner of Haloid and Rutter Streets.

January 3, 2003: **Hortense Greatheart,** forty-five, was found strangled in her apartment in Rochester, New York.

Robert Bruce Spahalski had lived off and on in that same building since the early 1990s, most recently in 2004.

November 8, 2005: **Vivian Irizarry,** fifty-four, was found bludgeoned and strangled in the basement of an apartment house in Rochester, New York, in the same building where Robert Bruce Spahalski resided.

Of the eight victims on this list, the Spahalski twins have confessed to killing only five. The murders of Gibson, Jobson, and Greatheart remain open cases, and Robert Bruce Spahalski is only one of several suspects police have investigated regarding those crimes.

PART ONE

1

Edgerton

Rochester, New York, lies along the south shore of Lake Ontario, about fifty miles east of Buffalo. Rochester is a medium-sized city, population about 250,000. It grew where the Genesee River flowed into Lake Ontario. Later it became the spot where the Genesee River crossed the Erie Canal. A large ninety-foot waterfall in the river—known as the High Falls—could be used to power mills, where grain was ground into flour. During the nineteenth century, Rochester was known as the Flour City. (Rochester maintains today the same nickname, but because of the annual Lilac Festival in Highland Park, the spelling has been changed to Flower City.) The original settlement was near the falls that marked the city's geographic center—only a few hundred yards from the courthouse where the trial in this case was held. During the nineteenth century, the city took root and grew outward.

During the twentieth century, the Erie Canal was moved to a new route, south of the city, and Rochester no longer existed because of water transportation. It found a new raison d'être in cutting-edge technology. Eastman Kodak (photography), Xerox (photocopying), Bausch & Lomb (lenses), all made their homes in Rochester. Like many cities in America experienced during the middle of the twentieth century, suburbs surrounded Rochester as old-time Rochesterians moved out and were replaced by newcomers, often poor minorities, who took their place in the city proper. Though the city itself had shrunk in population, from 350,000 to 250,000, the metro Rochester area (which included most of Monroe County) had grown by the first decade of the twenty-first century to a population of close to 1 million. The crime rate in the suburbs was only a fraction of that which law enforcement had to battle in the city.

The Edgerton section of Rochester, New York, where most of the murders in this book occurred, was bordered on the east by Lake Avenue, which had been that city's main north-south thoroughfare before the expressways were built. Lake Avenue was so named because it took motorists from downtown to the lake, where there had been for decades a major recreation area called Charlotte, Rochester's own Coney Island.

Another factor that took the shine off Lake Avenue was the shrinkage of the Eastman Kodak Company. Lake Avenue was the route one took to Kodak Park, a massive industrial region where film and cameras were made. It was four miles from one side of Kodak Park to the other. In its heyday, before 1980, Kodak employed 64,000 Rochestarians. In 2009, less than ten thousand work there, and much of Kodak Park is closed.

Despite all of this, Lake Avenue was still a main drag with a few stores and some hustle and bustle. It was one of the first streets to be plowed when it snowed, and in the winter, that was often. To the north, between Edgerton and Lake Ontario, there were spacious homes along sycamore-lined streets—once homes to the rich, but now available cheap, because of the same urban blight that had rocked most of Rochester.

The Edgerton section was bordered on the south by Lyell Avenue, a main east-west drag before the expressways, now known mostly for its drug deals and prostitution. In fact, the epicenter of Rochester's hooker activity was unofficially at Lyell Avenue and Sherman Street, due south of Edgerton Park, and the location of a strip joint. The neighborhood was bordered on the north by Lexington Avenue, and on the west by the New York Central railroad tracks.

Older Rochesterians still sometimes called it the Edgerton section; although, truth be told, Edgerton Park had not been its focal point for half a century.

That park—originally called Exposition Park, then renamed after Hiram Edgerton, the beloved mayor of Rochester, from 1908 to 1922—was once one of Rochester's proud points, a hub of activity throughout the year.

Sadly, it had for decades been little more than the unusually large, forty-acre grounds behind the former Jefferson High School. There were tennis and basketball courts, baseball diamonds and the football field, but it had been a couple of generations since it was a place where huge crowds gathered.

When the circus came to town each year, the tent was set up in Edgerton Park. When a traveling rodeo show passed through, they performed their tricks in front of the football stands in Edgerton Park. Before the new Rochester Museum was built on East Avenue in 1942, the museum was in Edgerton Park, and was recognized by schoolchildren of the time for its dark and spooky hallways.

The park once held the bandstand where the city's summer concerts were played. It held the football stadium where the city's biggest games were played. It was the home field of the Rochester Jeffersons, a pro football team named after the high school that was even then a neighbor. The Jeffs played from 1908 to 1925.

During the last five of those years, they were a franchise in the National Football League (NFL).

The park was also the site of the Edgerton Park Arena, an ancient crate of a building that had been originally used as the drill house for Rochester's bad boys during the nineteenth century when the park was the site of the city's juvie facility, known as the Industrial School. The spooky old arena was the home of the Rochester Royals pro basketball team from 1945 to 1957. The Royals played at first in the National Basketball League, which later became the National Basketball Association (NBA).

Yes, there was a time when Rochester, population approaching four hundred thousand, was big league. But that was a long time ago. The Edgerton Park Arena was torn down in the late 1950s, replaced by the city's War Memorial Arena downtown, now known as the Blue Cross Arena. The football field is still there, but the large roofed grandstand is long gone.

And by 1990, Edgerton Park was a memory held dear by Rochester's older citizens—most of whom now lived in the suburbs—and the neighborhood that still bore its name was among the most crime-ridden neighborhoods in America.

Not that there weren't other sections of the city that were almost as bad. It was merely the worst of several Rochester neighborhoods that had been collectively named "the Crescent" by police, because they formed a crescent shape around Rochester's center.

During the late 1980s and early 1990s, *at least* three serial killers operated in the Edgerton section of Rochester. If you'd based a fictional movie on such a premise, it would have seemed ludicrous.

Homicide detectives, overloaded and pressured from every side, got tough or burned out. It was a full-time job just trying to figure out which kills belonged to which killer—or killers.

The nightmare of multiple maniacs who killed for

kicks was exacerbated by a drug war. A Jamaican crew had moved into town and sought exclusivity when it came to Rochester's cocaine trade. If you dealt sniffable coke or smokable crack, and you didn't have dreadlocks, your life expectancy could be measured in weeks. According to a retired member of law enforcement, "The Genesee River ran bloodred for a few years."

But this is not a story about a drug war. It is about the murders of mostly women. Many, many women. Most of them addicted to crack.

If a woman was working the streets, johns were expected to supply the drugs during a trick. Trouble sometimes came when the woman expected to get paid in cash, in addition to getting high—and the johns thought that the drugs were sufficient as payment.

For years it was very dangerous to be a woman anywhere near Edgerton. Like the crime spree of "Jack the Ripper" in London, the murders in Edgerton brought public attention to Rochester's underbelly, its strips of streetwalkers and drug dealers. The victims were all women, most of whom were down on their luck, some turned out by their boyfriends, their mouths never far from a glass pipe and a crackling rock.

The evening news had a nightly feature on the plight of some of Rochester's most vulnerable citizens, its nocturnal streetwalkers. Television cameras videotaped the scene along Lyell Avenue, the sunken faces of the crack-damaged women covered with blue dots.

One by one, these women climbed into a pickup truck and were never seen again. Journalists interviewed the survivors. Filmed now from the neck down, the women all chanted the same mantra: "We're careful. We never got in a car with a john we don't know and trust."

And then another one would disappear, only to be found discarded somewhere in the desolation of Rochester's growing urban wilderness. Murder victims were last seen within blocks of each other. A cluster of victims had been found in their homes—one here, one across the street, another down the block.

It is rare for even the largest cities to have two serial killers active at once. Three in one 'hood was off the charts—unprecedented before or since. Multiple killers. No way to tell the number of killers, really. The methods of operation, the signatures, were too variant for it to be one. At least two. Probably three. Maybe more. Who knew? Homicide investigators developed circles under their eyes. There was no place in America where life was cheaper.

It was as if Rochester had been infiltrated by a cult of misogynists, as if killing women had become a fad— a savage pastime for hellish enthusiasts.

Then—early in the game, as it turned out—police caught a break, and the number of serial killers working in Edgerton decreased by one.

2

The Genesee River Killer

In January 1990, one of these killers was caught. He was the "Genesee River Killer" (GRK), the guy who liked to dump his bodies near water. Many of his victims had last been seen walking Lyell Avenue at night. GRK's Rochester crime spree officially began during the fall of 1989 when the bodies of Dorothy Keller and Patricia Ives were discovered dumped in a remote area at the bottom of the Genesee River Gorge. The crimes were eerily similar to the unsolved murder of Dorothy Blackburn, whose body was discovered in the spring of 1988. When police started to keep an eye on the gorge, the killer simply moved his dumping ground. The bodies of downtrodden women decomposed along other county waterways.

January 3, 1990, was an icy winter day, the ground white with "lake effect" snow. On that day, police found a pair of female jeans and the ID for a missing woman in Monroe County's rural outskirts, but they didn't tell the public. Instead, they staked out the area in hopes the killer would return to the scene. It wasn't long before they hit pay dirt.

On January 5, a policeman with binoculars aboard a police chopper spotted a man standing near the spot where the items were found. The man stood beside a creek, with his penis out. Seeing the helicopter circling overhead, the man put his member back in his trousers, got in his car, and left the scene. He didn't get far. He was soon tracked down by police on the ground. When asked what he was doing with his penis out, he said he was "trying to pee in a bottle." Police asked him to come downtown and answer a few questions, and he said okay. He told police his name was Arthur J. Shawcross, and he was subjected to intense questioning.

At first, the FBI profiling team working the case said Shawcross didn't look like the guy. Their profile said it had to be a younger man. This guy was forty-five.

Despite FBI skepticism, Shawcross eventually signed an eighty-nine-page confession. Present at the confession was homicide investigator Tony Campione, who recalled Shawcross being handed a stack of photos, each of a murdered or missing woman. The suspect was asked to divide the pictures into two piles, those he did and those he didn't do. When he was done, there were eleven images in the "did" pile. Campione and the other investigators had hoped for more.

The FBI profilers amended their thinking because of Shawcross. They said, since men did not emotionally mature while in prison, the "age" of an unknown perpetrator—based on the nature of his crimes and other known activities—could only count the number of years he was out of jail. Or so the new FBI theory went.

Shawcross's confession included admissions of abhorrent postkill rituals. He didn't just murder his victims, he said. He sometimes used a knife and sexually mutilated them. He shattered another taboo when he cannibalized them as well.

Years later, Campione had a bone to pick with the experts in Quantico regarding the Genesee River Killer case:

"The FBI profilers said the guy couldn't be gainfully employed, but it turned out he had a job. They said he was not involved in a meaningful relationship and it turned out he was married—with a mistress on the side. The only thing the FBI got right about Shawcross was 'white male.'"

A quick look at Shawcross's background revealed that the Rochester prostitutes were not his first murder victims. He was born in Maine, raised in Watertown, New York, which is in the northernmost part of the state. As a kid, he didn't get along with others, had a reputation as a bully, and developed into a loner. He dropped out of school, floated around for a couple of years, and then enlisted in the army, where, although doing a stretch in Vietnam, he saw no combat.

Later he told a shrink that he learned to kill in Vietnam, but all of his claimed wartime kills were of young female Vietcong—enemy agents. All female. Since he only saw duty as a cook in Saigon, it was believed that he fantasized these killings to boost a possible post-traumatic stress defense. It was also possible that these stories of knifing female members of the "enemy" were simply bastardized versions of real murders he'd committed as a young man in the United States, murders with which he had never been connected.

In 1972, he committed his first known murder near his hometown of Watertown when he took ten-year-old Jack Owen Blake into the woods, sexually abused him, and then killed him. Later that year, he raped and killed an eight-year-old girl named Karen Ann Hill, who was from Rochester.

For the two Watertown murders, Shawcross got off easy, bizarrely easy. Because of sloppy paperwork, he served a shortened sentence. It turned out that Shawcross had never been formally charged with one of his child killings.

Shawcross served fifteen years in prison and was freed in 1987. He was placed first in a small upstate New York town, but word got out as to who he was. He was then driven from the town, forced to move to Rochester, where he could better assimilate with society without sticking out like a sore thumb because he was a newcomer.

Soon thereafter, he began to kill again. And again. His victims were now predominantly prostitutes instead of children. He had grown strong and burly; he was confident he could control larger human beings now.

Shawcross was a celebrity at the time of his trial, which was broadcast gavel-to-gavel by RNews, the local all-news TV station. Because of the subject matter—prostitution, sexual mutilation, cannibalism—the trial became the most popular TV show in Rochester, and many Rochesterians heard things coming out of their television sets that they'd never heard before. Beatings, stranglings, asphyxiations—the whole city sat transfixed.

Shawcross claimed he was nuts, and attempted an insanity plea. One defense shrink testified for nine days, saying Shawcross suffered from multiple personality disorders, post-traumatic stress from Vietnam, and was the victim of horrible child abuse.

Acting insane, for Shawcross, took his behavior even further through the figurative looking glass. A hypnotist had put him into a trance with a video recorder going and Shawcross "remembered" previous lives dating back to the thirteenth century, when he was Ariemes, a medieval British cannibal.

But the reality was that Shawcross was a cool and cunning hunter. He worked for a food distributor and supplied food to the streetwalkers who populated the shoulder of Lyell Avenue, just west of Lake Avenue.

The group of ladies who became his victims—Patricia Ives, Frances Brown, June Cicero, Darlene Trippi, Anna Marie Steffen, Dorothy Blackburn, June Stotts, Marie Welch, Elizabeth Gibson, Felicia Stephens and Dorothy Keller, many of whom walked the streets—trusted him. Long after *everyone* knew someone was systematically killing Rochester's hookers, women in that area happily continued to trust Shawcross.

After a three-month trial, the longest in Rochester history, the jury took only six and a half hours to convict him. When it came to Shawcross, the black eye for law enforcement was that he should never have been allowed to walk the streets of Rochester in the first place.

How could a man who had raped and killed two children be released from prison? *Ever?* It is a question Rochesterians and others are still asking.

He was convicted and sentenced to life. Even in prison, Shawcross made news. He took up painting, and his paintings acquired infamy when they were included in an annual inmate art show at the Sullivan Correctional Facility in Fallsburg, New York. Some folks wanted to buy his art because of his notoriety, and others squawked that the human monster should not be allowed to profit from his evil.

3

John White

Investigators, of course, had hoped Shawcross would take credit for about thirty murders, so they could clear their books. But he only claimed eleven, and there was no reason to believe he had been responsible for more.

The FBI advised that these crimes that appeared to be those of a serial killer might have been committed by separate individuals, either copycats or crimes of opportunity. Perhaps the murders were by many different killers, all of whom were taking advantage of the overworked homicide detectives and taking care of a personal problem. "Do you know what the odds are of having two serial killers in the same city?" the FBI chimed in.

But Rochester and Monroe County law enforcement knew better. One suspect—the only one, really—for one of "the other guys" was a man named John White. He was the prime suspect for six more murders. White's presumed crimes started up just about the time Shawcross was captured, so Rochester's homicide detectives didn't even get a well-earned chance to catch their breath.

White was a black male, and many of the unsolved
cases had been black hookers working Lyell Avenue.
Some of the remains were found in Wayne County,
where White once lived; others were discovered up by
Lake Ontario in Hamlin Beach State Park.

He lived in the town of Gates, just west of Rochester,
and several of the bodies were found near railroad tracks
directly between where the victims were picked up and
White's home.

Police first keyed in on White when his car was stopped
on the Hamlin Beach Boulevard at about the time of the
Hamlin Beach murder, but before those remains had been
found. His odd behavior hadn't registered as anything
dangerous, until it was realized that he'd been behaving
peculiarly in the vicinity of a freshly dumped murder
victim.

It was said that White believed that it was everyone's duty
to purge the world of its evil, to cleanse the streets of the
filth. He recruited some of his presumed victims from the
same Lyell Avenue strip where Arthur Shawcross picked
up his. Each had stuck pretty much to his own race.

When a photo of John White was shown around, up and
down Lyell Avenue, several witnesses placed him with girls
who had eventually disappeared.

As with Shawcross, the FBI profilers were skeptical about
White. Black guys didn't become serial killers. Oh sure,
there'd been a few, Wayne Williams, Coral Watts, others.
But it was rare.

Local cops stopped listening. They had their man.
They just had to develop a case against him, hope he
grew a conscience, or otherwise messed up.

Police suspicion was so strong that they set up constant
secret surveillance. When White was home, he was watched
from a surveillance point across the street from his house,
on the other side of the railroad tracks in Gates Lions
Park, close to the basketball courts and pond there, in the
shadow of two tall apartment buildings called Dunn

Towers. Investigators brought a basketball along and sh
hoops while one always kept an eye on the house. If the
saw White leave his house and get in his car, they radioe
that information to the mobile surveillance team and h
would be followed.

(It was because of this surveillance that investigato
and the public knew some murders, which otherwis
might have been tossed into John White's basket, had
have been committed by someone else.)

The late homicide investigator William "Billy" Barne
was in charge of the White case. After the surveillanc
revealed nothing helpful about White, Barnes decide
it was time to pick him up and question him.

Unlike Shawcross, White kept his mouth shut. Despit
many hours of interrogation, the suspect denied ever
allegation hurled at him. Barnes had no choice but to l
him go.

Police felt "pretty confident" that White killed at lea
a half-dozen women. Yet he died a free man. He suffere
a fatal heart attack at age forty-eight in September 199
before a solid case could be developed against him, an
he was never charged.

Even if White was guilty, that left about fifteen mu
ders of females unsolved. *At least* one serial killer r
mained free. Almost to emphasize that point, to ru
investigators' noses in it, the murders of women from
the Edgerton Park area did not stop.

The 1990s looked to be just as bad as the late 1980
even with the Genesee River Killer off the streets. Mor
than a dozen homicides remained unsolved, and severa
of those had a strong list of common factors.

4

Moraine Michelle Armstrong

Tony Campione, present at the Shawcross confession, began his career solving murders just as the murder problem in Rochester exploded. He first investigated homicides in 1989 when Rochester was averaging about two dozen murders per year, less than one every two weeks.

Back in those days, most of Rochester's murders were domestic in nature. They were relatively simple cases. If the wife was dead, the husband did it. And if the husband was dead, the wife did it. Maybe she hired a guy to do it for her, but she did it.

But just about the time Campione took on murder duty, the serial killers got busy and there was an influx of crack into Monroe County, spawning its own bloodbath. Dealers were setting up shop, infringing on each other's turf, starting drug wars.

The road from Elmira to Rochester was well-worn. Jamaicans who'd previously lived in Elmira were behind much of the violence. The number of murders more than *doubled.* By the early 1990s, Rochester had sixty or seventy murders per year.

"When I started in homicide," Campione recalled, "there were six investigators and one lieutenant. A few years later, there were ten investigators, three sergeants, and a lieutenant." But they still couldn't keep up. A new murder would be called in before they could get a handle on the last one.

Campione was a Rochester boy, born and raised. He grew up in Dutchtown, on Campbell Park, between Jay Street and Lyell Avenue, both of which were very pleasant streets at the time. He went to grammar school at Holy Family, at the corner of Jay Street and Ames Street in Rochester's Dutchtown section. (Campione and the author both attended Holy Family at the same time for a year, 1961 through 1962. Also a student there at that time was Kenneth Bianchi who would later move to Los Angeles and become one of the "Hillside Stranglers.")

After grammar school, Campione attended Kings Prep High School. During his sophomore year, the school closed and he transferred to Cardinal Mooney High School. As a symptom of Rochester's problems, as of 2009 none of the schools Campione attended were still open.

By the time he graduated from high school, he knew he wanted to be a cop. He attended Monroe Community College (MCC) for criminal justice. Before graduating from MCC, he took and passed the New York Police Department (NYPD) test, the Rochester City test, the Monroe County civil service test, and the New York State Police (NYSP) test.

His first job in law enforcement came in 1974 when he became a deputy with the Monroe County Sheriff's Office (MCSO). He switched to the Rochester Police Department (RPD) in 1980, and by 1989, he had worked his way up to homicide investigator.

One early case he would never forget was the New Year's Eve, 1990, murder of Moraine Michelle Armstrong.

An African-American, Moraine was born October 1, 1966, in Rochester, graduated from East High School in Rochester, and had almost two years of college at Buffalo State, where she studied business administration.

During the 1980s, she had a steady boyfriend named William Scopes (pseudonym), who twice impregnated her. They began dating in 1983 when she was still in high school. In 1988, she suffered a miscarriage, and in 1989, she had an ectopic pregnancy, which left her unable to have children.

Moraine's best friend for a couple of years was a young woman named Tina Blocker. They met through a mutual friend in 1984 and enjoyed drinking Champale Golden together. Then, all of a sudden, Moraine changed, and Tina didn't see much of her anymore.

That change came in 1986 when Moraine started smoking crack. Her mother blamed her boyfriend for that. It was after she was told she was barren that the drug usage got really bad. Moraine stopped doing normal things, like going to the movies. All she wanted to do was smoke, and she was smoking away $100 a day. Sometimes crack, sometimes freebase. Wherever she went, spoons mysteriously disappeared. She was twice arrested, both times in the town of Greece, just west of Rochester, both times for trying to pass a bad check. In 1990, her mother, Dorothy Hickman, took her to a counseling program called ReStart, designed to get Moraine's life back on track, but it didn't work. She also spent thirty days in rehab, which was also unsuccessful. Most of the time she was on welfare. She had several short-lived jobs, mostly restaurant work. With each job, she frequently failed to show up and was eventually fired. Her last job was at the Sibley's department store at Marketplace Mall.

Up until 1990, according to her mother, Moraine was a family-oriented daughter and cheerful. But that year, she changed. She turned tricks, smoked crack. Arthur Shawcross was arrested, so the girls on the street thought it was "safe" once again. From the summer of 1989 until the summer of 1990, Social Services placed Moraine in an apartment on Tulane Avenue. Her landlord there noticed that she had a "lot of boyfriends." Most of them were white, but there was a Jamaican, too, who looked like trouble. He suspected that she was into drugs, but he never saw any. Once she called her landlord at three in the morning and said she was at a motel on an expressway, and would he come get her and bring her home? He said no.

During the summer of 1990, she lived in a downtown motel known for its drugs and prostitution. In October, city housing placed her in an apartment on Lake Avenue. Her mom would call her and she wouldn't want to talk.

"I'm busy," she would say. "I'll call you later." But she didn't call back. Dorothy would try to visit her in person, but Moraine wouldn't let her in the door. The last time Dorothy went there was Christmas Day, 1990. She knocked on Moraine's door, but no one answered.

By this time, Moraine had a new boyfriend named Dwayne. "He bought her things, and when he left her alone at night, he would leave her a gun," Dorothy said.

A man she stayed with, from time to time, last saw Moraine on Christmas Eve, 1990. His nickname was "Jesse James," and he said she was alone and driving a ten-year-old Buick. She looked like she'd come into some money. She was wearing a long denim jacket, a dark sweater, jeans, and brand-new boots. When the man mentioned the car and the clothes, she said she was into selling now—referring to cocaine.

Jesse James tried to warn her of the dangers, and she said, "I won't listen to you or Mama!"

She drove away.

William Scopes, Moraine's old boyfriend, heard

through the grapevine that Moraine had become a hooker and her drug habit was worse than ever.

"Your ex-girlfriend is looking bad," people on the street told him.

Melanie, Moraine's younger sister, said that Moraine was always independent-minded, and always wanted to stay out late with her boyfriends rather than do whatever it was that she was supposed to do. Working real jobs was a drag, she thought, because of the hours. Mornings were for sleeping. She dug the night life. She liked to go out clubbing, frequenting nightclubs like City Limits, Black Orchid, and the Oak Tree in Rochester.

Now that Moraine was a hooker, she had new friends, like "Oogie," who said Moraine both "had regular johns and went to the street." Oogie said Moraine's coke habit had steadily increased and had gotten "real nice."

On Saturday, December 29, 1990, Oogie encountered two white men who were looking for the girl who "ripped them off." They said they knew where she lived. The men frightened her so much that she called out their license plate number to another street girl named Kathy Williams (pseudonym). At one o'clock on late Sunday night/early Monday morning, Oogie said she heard screaming coming from Moraine's building.

A little more than twelve hours later, at 1:30 P.M. on New Year's Eve, 1990, 911 received a call of a "naked woman hanging" in a first-floor apartment on Lake Avenue, a two-story apartment building at the northwest corner of Emerson Street and Lake, a distinctive gray building that had a matching upstairs balcony and downstairs front porch.

The building faced Lake Avenue, but the driveway and four-car garage in the rear faced Emerson Street. To the north on Lake Avenue were a couple of commercial buildings, housing small insurance companies and a smattering of familiar fast-food restaurants.

The caller said her name was Christine Walker, but everyone knew her as Oogie. For the police operator, getting clear information out of her was not easy. She was "intoxicated, belligerent, and abusive."

Oogie identified herself as a neighbor woman who checked on the victim after not hearing from her all day. After a couple of false starts, police received coherent info from Oogie. She found the victim's door ajar, saw the victim with a cord around her neck, ran back out of the apartment, and called 911.

The responding officer found the woman's body in the bedroom. She was not hanging, but rather lying across a daybed, naked except for a white sock hanging off the toes of her right foot. There were several items, which appeared to be wires, wrapped around her neck. The body was cold to the touch. The officer requested an ambulance, technician, and supervisor.

The most obvious clue was a threatening message on a torn piece of cardboard, perhaps written by the killer, that said, *Disturb and Die how's that asshole.* The note, of course, could also have been written by Moraine herself, warning those who might seek her company that she was already otherwise occupied.

As the investigation began, twenty-two-year-old Melanie Armstrong, the victim's sister, came to the scene, and ID'd the victim as twenty-four-year-old Moraine Michelle Armstrong. In life the victim had been five-four, 110 pounds.

How did Melanie learn the bad news? Earlier two men came to her house on Bergen Street.

"What's going on? What's going on?" Melanie asked, coming out onto her front porch.

The men asked if her sister Moraine lived on Lake. Melanie said she did.

"The person who lives in that house is dead," the men said. Who were the men delivering the bad news? One was Dwayne, Moraine's boyfriend.

Police wanted to talk to the two men who had gone to Bergen Street to see Melanie. As it turned out, they weren't hard to find. They were standing in front of the building. The men admitted they had seen the body before police arrived and had gone to tell Melanie the sad news. Both men seemed very upset—in fact, grief-stricken. They did not know Melanie but knew where she lived, because Moraine had once pointed out the house she grew up in, the house where her mother and her sister still lived.

Moraine Armstrong's apartment was secured; within minutes the entire building was a swarm of police activity.

Crime scene technicians went over the apartment thoroughly. Everything was both photographed and videotaped. The video cameras were comically large by today's standards, and they needed to be rested on the cameraman's shoulder while in use.

There was no sign of forced entry. The TV set in the bedroom was on. There was a white substance later ID'd as cocaine on top of the dresser.

In the top dresser drawer, police found a plastic case with birth control pills. One pill was missing. It was a mystery why a woman who was barren had the Pill. Perhaps they belonged to a girlfriend. Several hookers turned tricks in that space. Fine metal wire was found both on top of the dresser and on the bathroom floor. Also on top of the dresser was a key ring, with four keys on it. One of those keys turned out to be to the apartment.

A gold bracelet lay on the bedroom floor near the bed. Sitting atop a stereo speaker against the bedroom wall was a paper bag. In the bag was a disposable lighter and an unused condom still in its sealed foil container. Also atop the speaker was a black purse containing several sticks of chewing gum, makeup, and a roll of Rolaids.

On the bedroom floor was a used pink Kleenex. A radio was on in the living room. Lights were on in the bathroom, living room, and bedroom. Both thermostats were set at 50 degrees Fahrenheit, and the temperature in the apartment was 52 degrees. All of the windows were closed, except for the one in the bedroom, which was open about three inches. The kitchen sink was filled with dirty water.

The victim was lying on top of a sleeping bag, which was on top of the mattress. On the victim's abdomen was a small amount of what looked like dried dirt. This was photographed and collected. There were clothes lying on the bed, a jacket at the foot of the bed, and a top and slacks near the pillow.

The victim's entire wardrobe was confiscated as evidence. Sadly, that wardrobe consisted of only a see-through white top with lace (which had adhering hairs and reddish-brown stains presumed to be blood), a red shirt with beads, an aqua-colored robe, a red-green-and-black top, white stretchy pants, a black leather jacket, with a bottle of Georgio perfume and $1.67 in loose change in the right pocket, and earrings with a woman's face on them. A single white pill was found under the victim's pillow. Also taken were a dark yellow blanket, floral-patterned bedsheet, and a floral-patterned pillowcase. From the bathroom police took a washcloth and two towels.

Technician Peter Butler located and bagged trace evidence throughout the apartment. He recovered fibers from the right side and back of the victim's head, around the victim's neck, abdomen, left thigh, sleeping bag, left shoulder, and chest. Particles were recovered from her abdomen, and swabs were taken of the victim's right outer thigh and lower left leg above the ankle.

When the medical examiner (ME) was removing the body, it was realized that a cord from the sleeping bag was also attached to the victim's neck. The cord was cut to separate the body from the bag.

The Black & Decker steam iron and the maroon curling iron were placed inside envelopes and removed with the body. The "disturb and die" note was confiscated. No prints were found on the note, but it was determined that it had been written on a piece of cardboard torn from a candy box. The candy box had been a one-pounder of Stefanelli's Candies, assorted milk chocolates.

Once the victim had been removed, the apartment was processed for fingerprints. Eight prints in all were lifted: one from a milk shake container and one from a grape soda can, which were both on the bedroom dresser, two off the phone in the living room, three off the medicine cabinet mirror, and one off a can of Glade air freshener.

The entire scene was sketched and measured. Before leaving, the crime scene investigation (CSI) team secured the apartment with evidence tape and the ME's seal. The investigators followed the body to the medical examiner's office and there processed it with a Luma Light, a high-powered light with wavelengths that cause blood and other materials to glow. A Luma Light can reveal the presence of blood even after an attempt to clean the bloody area.

The cords to the steam iron and curling iron were cut away from the neck. The irons themselves remained in their paper bags, and the body was again photographed, with particular attention paid to the ligature marks on the neck and a red patch on the abdomen.

The processing of evidence continued until 11:00 P.M., at which time the property clerk locked up for the night, said "Happy New Year," and split. The process continued first thing on the morning of January 1, 1991.

Back at the murder scene, the building's other residents— as well as neighbors up and down Lake Avenue, and around the corner on Emerson Street—were interviewed. Although some tried to be helpful—one saw a man who needed a jump start, another saw a woman arguing with a snowplow driver—none had seen or heard anything useful. Some said they knew the woman in the murder apartment as "Nicky" or "Nicole," and that she was a prostitute with a very likable personality. (Moraine had a name for every occasion and was also known as "Michelle," "Mikki," and "Choochie." Her killer would later refer to her as "Marissa.")

Dorothy Hickman, Moraine's mother, was located, notified of her daughter's death, and was interviewed. She said she had last spoken to her daughter by phone on the afternoon of Christmas Day. The mother reported that Moraine told her she'd had an argument with her boyfriend about spending time with a man that the boyfriend didn't like. She didn't know the boyfriend's name, but she thought he drove a dark Buick or Pontiac.

Investigator Tony Campione was assigned the case and showed up while the body was still where the killer had left it. He talked to the woman who lived in the adjacent apartment. She said she heard raised voices coming from next door on the night of December 29, but they were followed by voices of a normal tone, so she'd assumed it was a brief argument.

He talked to Dwayne, the victim's boyfriend, who said he'd spent a couple of days in a motel out on Ridge Road West with Oogie, the woman who'd called the cops, and Kathy Williams, another girl with whom Oogie was "partying."

Oogie backed up Dwayne's story. Police asked Oogie if anyone else used Moraine's apartment, and she said there was a girl known as "Honey," who turned tricks there, but last she heard Honey said she was going to leave town.

Investigators took a close look at the body and made a rough estimate as to time of death. She'd been killed approximately twenty-four hours earlier, they figured. It appeared that the life had been squeezed out of Moraine Armstrong while she and her killer were having sexual intercourse.

More neighbors would have to be talked to, but Campione didn't have high hopes. People there didn't like talking to police, ever.

On the other hand, Campione knew that the instant they started putting the yellow tape across a front yard to keep pedestrians off the property, a rubbernecker crowd would gather. When it came to arson and murder, investigators learned to scan the faces of spectators for expressions of acute curiosity.

And that was what Tony Campione did. And on January 1, he got a hit. There was one guy on the sidewalk who seemed unnaturally interested in the investigation—kind of a dirtbag crackhead type, but curious, *real* curious. Hovering.

"This guy was a strange dude, man," Campione recalled.

Campione began to ask questions of the crowd, *not* starting with the hinky guy. *Hey, anyone know the victim? When was the last time she was seen around? No. Don't know.* Then he turned to the curious fellow.

"What's your name?"

"Robert Spahalski."

"Age?"

"Thirty-six."

"Where do you live?" Campione asked the guy.

He gave his address on Lake Avenue.

"Across the street?"

"Yeah, or on Phelps Avenue." That was around the corner.

Spahalski needed a bath. His skin looked stretched across the bones of his face. He had dark hair, thinning and in need of a trim.

"Did you know Moraine Armstrong?"

"Not really," the man said.

"What's that mean?"

"She wasn't a friend or nothing. I seen her around," the man said.

"See or hear anything unusual lately?"

Spahalski paused for a second, like he was considering the matter, then shook his head.

There was no concrete reason to suspect this guy. But Campione was always suspicious of bystanders who seemed

unusually curious about police activities following a crime.
He put Spahalski's contact info into his written report.

Back at the crime lab, two hairs were removed from
the curling iron. The steam iron and the curling iron
were processed using a superglue. One fingerprint was
found on the steam iron. The cigarette lighter and
condom found at the scene were dusted for prints, with
negative results.

Another possibly interesting lead came from a witness
named Kathy Williams, one of the women who had been
partying in a motel with the victim's boyfriend at the
time of the murder.

Like Robert Spahalski, Williams had two addresses.
She lived either on Lorimer Street or Ambrose Street,
and at the time of the murder, she was staying on Lake
Avenue, next door to the murder scene, with a friend
whom she ID'd only as "Rose."

She corroborated Dwayne's story that he, Kathy, and
Oogie had been partying in a motel out on Ridge Road
between the last time any of them had seen the victim
alive and the discovery of the body. (A police trip out to
the motel itself further verified that the threesome had
been there.)

After Dwayne, Kathy, and Oogie got back to Lake
Avenue, they knocked on the victim's door a few times, but
there was no answer. Kathy said she didn't give it much
thought. Either she wasn't there or maybe she didn't want
to talk to Dwayne. Like all boyfriends and girlfriends, they
fought, and sometimes they weren't speaking.

Williams told Campione that she'd seen the victim at
about 3:00 or 4:00 A.M. on December 30 in the driveway
to the Lake Avenue residence, which was behind the
building leading to a multicar garage, and could only be
accessed via Emerson Street. She was with an unknown
white male in his late twenties. The guy had dark hair and

was clean-shaven. She saw Nicky and this guy go behind the building and get in a car together. She couldn't tell what kind of car it was.

Kathy was taken to police headquarters and sequestered with a police composite artist, but the results of their collaboration were disappointingly generic.

A second witness, a woman named Olivia, also worked with the composite artist, again with disappointing results. The composites were not released to the public, but copies were distributed in the Rochester Police's Physical Crimes Bureau.

Oogie was requestioned, and more sober than before, she remembered new details. About fifteen minutes before she discovered the body, she went outside and walked around to the victim's bedroom window. She'd pounded on the window and shouted, but she got no response.

Moving back to the front of the building, Oogie saw a short white male wearing a black leather jacket leaving the building. Subsequently a man named Terry Barnes (pseudonym)—a short white male—who lived upstairs from Armstrong on Lake Avenue, was interviewed. Barnes told police that he had left the building at about 1:15 P.M. on New Year's Eve to go to the supermarket, and, yes, he was wearing a black leather jacket at the time. He further stated that on his way back from the supermarket, he ran into Oogie in front of a Pizza Hut and she told him about discovering Nicky's body—an incident that Oogie had apparently forgotten.

On the afternoon of January 1, items removed from the body by the medical examiner were processed: two electrical cords, a silver earring, a rubber band with hairs attached, the white sock, and the sleeping bag's cord.

On January 2, the crime lab received an envelope containing the victim's hair (head and pubic) to be used for comparison purposes. The cocaine found on the bedroom dresser, the sleeping bag itself, and other fibers found at the scene were processed.

These were the days before DNA technology, and the victim was a prostitute. Processed evidence was not expected to help formulate a suspect list, but it could later be used to verify that a suspect had been at the scene.

Campione spoke to a man named Jesse, not Jesse James but another individual. This Jesse said that he and his son both knew Moraine and had helped her move into her apartment back in the fall. They knew her because they'd had sex with her when she was staying at the Downtowner Motor Inn on South Avenue. Jesse said he didn't know Moraine to have any enemies; he thought she might have had a pimp. He didn't know the pimp's name, but Jesse said his son might know, but he was in jail on a parole violation.

During the afternoon of January 2, technicians returned to Armstrong's apartment and used the Luma Light there. They looked at the walls, the headboard to the bed, and both sides of the apartment door. This search discovered just one fingerprint, on the east wall of the living room. After a two-hour search, the apartment was again taped and sealed shut.

At 8:30 A.M., on January 3, Crime Stoppers received a phone call from an anonymous prostitute saying that sometime around 2:00 A.M., on December 28, she'd been with two Italian-looking men in their twenties. She called them "John and Johnny." They said a hooker named Michelle (one of Moraine's common noms de guerre) had ripped them off for $800, and she was going to get hers.

John and Johnny offered cash to anyone who could tell them where Michelle was. They showed the anonymous prostitute a silver long-barreled handgun. She spent between a half hour and three-quarters of an hour with the two men.

During that time, John and Johnny switched cars. hey'd picked her up in a white four-door vehicle, and arking at a bar on Lyell Avenue, they switched to a ggedy blue Mustang. The report was of definite inter- t, but it was not enough to identify John or Johnny.

During January 1991, forensic chemists Harvey Van- oven and Harry D. Fraysier, of the Public Safety Labo- tory, analyzed the evidence that had been recovered at e Armstrong murder scene—with mixed results.

A hair adhering to the crumpled pink facial tissue und on Armstrong's bedroom floor was found to match ntrol hairs from the victim herself. A "fiber" lifted from e victim's body, however, turned out to be a one-eighth- ch light-brown hair from a white male.

The reddish brown stains found on the see-through hite top, as suspected, were determined to be human ood. A Caucasian hair found on the curling iron was ree inches long.

It was no surprise that pubic hairs from multiple per- ns were found, eight of them from white men, varying color from light to medium brown. The swabs taken off e victim's body tested positive for spermatozoan cells.

There was no further activity in the case until August 1991, when Gail Sofia, a probation officer, spoke to e prostitute named Honey, who'd turned tricks out of oraine's apartment. Honey said her real name was nine, and that she'd seen Moraine in the company of man she knew as "Up Jump the Bump." She had pre- ously met the man through Oogie and had been arned that he was a bad and dangerous man. It was etermined that Honey had "severe brain damage from caine use," and her report was mostly fantasy.

The investigation was going nowhere fast.

5

Damita Gibson

Damita Jo Bunkley was born in 1969 in a country tow
called Adel, Georgia. It was small compared to Rochest
but it was still the largest town in Cook County, abo
twenty-five miles north of the Florida Panhandle.

While her mother, Ethel, just sixteen at the time, w
seven months pregnant with her, Damita's father, Josep
Bunkley, was killed in an on-the-job accident. He was ru
over at a construction site while pouring concrete—
Ethel had the baby alone.

The death hit Ethel hard. She had always thought the
was something magical between her and that man—h
was fifteen years older than she was. Part of the mag
stemmed from the fact that they shared the same birt
day. He was born on that April day in 1938, she in 195
Kismet! Ethel recalled going to his grave site and seein
her own birthday on the gravestone. Different year, b
still . . . She still got goose bumps, thinking about it.

Things were so tough, and her despair so great, sh
knew it was time for a drastic change. In 1975, whe

Damita was six, Ethel's mother, Annie Mosley, who lived in Rochester, New York, came and got Damita. As soon as she could, Ethel would join them.

Ethel found keeping a man in her life to be cruelly difficult. She did get married again, but when Damita was ten, her stepfather also died in a job accident—this time in a factory explosion.

"When my second husband got killed, it really floored me," Ethel recalled.

If something like that happened today, Ethel would know to at least contact a lawyer and discuss the possibility of suing. But back then, she was so young and lawsuits seemed nowhere near the realm of possibilities. She did get some workman's compensation, but that was it.

Ethel had it in the back of her mind that living in upstate New York was just a temporary thing, that one day she would return to Georgia. That notion faded as Damita grew up in Rochester and clearly considered it home. It evaporated altogether in 1986 when the twice-widowed Ethel met a man named Mason Dix.

She first saw Mason at her mother's house, as he was a friend of her brother's. They hit it off, and had been together ever since. Although Mason had been around since Damita was still little, he became an official stepfather from the time she was sixteen, and he had a strong hand in raising Ethel's grandchildren as well.

Damita grew up well and seemed to have a bright future, despite her early hardships. She attended Number 17 Grammar School on Orchard Street in Dutchtown, Charlotte Junior High School on Lake Avenue, up toward Lake Ontario, and Jefferson High, the school on the edge of Edgerton Park.

Damita was a beautiful black girl, and for a time after high school, she worked as a professional model. She married and had three children, but things took a turn for the worse when her husband got on drugs. Damita

Gibson, her married name, and the children came
home to live with Ethel and Mason.

During the early days of 1991, William—Damita'
oldest—was four. Tanaya was eighteen months, an
Joseph was the six-month-old baby. It was during thos
weeks after the New Year celebration that Ethel saw he
daughter with a man several times, a tall guy with mus
cles, a powerful individual.

Once, she saw Damita talking to the man at a smal
grocery store on West Main. After that, several times, th
man came to the house and talked to Damita.

The guy was throwing off bad vibes like a sparkle
throws off sparks. Damita's stepfather Mason had t
come to the front door and run him away from there.

"Damita said that the man was looking for a friend o
hers, a girl by the name of Tina. She was his friend, bu
he couldn't find her. I'll never forget what that ma
looked like," Ethel said. "Every time he came over, h
would try to talk to Damita—and Damita would alway
brush him off. I was always skeptical of that man.

"I could tell that he didn't mean Tina or my daugh
ter any good. My daughter didn't like him. He was kin
of high. She thought he didn't look right," Ethel remem
bered. Years later, when Ethel saw Robert Bruce Spahal
ski's picture in the papers and on TV, she recognize
him right away.

During the late 1980s and early 1990s, poverty re
mained a major problem for Ethel and Damita and thei
children. Times were bad. They got by on governmen
assistance and charitable neighbors. The nice woma
who owned the grocery store allowed Ethel and Damit
to buy groceries for the kids on credit.

Sometimes they didn't have enough pairs of shoes fo
everyone, so shoes were shared. Thomas, Damita'
brother, allowed Damita to wear his lace-up boots to g
outside in the winter.

They lived in a very small space on King Street. In 2009

Ethel no longer remembered the exact address, although it had a fraction in it. She called the accommodations, "That house in the alley."

Then came the fateful day: Thursday, January 24, 1991—three and a half weeks after Moraine Armstrong's murder. Damita left her home on King Street, just west of Rochester's downtown area, to get her food stamps. She wore Thomas's boots. Her destination was a Freddy's store on Genesee Street, just south of Bull's Head, so called because there was the sculpted head of a bull protruding from the precipice of a building on West Main Street. Bull's Head was a transportation hub, where West Main, Genesee Street, West Avenue, and Chili Avenue all, more or less, came together like ill-spaced spokes on a bent wheel.

As was their ritual, when Damita was out by herself on Rochester's tough streets, she stopped frequently at pay phones to call home to let her mother know she was okay.

Damita managed to pick up her benefits and called her mother twice on the walk home. (These were the days before cell phones.) Then the phone calls stopped. Damita never arrived home.

During the five days that followed Damita's disappearance, another woman's body was found on Rochester's west side. Ethel became convinced that her daughter was dead. After about two days, Ethel began to search by car between their home and the last pay phone Damita used, desperately looking for something, anything, that might help her find her daughter. Damita's friend Tina had a car and drove Ethel all around.

Sometimes Ethel went out by herself and sometimes she was accompanied by Damita's friend Tina, the woman for whom the tall, drugged-out man had repeatedly been looking.

She drove up and down Genesee Street, the Bull's Head area, West Main Street, King Street, but nothing. Then one day, her father-in-law gave her some money so she could buy milk and food for Damita's babies when she drove over toward the area where the other body had been found.

One of the streets she searched was Jay Street, which was the next main east-west street south of Lyell Avenue. There were stretches of old factories and lots that stored equipment.

The gaps between the buildings featured objets d'art of sumac, scrub brush, bulldozed clay, and salt-corroded sheet metal. Curved spurs of railroad tracks, once used to deliver supplies to those factories, still marked the desolate cityscape like rusty scars. As was typical of Rochester in January, snow covered everything except the streets and the sidewalks.

Among the places Ethel looked was across the street from the J. P. Meade Building, just out past Hague Street, where the railroad tracks crossed Jay Street. She saw nothing. Felt nothing. As it turned out, she had been only the length of a football field away, and yet . . . *nothing.*

On January 27, during the time Damita was missing, the New York Giants defeated the Buffalo Bills, 20–19, in the Super Bowl in Tampa, Florida.

On Tuesday, January 29, 1991, five days after she disappeared, the body of twenty-one-year-old Damita Jo Bunkley Gibson was found by a worker behind a building on Jay Street. Her body had been dumped practically in the shadow of a huge water tower with a picture of the Gerber baby painted on it. The Holy Family Church steeple was visible to the east.

The body was found among the weeds and pricker bushes, supine beside the railroad tracks. Only Damita's nose stuck up out of the snow. A tight ligature turned out to be the laces from her brother's boots. She had also been repeatedly stabbed.

The detectives came to tell Ethel that they'd found Damita. Even though she knew already, deep down inside, that Damita was gone, the news still hit her hard.

"It was something like the day the Earth stood still," Ethel recalled. They took her to the crime scene and she "almost fell out." She realized how close she had been to finding her daughter's body.

Damita's brother felt guilty about Damita's death. He felt it was all his fault because he had loaned Damita his boots, the laces from which had been used as the murder weapon. He kept saying, if he hadn't given her those boots, she would still be alive. Ethel got the boy counseling to dissuade him of his guilt feelings.

Assigned to the case was homicide investigator William "Billy" Barnes.

With Damita dead, the father of her children tried to get custody. As it turned out, he was successful with only one child, the baby who went to live with his aunt, his father's sister. Then the aunt got married and moved to Youngstown, Ohio, taking the baby with them. Ethel went to court about it, but the family remained divided. It wasn't until the baby got shot, putting a groove in his belly, that Ethel got him back. The baby had apparently found a gun belonging to his aunt's husband. He shot himself with it. Luckily, he didn't kill himself.

Rochester is used to tough winters. Each year it is among the country's leaders in snowfall. But Rochester was not prepared for the troubles Mother Nature brought on March 3 and 4, 1991, about five weeks after the discovery of Damita Gibson's body.

An ice storm left the entire region covered in a thick layer of heavy ice. Trees fell. Power lines tumbled. Rochester Gas & Electric reported 150,000 people in the area without power, some for as long as ten days.

So many trees were killed by the ice that Rochester's natural landscape changed forever, and it would be years before the wounds from the storm stopped being obvious.

6

Adrian Berger

Two more women were murdered in the same area in 1991, one at about the same time as Damita Gibson. Cassandra Carlton, twenty-six years old, and Katrina Myers, twenty-five, were found dead.

They were found separately, but almost at the same spot—near the railroad tracks along Ferrano Street, west of Edgerton Park, almost to the canal and the city line. One was found next to the tracks. The other body was draped over the tracks, a bag tied over her head.

Both women were known to frequent the stretch along Lyell Avenue associated with so many other female victims—and both were found naked and strangled.

A geographic profiler would later peg these as John White murders. Those two bodies were more or less on the way home for White, if he had picked them up along Lyell Avenue and had taken them somewhere secluded to kill them.

White lived in a house on Trolley Boulevard, which ran right along the old trolley tracks off Long Pond

Road, which once took commuters from as far away as Brockport into the city. Geographically, Trolley Boulevard and Ferrano Street lined up perfectly, but both dead-ended on opposite sides of the Erie Canal, necessitating a southward zig to cross the bridge at Lyell Avenue, or a northern zag on Colfax Street to cross the Erie Canal on Lee Road. Either way, the wilderness of Ferrano Road would have been a convenient place for White to find some privacy.

There was very little light at night. If a driver turned off his headlights, the only illumination came from distant city lights and the red blinkers atop a radio tower, a few hundred yards to the west.

During a blistering heat wave that summer, on Sunday, July 21, 1991, another body was found—this one indoors.

The police investigation began almost by accident. Officer Gerald Smith parked in front of an Emerson Street home, at about 9:00 P.M., to follow up on a harassment case.

The block, just east of Edgerton Park, was bleak. Many of the houses sagged with deteriorating infrastructure. Abandoned houses awaiting demolition were boarded up. In the next few years, many of these houses would be torn down, thick wooden stakes driven into the resulting lot just inside the sidewalk to prevent motorists from dumping.

Officer Smith rolled down Emerson Street and pulled up in front of the house. Before he could even get out of the car, he was approached by three neighbors. A couple, Shire and Thomas Brown, along with Cassandra Williams, walked up to Officer Smith's patrol car with grim expressions and an unmistakable urgency in their steps.

"What's the matter?" he asked.

"There's a foul odor coming from that house—from the front apartment."

Smith winced. His stomach churned. Foul odors were

never a good sign. Even worse, when the "real-feel temp" was in three figures. Because the house in question had no back entrance, a pair of flimsy fire escapes had been attached to its sides, offering an escape route from the rear top-floor windows. The officer noticed a mass of flies on and around the windows to the front apartment—another very bad sign.

"And I haven't seen the lady who lives in that apartment since Friday," Shire Brown said.

Still another wince. Smith oriented himself. One block farther west, Emerson Street ran along the north edge of Edgerton Park. One block east and there was Lake Avenue.

One block east and there was also the back of the building where Moraine Armstrong had died.

Officer Smith walked down the driveway, then completely around the house. He was looking for signs of forced entry. The swarm of flies at the ground-floor north apartment further twisted his intestines. The unmistakable stench of decomposition clung to humid heat.

The house appeared secure. He pushed at the front door. Locked.

"Does this door lead directly to the front apartment?" Smith asked.

"No," Shire Brown replied. "That leads you to a foyer. There's another door to the apartment."

Officer Smith called for backup, which quickly arrived. The landlord was located and told to come to the scene with a key to all doors. He arrived about ten minutes later and unlocked the front door.

The landlord entered the building and approached the apartment door with key in hand, but Officer Smith pushed in front of him. Smith turned the doorknob and pushed. The apartment wasn't locked.

Smith looked at the top of the door and saw pry

marks, which might have indicated a forced entry. A closer look revealed that the marks did not appear new, and Smith decided they probably represented old damage.

The horrible stench was now overwhelming, and the landlord was escorted from the building without being allowed to enter the front apartment.

Smith and another officer entered the apartment and saw a body, maybe a white female, in an advanced state of decomposition. She was lying facedown on the floor next to the bed in the front bedroom area, naked from the waist down, wearing only a cotton T-shirt.

The front part of the house was sealed off with police tape, and Smith kept a log of everyone who entered the apartment. The victim's two cats were alive in the apartment and had compromised the possible crime scene. Animal Control was called to take them away.

The crime scene technicians first arrived eleven minutes after the body was discovered, and the cats were picked up at the seventeen-minute mark, or 9:31 P.M.

At 10:15 P.M., a crew from the medical examiner's office arrived: Senior Investigator William Campbell, Investigator James Brenner, Dr. Jacqueline Martin, Investigator Robert Walker, and Medical Examiner's Office photographer Andy Treitler.

Physical Crimes Bureau investigators Terry Sheridan and Tony Campione arrived at 10:20 P.M. and were joined ten minutes later by Sergeant Dom Perone. The case was drawing interest from top brass, as well as from state and federal police. Soon to arrive were Captain Lynde Johnston, of the Rochester Police Central Investigation Division, Investigator Eddie Grant, of the state police, and Special Agent Gregg McCrary, of the FBI.

It's safe to say that the small front apartment on Emerson Street was starting to get a little crowded. The body was presumed to be that of the resident, thirty-five-year-old Adrian Berger. The medical examiner's team was

frustrated by the extent of the decomposition, accelerated by the intense heat within the apartment. They
could find no obvious cause of death.

One of the investigators assigned to the case was Tony
Campione, the same man who had seven months earlier
processed the Moraine Armstrong murder and run a
background check on Robert Bruce Spahalski for being
too curious.

Years later he still remembered the brutal assault on
the mind and body that was the Berger death scene.

"It was a freakin' hot day," Campione recalled, the
latest in a long line of extremely hot days. It was a very
small apartment, a studio-type place.

Two rooms: a small kitchen and a room with a pullout
bed. A pillowcase had been pulled over the victim's
head. The victim's car was missing. A quick check with
the Motor Vehicle Bureau revealed that the vehicle was
a 1982 four-door Mercury sedan.

If she committed suicide, who took her car?

At 10:30 P.M., with the muggy heat only slightly more
bearable than it had been at midday, a canvassing of the
neighborhood began. Officers walked up and down the
street, knocking on doors, looking for people who had
seen or heard something unusual in or around the vicinity of the house.

Officer T. C. O'Halloran, sweat soaking through his
uniform shirt, was one of the men asking the questions.
He talked with neighbors Shire Brown and David Huslander. Both said that on Friday, July 19, they heard the
victim arguing with her boyfriend. Huslander said he
saw the boyfriend leave in the victim's car at about two
o'clock on Saturday morning. What was the boyfriend's
name? They didn't know. What did he look like? Tall,
muscular, nervous. One of those guys with veins protruding on the arms, meat on his bones but zero fat.

* * *

On July 22, the day after Adrian Berger's body was found, a call came into the police operator switchboard from a woman named Nancy Johnstone (pseudonym), who lived in the northeast part of the city. She said that she had seen the story about Adrian Berger's death on TV and had information she thought might be helpful to the investigation. Officer Cheryl L. Embling was sent to Nancy's home to take her statement.

Nancy said she knew Adrian because the victim "picked her up from work." Nancy and Adrian had once been neighbors on Phelps Avenue, a street that ran between Lake Avenue and the east edge of Edgerton Park. They spoke at least once a day.

The witness said she'd last spoken to Berger at about 6:20 P.M. on Thursday. Nancy told Embling that it was probably Adrian's boyfriend who had killed her. Berger had known her boyfriend for more than a year, Nancy said, and that they had broken up but had gotten back together on Tuesday.

"She told me she was concerned about her boyfriend's addiction to cocaine," Nancy said. "Just last week, she gave him eighty dollars, which he went and smoked, then returned, looking for more money."

"What's the boyfriend's name?" Officer Embling asked.

"Bruce," Nancy said.

"Last name?"

"I don't remember," the witness said. "But I'm pretty sure it's Polish."

"Think hard."

"Sorry."

"What else do you know about him?"

"He lives on Lake Avenue. He shares an apartment with a guy named Steve. Steve is the guy who collects the rent for the building."

She went on to say that Bruce had a criminal history and had just recently completed parole with New York

State for a felony. He'd served time, she said, at correctional facilities in Elmira, Clinton, and possibly at Attica.

Nancy told the officer that if Bruce took Adrian's car, he probably took other stuff as well, like her checkbook, her savings account book, and her bank card.

The victim, Nancy said, worked for Dynalab, her boss was named Sandy, and her next check was scheduled to be deposited into her account on July 23.

"You should talk to Sandy. Adrian and her were close friends," Nancy said. "She'll be able to tell you more about Adrian—and Bruce."

"You remember anything else about the boyfriend?"

"He's got a brother, I don't remember his name, who lives in Elmira."

Nancy then offered a more detailed description of Adrian Berger's missing car. She said it had a dent in the right rear fender by the gas tank and a crease-type dent along the left-side doors. There was a sticker on the right rear bumper that read YO DUDE and the license plate frame was neon blue.

At 2:15 P.M., on July 22, the victim's car was spotted by a patrol car. The 1982 four-door Mercury with a YO DUDE bumper sticker was parked on the street in front of a home on Ravine Avenue, just a couple of blocks away from the crime scene.

The car was towed to the police pound on Colfax Street and secured inside the Impound Evidence Building. It had been found locked, and remained so. Police asked around. The earliest anyone remembered the car being there was Friday morning. No one saw who had parked it there.

At about that same time, working on information supplied by Nancy Johnstone, Investigators Billy Barnes and Gary J. Schultz went to the Lake Avenue building, with its rear nestled tight up against the cliff that overlooked a Rochester Gas & Electric generating station and the Genesee River Gorge. The location was across the street from the Moraine Armstrong crime site. There, Barnes and Schultz located Adrian Berger's boyfriend, whose full name turned out to be Robert Bruce Spahalski.

In order to gain home turf advantage, they asked Spahalski to come downtown with them to the Public Safety Building (PSB), the police headquarters. He agreed.

Once there, the questioning began. Spahalski verified that he had been Berger's boyfriend.

"When did you last see her?"

"Thursday. Thursday night."

"Tell us about that."

He told the cops that between 5:30 and 7:00 P.M. he visited Berger at her apartment. During that visit, he went with her to Tops Friendly Market on Lake Avenue. They went in her car. Berger's neighbor Shire Brown and her husband were also in the car. "I rode in the backseat," Spahalski added. He returned to her apartment at nine-thirty, driving his own car.

"What type of car do you drive?"

"Pontiac—1976 station wagon."

"Color?"

"Blue."

"What did you do with Adrian?"

"Played dice on her front porch, until about ten-thirty, then I went home."

"You didn't see her on Friday?"

"Nope."

"What did you do?"

He told them that he got home from work at 3:30 P.M. and stayed home.

"Didn't go out?"

"Nope. Not at all. Well, I didn't leave the building. I went to another apartment in my building and did a carpet job." He was a jack-of-all-trades type, he said, and sometimes he cleaned or installed carpets.

What about Saturday and Sunday? He worked, went straight home, and didn't go out at all on either of those nights.

Spahalski was asked about his legal situation. He said that he had last been in prison from 1987 through 1989 for attempted burglary, was placed on inactive parole on June 30, 1991, and that his parole officer was named Mike Lester.

"You have an argument with Adrian?"

"No."

"You take her car?"

"No."

"Did you kill her?"

"I want a lawyer," Spahalski said, pressing his lips together firmly. That ended the interview.

Police gave Spahalski a ride home, and, while there, they picked up his roommate, Steve Hunter (pseudonym), who gave a slightly different version of Spahalski's activities during the last days and hours of Adrian Berger's life. Hunter said Spahalski had been a real homebody, hardly out at all since Thursday night.

On Thursday night, Hunter said, Spahalski was "out all evening" and came home about 12:30 A.M.

"I asked him where he was, when he got in, and he told me he was out hustling for money," Hunter said. The police understood this to mean that Spahalski was prostituting himself.

"What is your relationship with Spahalski, Mr. Hunter?"

"We have a homosexual relationship," Hunter replied.

"Where was Spahalski on Friday night?"

"Home, although he did leave the apartment for a while to do a carpet job."

Because Spahalski appeared to be draped all over the suspicious death of Adrian Berger, he became a stronger suspect in the murder of Moraine Armstrong.

Campione noted the proximity between this crime and the murder of Moraine Armstrong, seven months earlier. Then he learned the boyfriend was Robert Bruce Spalski, bells went off. He remembered the twitchy guy outside the Armstrong murder scene—the guy with his belly pressed against the police tape, so to speak.

But Campione also knew that they weren't going to be able to charge anyone with Adrian Berger's murder until they could prove there had been a murder, and from the looks of things, that was not going to be easy.

The medical examiner's frustration with this case did not subside with the autopsy. The body had parboiled in the heat. The postmortem failed to reveal method or cause of death. Following the autopsy, the case could not be called a homicide and was, instead, labeled suspicious.

Campione interviewed Adrian's mother and father, Phoebe and Martin, both of whom had traveled from their now-separate homes to Rochester when Adrian's body was found.

Adrian's mother told Campione that her daughter had an on-again, off-again boyfriend named Bruce. Sometimes they lived together. The mother spoke to her daughter about this man. Phoebe gathered from Adrian's comments that Bruce was "no good."

It was tough for a mother to keep too close of a tab on her daughter's love life. Adrian lived in Rochester. Phoebe, her mom, lived in Utica, about 120 miles east.

Adrian's dad, Martin Berger, who was divorced from Phoebe and lived in the suburbs of Philadelphia, told investigators that his daughter had had trouble finding steady employment in Rochester, and she had bounced around from job to job.

Adrian, her father recalled, had attempted to enlist in the U.S. Army, but it turned out she was 4F. During the induction physical, she couldn't read the eye chart.

"I guess if she had gotten in, it would have saved her life," Martin Berger said.

What about Bruce? Adrian told her mother it was o
and then off. Last Phoebe heard, it was off. Bruce an
Adrian had a fight about a week or so before poli
found her body. Phoebe said she'd only met Bruce onc
but she could describe him. Her description matche
perfectly with that of Robert Bruce Spahalski.

When Campione ran a background check on Adria
Berger, he found her record to be relatively clean-
although she had once been picked up on suspicion
a minor crime.

Spahalski's fingerprints were found in Adrian's apar
ment, which would have been gold for investigators if l
and the victim were strangers. But he freely admitted
once living in that apartment. His prints could hav
gotten there at any time.

David Huslander, the man who saw Adrian's boyfrien
leave Berger's apartment building during the ear
hours of Saturday morning, was shown an array o
photos of men with similar facial features, and asked
anyone looked familiar. He chose Spahalski's photo.

Law enforcement might have been flummoxed—for a
they knew, the woman's death might have been suicid
or due to natural causes. Although, to be fair, very fe
people died of natural causes with pillowcases over the
heads. Berger's family was positive it was murder, and th
her "no-good" boyfriend, Bruce, had "done Adrian in."

Following up on information supplied by the victim
work buddy Nancy Johnstone, Investigator Schultz inte
viewed Berger's boss at Dynalab, Sandy Smith (pseud
nym). She offered little in new information. Smith sa
that the victim had an erratic personality and had bee
known to make hang-up phone calls to people wit
whom she was irritated. Berger had been arrested on
for harassment in connection with this tendency. She sa
Berger last worked on Thursday. Berger told her boss sh

wanted to take Friday and Monday off, because she was
planning to go to a nightclub on Thursday night and had
made plans to go camping and visit her friend Micki in
Gloversville. She said Berger's boyfriend was Bruce Spa-
nalski, whom she'd never met. According to Berger, however, he was a coke addict who stole money from her.

Time passed. In early September, Martin Berger took
on the task of going to his daughter's apartment and
going through her personal belongings. He found her
diary and turned it over to police. They found an entry
that said Adrian planned to go to Gloversville (she wrote
it as "G'ville") to visit her friend Micki on the weekend
following her death. There were also several notations
that read, *Had sex with Bruce.*

Investigator Campione traveled to Gloversville to talk
to Micki Green (pseudonym) about the victim. Micki said
that she was Adrian's best friend and had been since high
school. She said that even though Adrian was bisexual,
she—Micki—was not.

"I am only into men," Micki said. "I been married with
kids in the past, and I live with my boyfriend now—in
case that was what you were thinking."

This was the first Campione had heard about the
victim being bisexual, and this was not at all what he had
been thinking, but he wrote it down, anyway.

Micki said that Adrian had planned to come visit that
weekend, but she had called to cancel, saying that she
had to work. This info, of course, did not jibe with Sandy
Smith's statement that Adrian was taking two days off
from work.

Micki said that Adrian was anti–hard drugs. She smoked
some reefer now and again, but she didn't care for the
hard stuff—coke, heroin, pills, or any other narcotics.

Even though it seemed like a contradiction, Adrian
was known to take money from her boyfriend, Bruce,

and, in exchange, take him on runs to buy coke. Apparently, Adrian's "anything for a buck" mentality was stronger than her anti-drug stance. That was the way Micki looked at it.

Micki did have a couple of things to say that Campione thought most interesting. She said Adrian did not carry a purse, but instead carried a wallet. Then she added that Adrian always slept in pajamas, with panties and a bra on underneath, no matter how hot it was. The fact, which she had learned from talking to Adrian's mother, that the victim was found wearing only a T-shirt, nude from the waist down, was a sign that something was wrong. Adrian was either having consensual sex at the time of her death or she was being raped.

Micki said she hadn't seen Adrian since Memorial Day, but she had spoken to her last on Thursday night when Adrian called to cancel her visit. She hadn't had a reason to believe anything was wrong.

And that was pretty much where the investigation stalled—for fourteen years.

7

Charles Grande

Charles Grande was born to a postal worker and his wife in Rochester in 1950. He had two sisters and a brother: sister Caroline (known as Carol) was twelve years older, brother Carmen was ten years older, and Rosary (named after her grandmother and called Rose) was two years younger.

His parents were Tony and Ann. They'd had their children in two sets of two. Carmen and Carol grew up as a pair—as did Charles, who was called Chuck, and Rose.

The mother was a good Catholic, and her children, even as adults, could not imagine her using birth control, so Chuck must have come as a major surprise after a full decade without a new baby.

Dad worked. Mom, for the most part, took care of the house and the kids, but she did do odd jobs, here and there, when they were in need of extra cash. It was a typical Rochester Italian family, boisterous and loving.

They could scream and yell at each other one second; everybody happy and laughing the next. It was a family filled with humor. The house was usually loud with people—family and friends in and out. The Grande home was a setting of joyful chaos.

They lived in the nineteenth ward, on Sherwood Avenue, an integrated neighborhood in the southwest corner of the city, south of Chili Avenue, between Thurston and Genesee Streets, eight blocks west of Bull's Head.

When Chuck and Rose were little, their grandmother owned a house off Lake Avenue, just north of Lyell. The house was on Cliff Street, which earned its name by running along the west side of the Genesee River Gorge. The children used to run up and down Lake Avenue, one block to the west, like they owned it, playing and chasing each other. Years later when that strip went downhill, they were slow to become fearful because it still felt like their old stomping grounds.

Many siblings in the world have ambivalent thoughts about one another. Some families develop a nasty, tearful tone. Brothers and sisters do mean things to one another. Life can be a constant game of one-upmanship. Sure, the members of these other families love one another, but they compete and taunt and get on each other's nerves as well. It was *not* that way with Chuck and Rose.

Rose thought Chuck was absolutely fabulous as a big brother. He was politically conservative, enjoyed arguing politics, and was nonstop funny. He was quiet, but when he got going, he could make people laugh so hard that they cried.

Chuck was in charge of the backyard garden at the house on Sherwood Avenue. He chose the plants carefully so that there were always flowers in bloom, from April to October. The yard, visible from the street, was so beautiful that strangers stopped to check it out. From inside the house, the family could hear the "oohs and aahs" of passersby.

He was the gentlest person Rose had ever met. If she

did well, he was happy for her. When things went less than perfect, he was sympathetic.

Chuck was very bright and an excellent student. His obsession was botany. He attended grammar school at St. Augustine's, McQuaid Jesuit High School, earned an associate degree at Alfred University, and then transferred to Cornell, where he earned his B.S. in horticulture.

Near the end of the Vietnam War, Chuck was drafted. He declared himself a conscientious objector and defended himself successfully before a rough draft board. It wasn't that he didn't want to serve his country. He just couldn't hurt anyone. Chuck agreed to do alternative service by working for Smokey Bear rather than Uncle Sam. He fought forest fires in the West for a year.

After college Chuck moved to Montclair, New Jersey. He worked a variety of jobs. He attempted a political career and ran for his local assembly. He had no money, so his grassroots campaign was exclusively door-to-door—and though he lost, he was proud of the fact that he ended up getting about four hundred votes.

He was a cabdriver for a time in Orange, New Jersey, but quit in the mid-1980s after he was robbed at knifepoint. He thought he was a dead man, but the robbers fled. The incident scared him so much that he left New Jersey and returned to Rochester. New Jersey was too violent, he told people.

Chuck lived with his parents for a while and worked as a stockbroker. Saving his money, Chuck bought a home in Webster, a middle-class eastern suburb of Rochester. It was a two-story farmhouse, once smaller but with a couple of additions built onto its rear—a plethora of room for a man living alone.

The home came with a couple of acres of land attached to it—room to plant all sorts of things. A row of pine trees ran along the rear of the property, and a copse of trees grew directly behind the house. When facing the front of the house, there was a barn, a dilapidated shed, and a carriage house behind and to the left.

What had once been the farmland behind the back lawn had been sold to the town by one of the previous owners and converted into a baseball/softball complex.

It might not have been a full-fledged farm, but for a lifelong city boy like Chuck Grande, it provided the perfect, and perfectly manageable, agrarian illusion.

Chuck helped the illusion by purchasing animals. He bought goats. Soon there were geese that wandered around and swam in his pond. His favorite goose was the one with the deformed foot, the one he called Big Foot.

Chuck started a landscaping business. As a career choice, it was perfect for him. Plants were not just a matter of science. They were a matter of art as well.

Plants were his paint; the earth was his canvas. He was never happier than when he was using nature to create physical manifestations of his artistic visions. He loved to make things beautiful.

He was the caretaker for a time for Maplewood Rose Garden on Lake Avenue, one of the most diverse rose gardens in America. His specialty was roses, and his work at Maplewood earned him an award. His dream, never fulfilled, was to be in charge of the greenhouse in Rochester's Highland Park, home of the city's annual Lilac Festival.

Chuck was a big trivia fan, with a near-photographic memory. He prided himself for having a head full of "worthless information." He loved game shows, his favorites being *Wheel of Fortune* and *Jeopardy!* He appeared on *Wheel of Fortune* as a contestant in 1989 and won $3,200 worth of merchandise. His ultimate goal was to be a contestant on *Jeopardy!* but never had the chance.

Also in 1989, Chuck's baby sister, Rose, married Scott Van Dusen, the radio personality. Scott was the host of the "Cruisin' with Van Dusen" radio show on WCMF-FM.

Chuck had some very classic tastes in entertainment. He

enjoyed Beethoven and Bach, Shakespeare and Poe. He
wrote beautiful poems, some of which weren't discovered
until after his death.

He wasn't all sophistication, though. He liked plain-
old-guy things as well. He loved local sports and tried
never to miss a Red Wings baseball game at Silver Stadium or a Rochester Americans hockey game at the War
Memorial. He once checked himself out of the hospital
early, following kidney stone surgery, because he didn't
want to miss an "Amerks" game.

When the ice storm hit Rochester during Chuck's last
winter, Chuck was one of the lucky ones who still had
power. He invited those he knew without power to come
stay with him until Rochester Gas & Electric got around
to fixing things. Among those houseguests were David
and Sharon Yates, of West Walworth, New York, in
Wayne County. They knew him from the ballpark and
called him Charlie.

Every now and again, he'd get a gambling jones and
head down to Atlantic City for a day or two. If there was
a poker game involving family or friends, deal him in.

But there *were* signs that Chuck had a secret. He could
be intensely private. His best friend, Mike Johnson, once
said, "He was a none-of-your-business type of guy with
certain things. He was not a mainstream personality. He
followed his own way of life."

In December of 1990, Chuck's father passed away, and
Chuck took it hard. Chuck and his dad had a strong
bond, understanding each other's emotions without
having to speak about them. Of course, they loved each
other—but they were also very fond of one another. They
were comfortable together.

After his father's death, Chuck stayed away from his
family more, and his behavior became increasingly unusual.

According to Rose, "He had been in love a couple of
times in his life, and it had always been with a woman. I

hate to use the word 'bisexual,' because there is a theory floating around these days that you either are gay or you're not, that there is no in-between. Well, there is an in-between, and that's what Chuck was. He had always been very, very quiet about his personal life—he never asked anyone else about their sex life and he never talked about his—but I knew more about it than most people. Still, I also knew that if Chuck had ever fallen in love and settled down with anyone, it would have been with a woman."

He was generally a happy guy, but that didn't mean he hadn't had hard times. His landscaping business, Horizon Landscape, which was operated out of his house, struggled at first. Business was tough.

But as Chuck's reputation grew, so did his business. By 1991, profits enabled him to afford a couple of full-time employees. Still, he didn't always have a wallet full of money. His love affairs hadn't worked out the way he wanted, but he didn't withdraw. He might have been quiet, but he wasn't shy.

Chuck was not afraid of people. Rose recalled when they went to New York City during the 1980s, a time when crime in the Big Apple was out of control. Instead of being afraid of the streets, which would have been normal, Chuck walked right up to people and talked to them, completely unafraid, convinced that everyone was good.

"He was intelligent but had no street smarts. None. He was almost childlike in that way," Rose recalled. It wasn't so much that he was a bad judge of character, it was that he never passed judgment in the first place. He had an absolute faith in karma. He intended no harm to anyone, so no one would intend harm toward him.

It only stood to reason, then, that Chuck would feel the same way about strangers when his bisexuality overwhelmed him. If there was danger, he might not sense it. He was naïve in just that way.

Rose wanted to make one thing clear: in 1991, a guy

who closeted some of his sexual behavior was not that unusual; it didn't make him a freak.

Rose had a gay friend once who told her that there were a lot of men, some of them married, with kids, who had gay sex on the side. No one in the straight world ever knew—and it was the most common thing in the world.

On the evening of Tuesday, October 1, 1991, about 8:15 P.M., Chuck, twenty-four days shy of his fifty-first birthday, called a landscaping client from his home, and that was the last anyone heard from him.

The next morning at nine, Alan and Dennis, Chuck's two full-time employees, showed up for work at his Webster farmhouse. A generation before, Phillips Road in Webster was exclusively farmland. But starting in the 1960s, the farms gave way to factories and large office buildings, with the Xerox Corporation being the prime developer. Chuck's neighbors now included the *Democrat and Chronicle* Distribution Center. The farmhouse was one of the last survivors of the area's rural past. The grounds once included a front lawn, but ever since Phillips Road was widened from a two-lane to a four-lane highway, Chuck's front door practically overlooked the shoulder of the road.

To the workers' surprise, Chuck's car wasn't in the driveway. No one answered the door. The employees gave the outside of the house and the grounds the once-over to see if there was a clue to his whereabouts. Maybe he left a note or something. Everything appeared okay, but Chuck and his car were not there.

As the two workers returned to the front of the house to wait for their boss, they saw Chuck's car on Phillips Road, slowing down to turn into the driveway.

For a moment, they breathed a sigh of relief. Apparently, Chuck had just been out running an errand or something, but the car didn't pull in. When the driver, who wasn't Chuck, saw there were men in front of the house, he turned his face away from them and accelerated down the road.

That was not good. One of the men, Alan Streeter, immediately went to the Webster police and told them what had happened. The men and a police officer returned to Chuck's house. The local cop looked for signs of a break-in but found nothing. The officer explained there was nothing further he could do at that point.

"What should we do?" the men asked.

"If he doesn't show up for two days, file a missing person report," the officer replied—and then left.

The workers did as they were told. They waited two days, and when there was no sign of Chuck or his car, they filed the report. Only then, during the evening of October 4, was a member of Chuck's family, Carmen, informed that Chuck was missing.

Carmen called everyone he could think of. No one had seen or heard from Chuck. Chuck's best friend, Mike Johnson, volunteered to be part of a search party. So Carmen and his son, Mike, along with Chuck's friend Mike and Chuck's mom, drove out to Webster.

At first, Carmen tried to make semi-jokes, saying he was going to be royally ticked at Chuck for ruining his Friday night, but the jokes soon faded to silence.

When the search party arrived at the house on Phillips Road, they pounded on doors, getting no answer. Mike Johnson volunteered to walk over to the nearest neighbor's house. The guy who lived there was a retired cop named Matt Zane, a friend.

Zane called Webster police. Minutes later, Officer Ernest Paviour pulled into the driveway in his patrol car. Paviour had disturbing news. At 1:00 A.M., on Thursday, he said, Chuck had been stopped in his car on South Avenue in Rochester. There had been a prostitute in the car with him and they appeared to be shopping for drugs.

"That's not Chuck," Carmen Grande said. "Not with a prostitute."

Additionally, Chuck wouldn't have been out at that hour, not when he had to work the next day. The incident was so bizarre, it terrified them.

Also frightening was the fact that Chuck's geese—even Big Foot—were running around loose, with no food or water.

"We *have* to get in the house," Carmen said.

As the Webster cop sat in his car in the driveway writing up a report, Chuck's family and friends circled the house, looking for the easiest point of entry. They decided upon Chuck's bedroom window, where an air conditioner could be removed. Once they had the AC out, Carmen's shoulders were too broad to fit through the window, so Mike Johnson volunteered to enter. Carmen gave him a boost.

Mike was only partially through the window, his legs still sticking out, when he screamed and pushed himself back outside. He was so frantic that he tore his shirt and cut himself.

"Chuck's in there. It's real bad," Mike said. "I . . . I don't think he's alive."

Carmen may not have been the best member of the search crew to crawl through small spaces—but when brute force was needed, he was the man. He ran to the side door, which led into the kitchen, and splintered wood as he kicked it open. He ran into the house, and the air in there was blazing hot, hot with a dry desertlike heat. Carmen ran to Chuck's bedroom, and what he saw seared into his brain. Chuck was on his stomach, on the floor, naked. There was a bloody towel nearby, what looked like a black pool circled his head. The back of his head and the side of his face—they didn't look like they should have.

Carmen ran back outside, screaming, "My brother's in there! My brother is dead!"

Mike Johnson ran to Ann, who was standing in the driveway next to the patrol car, to make sure the distraught mother did not enter the house.

For the rest of their lives, all of their memories would be divided into two groups, things that happened before that moment, and things that happened after.

At first, the timing hadn't been worked out. Police theorized that Chuck was cruising the bad streets of Rochester with a hooker, looking for drugs, which they'd eventually scored. They returned to his house, and she'd killed him. This was the theory related to local reporters and quickly and erroneously became "historical fact."

The published theory, however, fell through when the medical examiner rendered a rough estimate as to the time of death, and the best guess was that Chuck had already been dead by the time his car was stopped in the city. (Investigators later determined that the murderer hit Grande repeatedly over the head with a hammer from behind. The killer was a coward, Rose would often think, unwilling to kill his male victim face-to-face.)

With the victim dead, the killer stole some personal items. Chuck's glasses were missing. The St. Joseph's medal around his neck was gone. It was on a gold chain and had been a gift from his dad. Also missing were the watch, which had been a gift from his brother-in-law, Scott Van Dusen, and Chuck's wallet.

Many of the missing items were all small and personal items that meant something to the victim, but would have limited value to anyone else. They were items that could easily be hidden on the killer's person.

There were other things in the house of value, but the killer left them behind. It was later determined that some money was missing, but if the motive was burglary, the burglar had not been thorough.

Perhaps the killer was scatterbrained, a person with

attention deficit, for whom being thorough was difficult. Maybe something had frightened the killer into leaving, taking Chuck's road-worn Plymouth Volaré, before the job was finished. Sometimes the phone frightened away home invaders.

Before leaving the house, the murderer turned the thermostat all the way up. That was an odd thing to do. Maybe it meant the killer had some smarts. The thermostat trick, as it turned out, hindered the medical examiner's ability to determine time of death—just as a summer heat wave had frustrated the Adrian Berger autopsy. The best guess was that Grande died sometime during the evening of October 2.

Police had no reason to connect Grande's murder with the murders of women near Lyell and Lake Avenues on the other side of the Genesee River. That would soon change, however.

There were few murders in Webster, so the local cops were eager to turn the scene over to county sheriff's personnel. Crime technicians from both the city and the county went over the Phillips Road home with a fine-tooth comb, but nothing of evidentiary value was found.

The sheriff's investigators asked around and quickly learned Grande's secret. Informants said that Grande had been known to visit Rochester's gay bars, which were mostly downtown.

City police canvassed those bars. Among those drawing canvassing duty was Tony Campione. The cops showed bar patrons a photo of Charles Grande. One guy said he'd seen the man in the company of a street dude named Bruce.

Bruce! Holy shit, could it be? Campione wondered. *Can it be the same Bruce that is a suspect in the Armstrong and Berger murders?* It wasn't such a stretch. After all, Bruce's roommate on Lake Avenue had admitted to having a gay relationship with him. It stood to reason that a guy who swung both ways might kill both ways as well.

Campione ran a background check on Charles Grande and hit upon the field report written by Officer John Penkitis regarding "Grande" and the prostitute on South Avenue. The report said that a man named Charles Grande had been stopped in a 1980 Plymouth Volaré, that he was in the car with a suspected hooker, and they seemed to be trying to buy drugs.

The thing about the report was that it was *probably* dated *after* Charles Grande was dead and his car had been stolen, but it was *before* Grande's body was found and the car theft reported. Campione realized the traffic cop had probably stopped Grande's killer.

According to the report, in the hours following the Grande murder, a cruising city cop—who'd only been on the job for a little more than a year—had pulled over someone on South Avenue, downtown, driving Grande's 1980 Volaré. Sitting in the passenger seat was a woman named Barb Brooks (pseudonym), who, the officer suspected, was a prostitute.

The officer asked the driver his name and he said Charles Grande. When asked for license and registration, the driver handed over Charles Grande's driver's license and other personal paperwork from the inside of a wallet.

The license not only had a photo of Charles Grande on it but listed his height as five-eight. The officer barely glanced at the ID, just took down the name and gave it back. He did the same with the prostitute.

As an adult, Grande was close to six feet tall, but at age sixteen, when he got his driver's license, he still had almost four inches of growing to do.

At one point, the officer asked the driver to get out of the car and so had ample opportunity to note that he was over six feet tall and well-muscled.

The officer ordered the driver back in the car, told the prostitute to take a hike, and let them both go their separate ways. Two days later, when Grande's body was discovered, police put out an all-points bulletin (APB) for the Volaré.

After having discovered Chuck's body, frantic older brother Carmen phoned his brother-in-law Scott Van Dusen and told him the bad news.

"I have to tell Rose," Scott said, shock in his voice.

Through his despair, Carmen exhibited some inspired wisdom. "Don't call her on the phone," Carmen instructed. "Go pick her up, because she won't be able to drive."

At the time, Rose was working the evening shift as a mail processor in a Rochester post office. She was trying to quit smoking, and was in her fifth day without lighting up.

Her workstation was deep inside the building, sealed off from the public area. No one from the outside could get in to see her unless it was an extreme emergency.

Processors were not allowed to take phone calls, not allowed to talk to visitors. It was like an assembly line, and it did not stop for anything routine.

She was "keying" letters, processing them on a machine. It was a job that doesn't exist anymore—now that everything is automated, computerized, and digitalized. On this evening, Rose's mind was on her niece who was in a really bad way."

As she performed her repetitive task, she wore headphones to screen out the noise. She found herself wondering if her niece could move in with Chuck, or maybe Chuck could move in with her niece, since both of them were alone and might benefit from a mutual support situation. Nothing permanent, maybe just for a couple of weeks until "things settled down."

Somewhere around 8:00 P.M., maybe a few minutes after, Rose's supervisor came up to her and stood near her. She took her headphones off to see what was up.

"Your husband's here," he said.

"Oh, really?" she replied. *That's great,* she thought, and

she turned around. Scott Van Dusen was standing at the end of the machine, which was fifty feet long. The instant she saw him, her heart leapt into her throat.

Scott had his hand over his mouth. *Uh-oh.* She knew something was very wrong. She got up and ran to him.

"What are you doing here?" she asked anxiously.

"Come on, we gotta go," he replied.

"What do you mean?" she asked, fighting back a panicky feeling.

"Just get your stuff. We have to go." He put his hand over his mouth again and said, "Your brother Chuck is dead."

She put her hands on his shoulders for support and her knees started to buckle. "That's impossible," she said. "What happened?"

"I think he committed suicide," Scott Van Dusen replied. He wouldn't be told it was murder till later that night.

Rose ran back to her station to grab her stuff, but in her panic, she dropped everything and it fell "all over the floor." She got down on her hands and knees to pick it up. As she did this, she managed to tell her supervisor that she was leaving, and that she wasn't going to be back for a while. "Why didn't Chuck talk to me?" Rose thought. "How could he do this to his family?"

The second they were outside, Rose grabbed her husband's arm.

"Scott, I'm going to need a cigarette," she said, and he bought her a pack. That was the last time she went as long as five days without a smoke.

When Rose and Scott arrived at Chuck's house, Carmen was talking to the police. At that time, she was informed that her brother had not committed suicide. He had been murdered with a hammer to the head. Some personal items and his car were missing.

Investigators searched the crime scene with various possible scenarios in mind. Maybe it had been a drug deal gone bad. Maybe it was a weird sex thing. Maybe it was

Devil-worshipping thing. They searched for evidence to support these theories, but they found nothing: no drugs, no porn, no weapons, no stolen property, no large amounts of money, nothing satanic.

Instead of a den of iniquity, what investigators discovered was that Chuck's radio was tuned to Rochester's classical station, on his turntable was a Beatles record, the walls were lined with bookshelves, and each room was decorated with plants.

Truth was, Chuck was against drugs. Oh sure, he might have smoked a little grass when he was young. Who didn't? But the hard stuff, the stuff the cops were looking for, no way.

Tony Campione has maintained that Spahalski's name first surfaced in the Grande case because a gay-bar patron said Chuck had been seen with a street guy named Bruce. And, to this day, Rose Grande still didn't believe it. As Rose put it, "I know what they said, but police went through every sleazy angle they could, and they found nothing."

When Rose learned which of Chuck's possessions had been stolen during the murder, she shuddered. "His glasses?" she exclaimed. "Really, his *glasses*? It's like somebody wants to *be* Chuck."

Once Campione discovered that a man impersonating Charles Grande was stopped for driving with a probable prostitute named Barb Brooks in his car, he had a solid lead to work. An all-out search for Grande's car ensued.

The car was found abandoned behind the old Empire College on Prince Street, about ten blocks east of Rochester's downtown. Campione and his partner went to where the vehicle was located and called in the evidence technicians. A city tow truck was summoned and the car was pulled to the Colfax Street pound, where it was processed.

Investigators were disappointed to learn that the Volaré had been wiped clean of fingerprints. No meaningful evidence was found.

Campione next worked the streets until he located the prostitute named Barb Brooks, who was brought in for questioning. She was shown an array of photos and asked if any of them were of the man she was with when the policeman stopped the car. She picked out a photo of Robert Bruce Spahalski.

Campione located the officer who had made the rookie traffic stop, and he, too, picked Spahalski out of the array as the man who'd been driving the Volaré.

Sometime thereafter, maybe "four or five days" after Chuck's body was found, the Grandes were taken to the Webster police station. They were shown six mug shots and were asked if anyone looked familiar. No. Rose only realized later that one of those photos had been of Robert Bruce Spahalski.

It wasn't until Chuck's funeral service that Rose realized just how popular he had been. Hundreds of hearts were broken by his death. The anguish was palpable.

"It was amazing," Rose remembered. "It was obvious that there were many people who felt about him pretty much the way I did. They loved him. He was a precious person."

And then even the ceremony was over, and the Grandes home, already quieter than it had been years before, now grew silent with a despair that would never lift.

Campione lacked the evidence to charge Spahalski with murder, but he figured he had a case for criminal impersonation and ordered that Spahalski be picked up. Spahalski was brought in and booked for the misdemeanor

At least it was something, a reason to arrest him and get another chance to talk to him.

As long as he had him, Campione didn't limit the interrogation to Grande, but brought up Armstrong and Berger as well. According to Campione, Spahalski was "very antagonistic."

Spahalski said to the investigator, "F*** you, I ain't saying shit."

Campione informed Spahalski that he was being charged with criminal impersonation, and then left him alone in the interview room. Spahalski may not have known that criminal impersonation was a misdemeanor. He may have thought he was in worse trouble that he was.

Using his unexpected and tremendous strength, Spahalski broke the handcuffs, just snapped the metal, and freed his hands.

"In my thirty years in law enforcement, he was one of only two men I encountered who had the strength to break handcuffs, and the other guy was a lot bigger than Spahalski," Campione recalled.

With his hands free, Spahalski revealed himself, in addition to being a man of great strength, to be a man of exceptional athletic skills as well. He jumped up onto a table, removed a panel from above, and, with a hoist and a wiggle, pulled himself up into the drop ceiling. He couldn't get far, because every time he reached one of the exterior walls, he encountered nothing but concrete. Another investigator heard suspicious noises up there and found Spahalski in the ceiling, with nowhere to go.

A charge of criminal mischief was added to the criminal impersonation charge.

Spahalski couldn't afford a lawyer, so one was appointed. That lawyer turned out to be the assistant public defender Richard Marchese. Spahalski told him that Campione had been pestering him about the deaths of Grande, Berger, and Armstrong. One was a client, one his girlfriend, and the third a hooker he barely knew, he said. They all died. Life was tough, but it didn't have anything to do with him.

Marchese was defending a misdemeanor here. He didn't need any of that murder talk from the cops. The lawyer wrote three identical letters to the Rochester, Webster, and Monroe County Police Departments. The letter to the RPD was addressed to homicide detective William "Billy" Barnes. The letters informed those agencies that he, Richard Marchese, was representing Spahalski and warned all recipients not to question Spahalski about any aspect of Charles Grande's murder—or any other murder, for that matter—unless he, Richard Marchese, was present.

At the end of 1991, the *Democrat and Chronicle* ran a long article about the year's murder victims in the area. Missing was the name of Charles Grande. This was the same paper that printed after Chuck's body was found that he had last been seen cruising downtown Rochester with a hooker, looking to buy drugs.

Rose couldn't have been angrier. She remembered "Given the brutality and viciousness of his murder, it was hard to believe there was no mention of it anywhere. Chuck's reputation, his value, his goodness, his reality had been destroyed by the media, and then his whole life and memory had been flushed down the toilet by them."

In April 1992, Rochester's International League baseball team, the Red Wings, began a new season on the city's northeast side. Opening Day, as it had been since 1929, was at Silver Stadium on Norton Street, and for the first time in years, Charles Grande was not there to root the Wings on.

But his ballpark buddies David and Sharon Yates, who had stayed out on Phillips Road with the man they called Charlie after the previous year's ice storm, bought a ticket for him, anyway.

The seat was in the front row of general admission, directly behind the Red Wing dugout, his favorite seat. On the empty seat, in loving tribute, his friends placed a seat cushion, a baseball cap, a Coke, and a sausage sandwich. On that Opening Day, there were tears mixed with the cheers.

During the summer of 1992, Spahalski's criminal impersonation trial commenced before a six-person jury and forty-one-year-old Rochester city court judge Frank P. Geraci Jr. Geraci, a 1977 graduate of the University of Dayton School of Law, had only been a judge for a few months. Before that, he had served as the deputy clerk of the city court of Rochester, worked as a young lawyer in the Monroe County District Attorney's Office, as an assistant United States Attorney in the Western District of New York, and in private practice. (In 1998, six years after this trial, he was elected a Monroe county court judge, a position he has held ever since.)

The prosecuting district attorney (DA) was Thomas R. Morse, the *R* standing for "Rainbow," who later went on to become a city court judge himself.

Among the spectators at the trial was Rose Grande, convinced that this wasn't just a man who had criminally impersonated her beloved brother, but who had murdered him as well.

"That man *threatened* to kill my husband and I, and a friend of my brother's at that trial—in court, in front of the judge and everyone," Rose remembered. "At the time, I weighed about one hundred pounds. And he was a lot bigger than me," she said. "Even though we all had

to go through a metal detector before we entered the
courtroom, they still let the defendant in with keys."

She was outside the courtroom in the smoking area
and she probably shot him a glare, because he walked
right up to her—a bully boy, locating and approaching
the weakest target.

"My brother, brother-in-law and my husband were
there and he walks up to *me*," Rose said. "He had the
keys in his hand, and the look on his face set everyone
else in the room just about running. And he gets right
up in my face with the keys in his hand and he says, 'You
want to tell me why you keep *lookin'* at me?' My brother
went nuts."

Carmen was the burly Grande, with large, rough
hands, and he had always seen himself as the family pro-
tector. He jumped between Spahalski and his sister and
said, *"Because you're a fuckin' murderer, that's why!"*

To this day, Rose believed that it was only the heavy
presence of police in the courtroom that kept the defendant from attacking her. "He was totally *out there.*
He would have gouged my eye out or something with
those keys."

Although there were cops all over the place, none of
them had made a move to protect her. Carmen had reacted, but the police hadn't. Still shaken she went to the
nearest cop and said, "Hey, that guy just threatened me,"
but the cop still didn't react. Rose later learned that the
policeman she had talked to was scheduled to testify at
the trial, and probably wanted to avoid doing something
that could have been used as fodder by the defense.

Spahalski was good at threats and not hesitant about
dishing them out. And why not? They were usually so
effective. His roommate, Steve Hunter, had been approached by the prosecution about testifying against
Robert in court, and Spahalski told him what a mistake
that would be. The roomie made himself scarce.

The woman Barb Brooks, who lived just down the street

from Spahalski and who had been in the Volaré at the time he was stopped, was, of course, someone the prosecution wanted to get on the stand, but boom!—crunch time came and no one knew where Barb Brooks was.

The woman had, in fact, been threatened, because after seven months of being underground, she reemerged and told police that Spahalski told her in no uncertain terms not to testify against him. But by that time, Robert Spahalski's trial was long over, and double jeopardy prevented take two.

Marchese did a great job for Robert Spahalski. His defendant was suspected by smart cops of being a multiple murderer, and yet, despite the testimony of Tony Campione, he got him acquitted on the impersonation charge.

As was often the case, the jurors were the least informed people in the room. The first thing Marchese did was make sure that the jury never heard a word that might imply that this case had anything to do with a murder. In fact, there was no mention that the impersonation was associated with *any other* crime. That information would have been prejudicial to the jury, Marchese argued. And the judge agreed.

The prosecution was not even allowed to refer to Chuck in the past tense, and by referring to him in the present tense, the implication was that Chuck was a living person.

What if the jury had known that Charles Grande was dead and that the defendant was the prime suspect in his murder? What if . . . ?

Likewise, the jury was not allowed to know that the defendant was a lifelong criminal.

During the trial, Rose hoped the jury would figure it out on their own. Maybe the jury would look around the courtroom and wonder why Chuck wasn't there. Maybe they would see the group of concerned folks sitting behind the prosecutor's desk and wonder who they were, and why this case was so important to them. Maybe . . .

But the jury focused instead on Marchese. The defense attorney pointed out repeatedly that in this case the RPD was sloppy. They were sloppy in their observations and sloppy in their paperwork. Reasonable-doubt sloppy.

Officer John Penkitis, the rookie cop who'd made the traffic stop, testified, but it didn't go well. When asked to identify the driver of the Volaré, he pointed at the defendant. Marchese then ripped him with a blistering cross-examination.

The cop was forced to admit that at the time, he'd really had no reason to remember what the driver of the Volaré looked like. When writing his report, he didn't describe Robert Spahalski from personal observation but rather copied down the information from the driver's license he'd been handed, which had Grande's height and weight at age sixteen.

Marchese said, "How could my client have been the one driving the car? He is six foot two. Charles Grande's license said he was five-eight. We are supposed to believe that the officer didn't notice a six-inch height difference?"

Without context the jurors saw the case as a no-brainer. The driver's license said five-eight, the defendant was six-two. How could he possibly be the guy?

On the day before the verdict came in, Rose was furious over what she felt was the inadequate prosecution of Robert Spahalski, the fact that the bastard had been allowed to threaten her and her family in the courtroom, the fact that Chuck had been omitted in the article on the year's murder victims by the local paper, furious over everything.

She decided to do something.

Rose wrote a letter to the *Democrat and Chronicle*'s editor in chief. The voluminous letter said, in essence, that she could read the writing on the wall. Robert Bruce Spahalski was going to walk on these charges of criminal

impersonation. The thing had been botched from the
get-go. Maybe if the newspaper had treated her brother
like a real person, as they did for the other Monroe
County murder victims of 1991, maybe then the prosecution and the police and the jury and everyone else in
the world would have taken this case more seriously and
Spahalski would be heading for prison instead of heading for his home, or his home on the streets, or whatever. To its credit, the paper reacted strongly to the letter
and immediately did a story about Rose and her battle
for justice.

   As anticipated, in August 1992, six of Robert Spahalski's peers set him free. It was the second-worst day of
Rose Grande's life. To protect Spahalski's civil rights, the
judge in the case ordered that all records of his arrest
and subsequent prosecution be sealed. Despite the acquittal, both city and county police remained convinced
that Robert Bruce Spahalski murdered Charles Grande
and probably others. The Grande case would still be
active fourteen years later.

   In September 1992, the *Democrat and Chronicle* ran an
article on the front page called FAMILY'S VOID, QUESTIONS
LINGER 1 YEAR AFTER WEBSTER MURDER. The article was written by Michael Wentzel, who, according to Rose, was the
paper's best reporter. He left the daily in 2006.

   The article quoted Webster police chief Alexander
Kirstein: *"We have a solid idea who did it. But we need to develop
solid evidence that ties this to the suspect. We need someone to come
forward with information. We have to think he knew the person to
let the person in the house. This case is still alive. We still follow up
on information. Maybe I'm an optimist but this really isn't a dead-
end case."*

   At that time, the murder of Charles Grande was Webster's only unsolved homicide.

   Wentzel talked to Rose, who was eager to set the

record straight. The same paper Wentzel wrote for had reported that Chuck had last been seen in the city trying to buy drugs with a prostitute. After it was learned that this was not true, the paper hadn't retracted the statement. In fact, when Robert Spahalski was arrested and tried for criminal impersonation, the newspaper didn't even mention it.

Rose told the reporter about the frustration she and her mother felt. The little old Italian ladies from the nineteenth ward read that Chuck had been with a prostitute, out in the middle of the night, buying drugs. Maybe he was asking for it, they thought.

She said that she still see the questioning look in people's eyes. People wondered if he was into something horrible. "You play with fire, you get burned," she said. The unfavorable picture put the focus on her brother. The focus should be on the murderer, she insisted. "He might do it again."

Chuck's best friend, Mike Johnson, agreed. "The newspaper reports bothered everyone. They cast aspersions on the family. The ignominy added to the effect of the murder."

Johnson gave the reporter a perfect conclusion for his piece by offering a poetic analogy: "I can still see the black dust all over the house from when the police were looking for fingerprints. The black dust settled over the house. It settled over everything about Chuck. It has never cleared away."

After Robert Spahalski walked on the criminal impersonation charges, he resumed his life on the street, sometimes buying and selling female sexual services, sometimes selling his own.

Every now and again, Tony Campione would be cruising by and see him standing on the sidewalk, somewhere downtown, and the homicide investigator couldn't help but get in his face, let him know he was being watched, that the cops were onto him. From that point forward, his movements were being closely scrutinized.

"Hey, Bruce, how's it going?" the investigator would shout from his car window.

Spahalski would inevitably flip him off.

Campione would stop the car and walk up to Spahalski, nice and slow.

"So, Bruce, you gonna tell me about Grande and those girls you killed?"

That always shut him up.

Like Campione, Rose Grande wasn't about to leave Robert Spahalski alone just because he'd been acquitted. About a year after the criminal impersonation trial, Spahalski was arrested on a minor charge and had a one-day trial. Rose found out about it and sat in the spectator section, again accompanied by her brother and her husband. After his conviction, the judge asked Spahalski if he had anything to say.

"Yeah, these people," he said, looking back at Chuck Grande's family, "think I did something I didn't do. I never killed anybody, and I better never see any of them again!"

To this day, Rose still shuddered over the vile aura that was coming off him when he spoke those words. A woman then escorted Spahalski from the courtroom and she pushed him so hard that he flew through the door; then she closed the door behind him.

Rose never did leave Robert Spahalski alone. She knew more about the "evil one" than she should. "That's what a curious mind will get you," she said.

Sometime in 1994, Rose put pen to paper and wrote a fourteen-page essay about Chuck, his murder, and the man she knew murdered him. She wrote about the press and the justice system and how each had wronged her brother. She wasn't sure what she was going to do with it but it was therapeutic to write.

About the impersonation trial, she wrote, *The jury wa. told by the defense attorney that the accused was an innocent mar and that he was "scared." They were also led to believe throug. crafty wording that the accused was a good member of society wit. no prior criminal record. By the time he was finished the jury had been rendered incapable of delivering justice. They were completel. ignorant of the pertinent facts they needed to make a fair decision Every word, manipulation and lie was allowable and legal unde. the laws as they stand today.*

The justice system today is perverted because it often works in favor of the criminal and against law enforcement and law abiding citizens.

She wrote sadly of what a dangerous city Rochester had become, and had a theory as to why: *Shortly after Shawcross was caught, it was reported that there were more than eight. paroled murderers in Rochester. How many convicted murderers and rapists and child molesters and repeat violent offenders ar. in this city now? We should not be a dumping ground for socio. paths who have no right to be paroled in the first place.*

She wrote that the justice system did not have its priorities in order: *The punishments all too often do not fit the crime. For instance, a basically harmless person who is caught using marijuana or stealing merchandise can get a stiffer punishmen. than a violent maniac who beats his young children half to death. The system needs to begin recognizing real danger.*

This is a controversial thing to say but I believe the laws should be changed so that attorneys are no longer allowed to lie in court. They can swear on the Bible that they don't, but I know some of them do because I have seen it.

The kid sister—who was dedicating her life to removing her brother's killer from society—would need to wait more than a decade before she could again feel optimism.

Meanwhile, the violence near Edgerton Park raged on.

8

Vicki Jobson

Vicki Jobson was born on November 12, 1961, the day after Veterans Day, in Syracuse, New York, a city a tad smaller than Rochester, ninety miles farther east along the New York State Thruway.

She had four sisters and one brother, three older siblings and two younger. Her father worked at General Motors, and her mother was a nurse's aide.

Vicki attended Salina Jefferson Elementary School, Grant Junior High School, and then George W. Fowler High School on Magnolia Street. And for a time, her life was going great. She met a man, stayed with him for more than a decade, and had two children. Like her mother, she worked as a nurse's aide. She also had a reputation as a fun girl, a party girl.

Then the partying got to be too much for Vicki, and things started to slide. At first, she just seemed to have a case of the blahs; then she was sulky; then she was caught in a deep-blue funk—clinically depressed.

Someone offered her a blast off a glass pipe and she

thrilled to the near-orgasmic rush of a first-time crack user. She liked it. She liked it a lot. And her life tumbled free fall into the abyss of drug addiction.

Vicki left her husband and her children and moved to Rochester, the next city on the Thruway to the west, where her mom, aunt and sister already lived. Vicki's younger sister, Kelly, was the last to follow Mom to Rochester, relocating two years after Vicki did.

It was as if the family were beginning a hesitant migration westward, but the mother and her daughters got to Rochester and stuck. Ask any of them, "Why Rochester?" and you'd likely get a shrug of the shoulders.

Life did not improve for Vicki. The change of habitat did nothing to help her depression—or her corresponding drug problems. Her rate of deterioration increased. Her next boyfriend was the kind who forced her to turn tricks.

Vicki's mom tried to come to her daughter's rescue, to pull her back into the safety of the family womb. She tried to get Vicki a job that didn't involve standing next to Lyell Avenue in hot pants. At night the mother would go out searching. She'd bring her daughter food and try to get her to eat.

"Sometimes she would just grab her and throw her in the car," remembered Vicki's sister Kelly. "She'd bring her home or take her to McDonald's."

Maybe the motherly attention did some good for the short term, got her warm and filled her belly. However, the slide continued long-term. Her habit ruled her life. Vicki was bad off, visibly strung out.

Vicki's mother was desperate. It really was a matter of life and death. Why couldn't Vicki see that? White girls like her were disappearing like ice cubes on a summer sidewalk. Clients were deadly. Diseases were deadly, her mom would emphasize, screaming sometimes. But Vicki was deaf to it, a slave to the pipe. Getting a "real job," as

er mother called it, or a "straight job," as it was known on
he street, was out of the question.

Rochester police ran a sweep. Vicki was arrested for
prostitution.

Miraculously, she wasn't homeless. By the fall of 1992,
he was thirty years old and lived in an apartment on
Lake Avenue, in the same building where Robert Bruce
Spahalski had dwelled at the time of the Moraine Armstrong murder.

Sometime during the month of October, she paid her
last visit to that apartment. She went out to work and
never came back. Vicki's home was directly across the
street from the apartment house where Moraine Armstrong had lived—and died—twenty-one months earlier.
Vicki's apartment house was near the corner of Emerson
Street and Lake Avenue, a little more than a block from
where Adrian Berger had been found dead fifteen
months earlier. There was a dark parking lot next to the
building, suitable for doing business, and the wire fence
behind the building kept pedestrians from falling off the
cliff and tumbling into the river gorge.

Vicki's thirty-first birthday came and went without a
word from her.

On December 7, 1992, the badly decomposed body of
Vicki Jobson was found nude and perforated with stab
wounds. The remains were one block north of Lyell
Avenue in deep right field of the baseball grounds in
A. R. Wilson Park, along a row of thick trees, near the
corner of Haloid and Rutter Streets, and by the New
York Central railroad tracks.

Across the street were crumbling tennis courts, the
nets for which were torn and drooping. Incidentally, a
2009 inspection of the site revealed a hole in the wire
fence separating the ball field from the railroad tracks.
Pedestrians could easily go through the fence and walk
along the tracks via a dirt service road to a secluded clear-
ing beneath a cluster of sumac trees, where a mattress

and box spring lay on the ground, next to a plastic chai
(Perhaps this was the "office" and "waiting room" for on
or more of the women from Lyell Avenue.)

In response to the discovery of the remains, the fir
policeman on the scene was Officer Mark Mariano, wh
had also guarded the exterior perimeter at the Morain
Armstrong scene, and wrote the initial report regardin
the discovery of Vicki Jobson's body.

The medical examiner determined that Vicki ha
been killed *much* earlier, and her body had just recent
been moved to the spot where it was discovered.

So many questions went through investigators' mind
With Shawcross incarcerated and John White unde
constant surveillance, there was a chance that Rocheste
police were still looking for two serial killers. Could it be
It seemed mathematically unlikely. Four serial killers a
choosing victims from the same 'hood? The recent vi
tims, it seemed, could be divided into two groups. Wa
there the guy who snuffed women in their apartmen
and then turned up the thermostat, and then anothe
who killed his women in one location and then, havin
access to a car, dumped his victims' bodies near railroa
tracks on Rochester's west side? In 1991, Damita Gibson
Cassandra Carlton, and Katrina Myers were found nea
tracks. Now, in 1992, Vicki Jobson joined the list. Th
apartment killer had taken Moraine Armstrong an
Adrian Berger. A strong suspect in Berger's death wa
also the prime suspect in the Charles Grande murder.

An investigator would be quick to assume that ther
were two or more killers, except for one thing: Rober
Bruce Spahalski had links to victims in both group
Maybe he was responsible for all the deaths. Mayb
sometimes Robert had a car and sometimes he didn't.

As homicide investigator Tony Campione was quick t
point out, "He certainly wasn't above stealing a car."

Was it possible that there were two killers, and the
sometimes worked as a team? Could that team be th

John and Johnny" who had been looking for Moraine Armstrong during the days before her murder? And if police were looking for a two-man team, was Spahalski one of those two men? In the eyes of a cracked-out streetwalker, Spahalski might have come across as an "Italian guy." Or, looking at it from another angle, was the two-man team a separate entity, while Spahalski was a free agent out killing by his lonesome?

For a long time, Vicki's family thought that John White might have been Vicki's killer, but police had already ruled him out. White was already under surveillance at the time Vicki's body was dumped.

Vicki—like Damita, Cassandra, and Katrina before her—had been disposed of by a man without a heart, without a soul. She'd been disposed of like a piece of tissue paper. Dumped naked.

But none of that could stifle the intensity of a mother's love for her daughter. The mother kept a lock of Vicki's hair next to her bed for all of her remaining years.

Years went by, but police never forgot about Spahalski, and they never passed up an opportunity to drag him downtown and ask him a few questions.

Just such an occasion arose during the summer of 1998 when a city bar proprietor called in a complaint that a man matching Spahalski's description was in his bar trying to sell a camera with a long zoom lens attached to it.

The barkeep thought the guy might be a junkie and the camera might be hot. Police came a few minutes later. The man had left the bar, but he wasn't far away. Police picked him up and brought him in for questioning.

Robert Spahalski admitted that he had been trying to sell the camera, but he claimed that it was rightfully his, and that he had sold it to someone the instant he left the bar. Without being asked, he told the Rochester

police, again, that they had the wrong guy when it came
to the murders that had occurred in his proximity. No
matter what they might think, he had a drug problem
and he was currently undergoing drug rehabilitation,
but he was not the sort of person who would hurt or kill
anybody.

His interrogators thought this unsolicited denial was
very interesting. After all, they had only asked about the
camera.

Sometime during 1996, Robert Bruce Spahalski went
to a clinic and had some blood work done. One key test
came back with startling results. He was HIV positive.

9

Hortense Greatheart

In 2003, Spahalski's name surfaced in connection with yet another murder investigation. The body of a forty-five year-old African-American woman was found in January 2003, strangled in her apartment on Lake Avenue, an apartment building only one block south of where Moraine Armstrong and Adrian Berger were killed. The building was on the west side of Lake, amidst a stretch of car washes and dealerships. It was yet another building in which Robert Bruce Spahalski had lived, off and on, since the early 1990s. The closest intersection was Lake and Phelps—Phelps being the street that once took travelers to the main entrance of Edgerton Park along its eastern edge.

Those who lived on the ground level couldn't afford real curtains to stifle voyeurs, and tacked up whatever was handy—a towel, a blanket, a pair of pajama bottoms.

The victim was identified as Hortense Greatheart and the medical examiner determined that she had probably died on January 3. It was a guess. A smart killer had

messed with the rate of decomposition and made deter
mining the precise time of death impossible by turning up
the thermostat in the victim's apartment—the same tech
nique used at the Charles Grande crime scene in Webster

The number one suspect in that case had been Robert
Bruce Spahalski. Investigators couldn't help but suspect
him in the Greatheart case as well.

Greatheart—date of birth, June 12, 1957—was survived
by her brothers, Troy and Brian Stanley, and her sisters
Rita Jones, Kathy Parker, Brigette, and Amy. Her wake was
held between 7:00 and 9:00 P.M. on Friday, January 10
2003, at the G. L. Dixon Funeral Home—Geraldine Dixon
proprietor—in the northeast quadrant of Rochester, on
North Street.

Funeral services were held the following day at noon
at the Fountain Missionary Baptist Church on Scic
Street in Rochester. Officiating at the ceremonies was
the Reverend John Sanders, an orator of such skill that
he sometimes worked as a guest speaker at other Missionary Baptist churches.

In the thirteen years since the rash of killings had
struck the Edgerton Park area, the homicide rate in the
city of Rochester had not improved. In fact, Rochester
was the deadliest city in New York State, per capita.

Hortense Greatheart was merely the first of fifty-seven
people who were murdered in Rochester in 2003. That
figure included eight children. The circumstances of
those deaths revealed that Rochesterian youth were all
too often growing up too fast.

The dead children included a thirteen-year-old girl shot
to death by her twenty-one-year-old boyfriend, a fourteen-
year-old boy who died in a bar fight, and a seventeen-year-
old boy who smiled at the wrong girl.

Of the fifty-seven murders in Rochester, only thirty-
four had been cleared at year's end. Greatheart's was

among the cases still open. The great majority of those murders occurred in the geographic arc of neighborhoods known as the Crescent. The city's record was sixty-eight murders in 1993, when the Jamaican drug war was at its peak.

Cedric Alexander, the acting police chief in the city, noted that each murder in Rochester revealed some sort of "societal ill."

"That's why this is not just the police department's responsibility. It's the entire community's responsibility," Alexander said.

Community activist Susan Costa noted that the majority of people who lived in Crescent neighborhoods, including Edgerton Park, were good people, concerned only with what was best for their area.

Criticizing the governmental support systems that had been set up to decrease crime in those areas, she said, "The resources aren't channeled in a way that makes them available at the grassroots level."

A lot of the violence was gang-related. A young man was murdered near Lake Ontario. Six days later, one of his pallbearers was also shot to death. Two weeks after that, a teenager who had witnessed the first killing was also murdered. And it went on and on.

On Robert Spahalski's fiftieth birthday, in December 2004, he began collecting Social Security disability payments, based on his diagnosed post-traumatic stress disorder stemming from a gang rape he endured in prison.

During the spring of 2005, the New York State Police squad for cold cases undertook a fresh look at the Grande murder. Luckily, evidence had been preserved—evidence that carried a new importance in the era of DNA technology.

10

"The matter is urgent."

In Rochester, police headquarters was in the Public Safety Building, close to the Genesee River's left bank, just upstream from the High Falls.

On Tuesday, November 8, 2005, at around 10:40 A.M., a tall man with thinning dark hair combed straight back entered police headquarters on Exchange Street. He was wearing an orange top and blue jeans. It had been a bit of a hike from his home on Spencer Street. Maybe a mile.

The man walked right up to the front desk. The receptionist on duty that morning was Officer Maria Graves. To her, the man appeared determined but agitated. Fidgety. He didn't look healthy. He was dried up, slightly mummified, with a parchmentlike complexion, and skin pulled tight over his bones. His lower jaw and nose were exceptionally close together, a sign that he was missing more than a few teeth.

Graves looked at the man's hands, which were stained with nicotine and covered with sores. She recognized the sores as a sign of crack abuse. Crackheads often burned their fingers while smoking crack cocaine. When their disposable lighters ran out of fuel, and they ran out of matches, they resorted to lighting their pipes on the open flame of the stove burner. High and numb from smoking cocaine, they often blistered their fingers before they realized they were torching themselves, as well as the sweet white rock. Then, while coming back down, they nervously picked at the wounds on their fingers.

The man said he needed to see a detective right away. His name was Robert Bruce Spahalski, he was fifty years old, and he didn't have an appointment.

"The matter is urgent," he emphasized.

"What's the problem?" Officer Graves asked.

"I killed someone," came Spahalski's chilling reply.

The receptionist asked the location of the murder.

"It occurred on Spencer Street," Spahalski said.

The receptionist ran a quick check and learned that no homicide had been called in from that location. Still, the man didn't seem to be joking. The receptionist called Officer Lourdes Baez, who quickly came out into the reception area.

The homicide supervisor that day was former officer, now Sergeant Mark D. Mariano. He and Detective Glenn Weather happened to be walking through the lobby as this was going on.

Officer Graves called out to them. Both recognized Spahalski as a suspect in several earlier killings. Mariano had been a young patrol cop back at the end of 1990 when Moraine Armstrong was killed, and had helped protect the scene while investigators processed it. He'd also been the first officer on the scene when Vicki Jobson's remains were discovered.

"Tell these guys what you just told me," Officer Baez said.

"I just killed my friend," Spahalski said. "It happened on Spencer."

"How come we don't have a report of the murder?" he was asked.

"Because I'm the only one who knows about it," Spahalski replied.

"Who is the victim?" Officer Baez asked.

"Vivian Irizarry," Spahalski said. "She was my very good friend." Vivian, Spahalski explained, had been a friend first of his girlfriend, and then a friend of his. Vivian and his girlfriend were related—cousins, he believed.

"How did you kill her?"

"I don't remember."

Mariano remembered thinking, *This can't be happening.* It was like a dream come true.

The officer asked when the murder had occurred. Spahalski said he wasn't sure because he'd been high at the time. After killing the woman, he went on a drug binge and had tried to commit suicide by taking an overdose of pills. So he'd lost track of the days.

"What happened?" Officer Baez asked.

"Me and her were smoking crack," he said. His girlfriend, Christine Gonzalez, was working, so he received a visit from Irizarry, his longtime friend, to get high.

After smoking for a while, Irizarry used a knife to cut open a new bag of crack, and he had "freaked out." He started to hallucinate and thought Irizarry had transformed into a demon. He said his head was messed up from a combination of the drugs and some "mental problems I have."

Thinking his companion was an evil being that needed to be vanquished, he hit her three times over the head with a blunt object. He wasn't sure what the object was. It was something he had "grabbed in the kitchen."

She fell down unconscious. When his crack high subsided, he could see that the demon he'd tried to vanquish was just Vivian, and he'd injured her badly. He checked and discovered that she was still breathing, but she had soiled herself.

"So what did you do?"

"I took off her clothes and washed her off."

"And then . . . ?"

"She was having convulsions or something. I thought she was dying. I couldn't bear to see her suffer. I knew that she was mortally wounded, so I choked her out and put her out of her misery," Spahalski said.

His interrogators felt their stomachs flip as Spahalski described the way Irizarry died. Not too much exertion was required for the choking this time, he said. Due to her sorry state, death came quickly, he added.

"How did you choke her out?" Officer Baez asked.

"I used a piece of twine."

"Where is she now?"

"I put her clothes back on and put her in the cellar," Spahalski said.

After that, he went back upstairs and indulged in a drug binge. He did little else but smoke crack for a week. When his girlfriend came home with money, he used it to buy more crack, Once, he went back into the cellar to check on Irizarry. Her body was still cold, so he figured she was really dead. After thinking about it for a while, he realized his guilt feelings weren't going to allow him to remain free. He turned himself in.

Sergeant Mariano volunteered to go to the Spencer Street address to see if, in fact, a crime had occurred. Spahalski was taken to Detective Weather's office on the fourth floor. Mariano called for a patrol car to go to the house and secure the scene until he got there, and Officer Stephen Boily complied.

During the transfer, Spahalski thanked Officer Baez for not putting handcuffs on him. Handcuffs hurt. Besides, the bondage made Spahalski jumpy, something like claustrophobic, like his nerves were going to jump right out through his skin.

Claustrophobia was something Spahalski knew about. A lot of guys who were facing life in prison felt claustrophobic.

After arriving in Weather's small office, room 450-1, several other detectives came in to participate in the interrogation.

Spahalski was answering the preliminary questions—name, age, address—but he was starting to act peculiarly. He stretched his arms in front of him, then over his head. He stood up and walked around the table. He bent his body at the waist, first forward, then backward.

"Something wrong?" he was asked.

"This room is small."

"You feeling claustrophobic?"

"Yeah."

"Would you like to move to a larger room?"

Spahalski nodded vigorously.

The investigators moved him to a conference room, right across the hall. Spahalski sat at the head of a long table, and the detectives took seats on either side of him—Weather on his right and Investigator Randy Benjamin on his left.

Benjamin began to read Spahalski his rights, but the suspect stopped him.

"You don't have to do that. I understand my rights," Spahalski said.

"It's just a formality. We have to do it," Weather said, and Spahalski shrugged.

Spahalski was advised of his legal rights, and when he asked, he was supplied with a pack of cigarettes and an ashtray. Spahalski said he was willing to waive his Miranda rights.

"I want to tell my story," Spahalski said. The detectives noted that he seemed sober and alert, and therefore deemed him competent to waive his rights.

"We want your whole story, Robert," Weather said. "Let's start at the beginning. Where did you grow up?"

"Born and raised in Elmira, New York," Spahalski said. He added that he'd graduated from Elmira Free Academy and moved to Rochester in the 1970s. He said that back in Elmira, he and his twin brother had been on the high-school gymnastics team, that they were so good that they'd trained with the U.S. Olympic team. He said that his mother and father had broken up when he was twelve, and that his twin brother was in prison for murder, kidnapping, and robbery.

"Murder?"

"Yeah, he robbed a guy and then stabbed him." And then he added, hyperbolically, "Stabbed him forty-seven times."

Killer twins, the investigators thought. That was a first, as far as they knew.

"What do you do for a living?"

"I'm out of work right now. I get disability." He added that he was receiving Social Security income for mental problems.

"What sort of mental problems, Robert?"

"Uh, I got anxiety. I got post-traumatic stress disorder."

"What was the trauma?"

"I got that from when I was in prison."

"Any other mental problems?"

"I hear voices—and I'm HIV positive."

"Take drugs for the HIV?"

"Ziagen."

He told the investigators about the extent of his education. He said he could read and write, and that when he was in prison, he had worked on getting his associate's degree.

"When were you in prison?"

"Off and on since high school. All for burglary or burglary-related."

By this time, Sergeant Mariano was on Spencer Street, parked in front of the building in question. The building was two houses attached at the side, containing four apartments. It had a maple tree out front and was the closest house to Plymouth Avenue, on the north side of Spencer Street.

There had once been a house on the corner, but that was gone, and wooden stakes were driven around the perimeter of the vacated property to prevent dumping. The corner house on the south side of the street was also gone, and dirt paths had been worn by pedestrians cutting the corners to head north or south on Plymouth. In addition to the pair at the front, the double house had two entrances in the rear that faced a pair of maple trees and an alley.

The house was locked up. Firemen arrived and were ready to knock in a door, when the landlord—Kevin Turner, who lived right nearby—came running up with keys. The instant the door was open, Mariano knew from the smell that Spahalski was telling the truth.

Sergeant Mariano and Officer Boily entered the house and went downstairs into the basement. In the portion of the basement farthest from the entrance, the chilly back room, there she was—naked, except for a sock on one foot, the left foot. (Oddly, Moraine Armstrong had also been found wearing only one sock.)

A single white sock—a match for the one still on the body—was found on the basement floor, next to the staircase. That sock appeared to be stained with blood. There was a radio in the basement that also looked to have blood on it.

Spahalski had lied when he said he had re-dressed Irizarry after washing her.

"There was a ligature around her neck, and she was obviously dead," Mariano recalled.

Mariano had seen corpses before. There was no confusing a living body and a dead one. When the spirit left the flesh, people changed in some indefinable way, animate to inanimate.

Seriously injured people needed quick attention, dead people could be dealt with leisurely, and the movements of first responders tended to slow rather than quicken when they found a corpse.

The police and firefighters on the scene didn't need a coroner to determine the victim had been beaten and strangled. Her face was bruised, her head covered with blood. There were cuts on her head, and there was still a piece of twine wrapped tightly around her neck.

Mariano saw drag marks, a trail of blood showing that the body had been dragged into that position from another location upstairs, and though the victim had been dead for several days—four, it was later determined—decomposition was retarded by the chilly temperature in the underground chamber.

Mariano touched nothing. He backed out of the basement. The perimeter of the property was taped off and secured. Officer Boily was posted at the basement door, with orders not to allow other officers entry until the technician's unit arrived to process the scene.

Back at headquarters, a few minutes into the interrogation, Weather's phone rang in his office across the hall. He got up to answer it. It was Mariano. The message was simple, "Body found."

Talking to Turner, the landlord, Mariano learned that one of the building's four apartments had been rented by Robert Bruce Spahalski and his girlfriend, Christine Gonzalez, for about four months. Turner's understanding was that the couple had been together for around ten years. He said that Robert was a quiet tenant, who had a cat.

"I never even heard him use a curse word," the landlord said, shrugging.

Turner signed a consent-to-search form, allowing police to search all of the public areas in the building, which included the basement.

Turner told Mariano that Spahalski did not pay his own rent. The bills were paid by DePaul Mental Health, a nonprofit agency that treated drug addicts and those with mental-health issues.

He said Spahalski's girlfriend worked at the Volunteers of America. The victim, if she was who he thought she was, was a relative, maybe a cousin, of Christine Gonzalez's.

"They all got along," Turner said. "I think they smoked crack together sometimes."

"When was the last time you saw Spahalski?" Mariano asked.

"Let's see. I woke up this morning about eight-thirty. I saw him walking across the shortcut on the other side of the street that leads to Lyell Avenue. People use that shortcut to go to the store. I assumed that's where he was going. Then I saw him coming back the same way. I shouted out, 'Hey, Robert,' but he didn't answer. He was stone-faced. I was calling him through my living-room window. When he got up on the front porch, I said, 'What's up?' He just nodded at me, which was unusual. He didn't talk much, but usually he'd say something."

Later in the morning, Turner said, he saw Spahalski walking southbound on Plymouth Avenue, apparently heading toward Lyell, and again saw him returning from that direction. This time he made no attempt to engage Spahalski in conversation. Turner said he heard no commotion and saw nothing suspicious, and had no idea that anything was wrong until emergency vehicles pulled up out front.

"When was the last time you were in the basement?"

"I don't know. Not today."

"Who has access to the basement?"

"Just me and Spahalski. I can get in through the side exterior door. He has access through steps that lead up to his kitchen."

"Could he have gotten into the basement through the exterior door?"

"No, you have to have a key to go that way, and I have the only one."

* * *

The interrogation of Robert Bruce Spahalski continued in the conference room on the fourth floor of the Public Safety Building.

"Tell us about the victim, Vivian. Where did she live?"

"I don't know the exact address. I think she lived off Norton Street."

"How old was she?"

"About fifty-three."

"We're going to be searching your apartment, Robert. Is there anyplace in particular we should look?"

"There is blood in the pantry—on the wall near the door and on the carpet."

"You want to be there when your apartment is searched, Robert?"

"Nah, that's okay."

The suspect again told Investigators Benjamin and Weather how he killed Vivian. He said he hit her over the head with an object. He didn't remember what the object was, just something he had picked up in the pantry.

"How many times did you hit her?"

"I don't know. At least three." It was like he was chopping her down. Her head got lower and lower, and he kept hitting until she was all the way down on the floor—completely prone.

Then he strangled her. Used a piece of rope. He did it out of mercy. It was a mercy killing. She'd been mortally wounded when he bashed her head, and he just wanted to end her misery.

As he told his story, the investigators noted that his eyes were welling up with tears. Whether he was crying for Vivian or himself, they couldn't tell. He was breathing heavily and biting at the sores on his fingers.

"Why are you confessing today, Robert?"

"I want to go to jail. I was going to kill myself for what did. I took a bunch of pills, but they didn't take."

The investigators asked him when he took the pills, and he replied it had been not long after the murder.

The police heaved a sigh of relief. The last thing the needed was to have the confession interrupted by a medical emergency caused by a suicide attempt.

"Did you drink any alcohol or take any drugs today? Benjamin asked.

The suspect shook his head. Spahalski then said, " don't want Vivian's body to decompose in that basement. I'm sick. I don't think I've got much longer to live and I want this to be known."

His confession regarding Irizarry had taken about half hour.

Weather asked, "Is it okay if I record your statement i written form?"

Spahalski acted like it was a stupid question. "That what I've been waiting for!"

Detective Weather wrote Robert Spahalski's detailed admissions down on a police confession form. He began writing down the statement at 11:34 A.M. The top part of the form was fill-in-the-blank: *I, _____, am __ years old an reside at _____. Investigator/Officer _____ has explained me that I have the right to remain silent.* The confessor didn have to say anything if he didn't want to, and anything h did say could be used against him. He would agree to tal about this matter without a lawyer present. Spahalski confirmed that he knew that once he started, he could sto talking at any time. He agreed that he'd read the state ment of his rights (or he had it read to him) and wa willingly making the following statement. In the blank Weather wrote, *Robert Spahalski, 51*—this was an error, Spa halski was still a month shy of his fifty-first birthday—an Spahalski's address on Spencer Street. He crossed out th word "Officer" and wrote his own surname in the fina blank. There were ruled lines provided for the body of th confession. The confession was so long that it require three sheets.

Robert Spahalski's story began on Friday, Novembe 4, 2005, about 2:00 P.M. A very good friend of Spahalski' named Vivian Irizarry came to his house on Spencer Street. Vivian was also a friend of his girlfriend, Christine. Christine lived with him, but she wasn't home when Vivian came over. Christine worked at the Volunteers of America on Canal Street.

Vivian gave Spahalski some money and he went and bought some crack cocaine. When he returned, he and Vivian smoked it—about $100 worth of crack.

"I was in the kitchen and she was standing in the pantry," Spahalski said.

They talked about smoking the last bag. Spahalski walked into the pantry to where Vivian was. The woman had a knife in her hand. She was cutting the small Baggie open, and all of a sudden, according to Spahalski, he began to hallucinate from the effects of the drugs. He saw Vivian as a "demon."

"I flipped out," Spahalski said. "It must have been a combination of the crack and some mental problems I have."

Detective Weather wrote fast, and his handwriting showed it. But he got the job done, capturing all of the details of Spahalski's murder scenario on the written confession form.

Spahalski had picked up something in the pantry—he couldn't remember what it was. What he did remember was he hit her over the head with the object, at least three times.

Vivian fell onto the ground. She lay there for a while, maybe an hour or so. Spahalski started to come down from the cocaine and began to realize what had happened.

He saw that Vivian was badly wounded and had soiled herself. Spahalski's phrase was she "shit herself." He then added that out of respect for her, he took off all her clothing and washed her. He threw her clothes away.

Vivian was still alive but having trouble breathing and having convulsions. He picked her up and brought her into his bedroom. He laid her on his bed.

"I couldn't bear to see her suffer like that, and I knew

she was mortally wounded," Spahalski said. "I have been around dying people before when I was in prison, and when I ran the streets. I could tell."

He went to the drawer in his dining room—he called it the junk drawer—and got out a piece of twine. He went back to the bedroom and tied it around Vivian's neck.

"I choked her out," he said. Spahalski claimed she died very quickly. He'd been merciful and had ended her suffering. He brought Vivian's body down into the basement and over into the far corner.

As he wrote, Weather was struck by Spahalski's coldness, by the matter-of-factness of his words.

Spahalski was alone with the body until Christine came home, about 4:45 P.M. Christine had just gotten paid, so Spahalski took the money and went out and bought a "bunch" of crack. He smoked and smoked.

He pretty much did nothing but smoke crack for the next couple of days, Spahalski claimed, and during that time, he never told anyone that he had killed a woman and stashed her body in the basement.

He was a haunted man. He visited Vivian's body a couple of times, and apologized to her remains. This went on until Sunday morning, November 6, when Spahalski woke up and felt just horrible.

He had to do something. He went down the stairs and into the basement to visit with Vivian one last time. He couldn't just leave her down there to rot. He had to do something while her body was in good condition.

"It was cool down there, and her body had not started to decompose," Spahalski said.

It was because of his bad feelings since killing Vivian that he walked to the police headquarters that Tuesday morning and confessed. He first talked to a couple of female cops and told them about the body in the basement.

Spahalski told the police officers how and why Vivian Irizarry's body was there. Investigator Weather, a cop Spahalski hadn't met before, asked him to come to the fourth floor with him and talk about what had happened.

"I would like to say that I am very, very sorry about what happened. I apologize," Spahalski said, and Weather wrote.

Robert noted once again that Vivian had been a very good friend of his. He was familiar with the legal system enough to understand his rights. He didn't want an attorney. He chose to plead guilty and do his time.

They gave the written statement to Spahalski to read, but he struggled because of the handwriting. The statement was read aloud to him.

"Is that what you said?" Weather asked.

Spahalski complimented Weather: "Good for you, you got everything right. You caught everything. You're very meticulous in your facts."

"Is there anything you'd like to add to the statement? Anything you want taken out?"

"Nope."

He was given a pen and shown where to sign. He scratched his signature onto each page of the document. As witnesses Weather and Benjamin also signed each page. It was twelve-twenty in the afternoon.

At about noon on Tuesday, Investigators Joseph Dominic and Tom Cassidy drove to Canal Street, where Spahalski's girlfriend, Christine Gonzalez, worked for the Volunteers of America. (The location was only a few hundred yards from where Damita Gibson had lived at the time of her murder.) They asked her to come with them to the Public Safety Building and she agreed.

"What's this about?"

"We'll tell you when we get there."

Once at the PSB, they informed her that her friend Vivian Irizarry was dead and that her boyfriend had just confessed to killing her. Vivian's body, they said, had been discovered in the basement of the building where Gonzalez lived. Vivian had been dead for a few days.

Though shaken, Christine agreed to cooperate with their investigation in any way she could. She signed a consent-to-search form, allowing police to look in the apartment she shared with Spahalski. It was 12:17 P.M.

"Do you want to be there when we search the place?"

"No, that's okay." It was the same response Spahalski had given. The less time spent in the same room with cops, the better.

"Will we need a key?"

"The door should be open."

"Did you pay rent on the apartment?"

"I live there. My boyfriend pays the rent."

"How long have you lived with him?"

"Twelve years. More than twelve years." Actually, it was more like fourteen.

She said they met in 1990 or 1991, something like that. Robert, known as Bruce, was living in a building on Lake Avenue; there were about fourteen units in the building. A Realtor allowed Bruce to be the building superintendent and collect the rent. When a new tenant moved in, Bruce collected the deposits, too.

When Christine moved into that building, Robert Bruce Spahalski was the first guy she met. He thought she was a real cutie-pie and liked the fact that she was a full-blooded Navajo Native American.

Both she and Bruce had back apartments, with back porches that overlooked the river gorge and had a beautiful panoramic view. She used to watch Bruce get on his ten-speed bike and disappear twenty or thirty times a day. At first, Christine didn't know what that was all about. Later she learned he was delivering drugs to "targeted clients who liked to smoke crack." Bruce said he made $20 or $30 per run.

He kept his stash in a spot on the cliff that led down

to the gorge. She loved to watch him effortlessly climb the fence between the building and the cliff.

They started out as friends, had sex, then eventually moved in together in the same apartment as boyfriend and girlfriend. Over the years, she had to learn to be more and more tolerant when it came to Bruce. He had a strong crack addiction and it became king. Once, early on, he sold her $40 in food stamps for $20, and then he stole the food stamps back. He spent it all on crack. Eventually he had her smoking, too.

As Spahalski remembered it, Christine laughed when she learned about his food stamp scam. She smoked crack, he recalled, but it was never her favorite thing. She was a beer gal.

"You never saw her when she wasn't sipping at a forty-ounce magnum beer. She'd choose that over crack any day," he said.

With Christine, Robert Bruce Spahalski got his only adult taste of domestic bliss.

"Christine and I had the pure and exquisite delight of helping raise her daughter's three grandchildren. I met those little pests when they were about three, four, and five years old," he remembered. "They called me 'Uncle Boo-Boo,' because I had a Band-Aid on when they first met me, and the name stuck for the next twelve years. Christine would give her life for those kids, she loved them that much."

Robert said he took the grandkids fishing, swimming, biking, and exploring roadside junk for hidden treasures.

"The youngest one once found forty dollars on one of our treasure hunts," Robert said. "I stole it for my drug habit."

On the day of Robert's confession, the investigators took a deposition from Gonzalez and then offered her options as to what she could do next. She wouldn't be allowed back to her apartment right away, but she was welcome to stay at the police station. They could take her to a friend's house if she liked.

"I would rather just go back to work," Gonzalez said. So they took her back to the Volunteers of America, where she arrived at 1:40 P.M.

Christine Gonzalez never again saw or spoke to Robert Bruce Spahalski, her live-in companion of a dozen years.

According to Robert, "She wasn't in a position to help me, anyways. She had her own problems to contend with—with the reporters and the news people. Christine is very private in nature and probably hates my guts for murdering her best friend."

In the conference room on the fourth floor, Robert was offered food, but he said he wasn't hungry. He was photographed and fingerprinted. At least an attempt was made to record his fingerprints. He didn't appear to have any. His fingertips were all scar tissue. Afterward, he was returned to the conference room for further questioning.

"Is there more?" Weather asked.

"Yeah, there's more," Spahalski said.

Perhaps already contemplating an insanity defense, Spahalski claimed once again that among the mental problems with which he had to battle was post-traumatic stress disorder. As had been the case when he was smoking crack with Vivian, he sometimes suffered from strong hallucinations, a complete loss of reality.

Earlier he'd said that he knew what death looked like because he'd been around dying people before. Now he elaborated. Vivian was not the first person he'd killed.

The investigators were all ears. They knew that there was one murder case, a case in Webster, in which Robert Bruce Spahalski had been deeply involved, a "person of interest," to say the least.

Knowing that there was more to get out of the man, Weather decided that the Webster case was the best place to start.

"Tell us about the murder in Webster?" Weather asked.

"I don't want to talk about that guy," Spahalski said, shaking his head.

"Why not?"

"It's that guy's family. They been hard on me. They f***in' stalk me. They're all angry and shit."

"All right. Why don't we take a break and let you think about it for a while."

The investigators left Spahalski alone for forty-five minutes while they looked up the case. He wanted to make sure he asked the right questions.

During the break, the interrogating investigators spoke with Sergeant Mariano and told him what Spahalski had said about Charles Grande's family.

Mariano suggested "that we tell Spahalski that we had located and talked to the Grande family. Further, I mentioned that it might help if we tell him that the family now only wanted to know what really happened and that they would pray for him and harbored no more anger as long as they knew the truth." He chronicled this in his report.

Investigators Benjamin and Weather thought that was a good idea, and when they reentered the conference room, which was blue from Spahalski's chain-smoking, they spoke to him just as Sergeant Mariano had suggested. The tactic worked.

Spahalski once again talked, starting at the beginning.

"I ran an escort service in the 1990s. Gay and straight. I was running it by myself," Spahalski confessed. "I had many customers."

"You turned out the ladies?"

"Yes."

"And turned tricks yourself?"

"Yes. Both."

Spahalski may have used the line about the family praying for him as a catalyst to unburden, but his sadism was intrinsic. He still planned to spin a yarn that hurt the Grandes the most.

He flashed back to the fall of 1991. He was walking the streets at the time of the Webster kill. The man Grande was a regular.

"When you say 'regular,' what do you mean by that?"

"He'd picked me up before."

"How many times?"

"I think this was the third time."

"Okay, go ahead."

Grande was crazy about him, the killer claimed. Completely smitten. Now Grande wanted him to move in upstairs. In his house. Be his boyfriend.

On the fateful night, Spahalski said, Grande picked him up at his usual spot in downtown Rochester, on State Street, and drove to his home. Spahalski forgot the name of the road it was on, but he remembered it was in Webster.

"Did you have sex?"

"Yes. Oral sex," Spahalski said.

He killed Grande with a hammer and left his body nude. He hadn't thought about it ahead of time. It wasn't part of any scheme or plot or anything like that. He just did it. He got mad and he did it. The hammer was simply handy.

"Why were you mad?"

"He said he would pay me sixty dollars. Then, after, he only paid me forty. I wanted the rest," Spahalski said.

Grande refused to pay the $20. Spahalski had kept his end of the bargain, but Grande was going to renege on him. It wasn't right. They argued, and while they were yelling, Grande punched Spahalski. That was when the male prostitute saw red, and, quoting one police report, "violence ensued."

The investigators noticed but chose to ignore the inconsistencies in his story. If Grande had truly had emotional feelings for Spahalski, and had genuinely wanted him to cohabitate, then he was worth far more to Spahalski than a stinking $20.

If Spahalski's confession was to be taken at face value, Grande was like an ATM for Spahalski. Why kill him?

He wouldn't have actually moved to Webster, of course, to live with the man. That would have taken him too far from his drug dealers. Everyplace Spahalski had ever lived in Rochester was within walking distance of his crack supply.

But he certainly would have strung Grande along for a periodic touch when the crack kitty went dry.

"I killed him for twenty dollars," he said.

He was that stupid.

The confession continued: No, Grande wasn't his enemy, Spahalski said. He didn't hate him. He kind of liked him. He'd been a regular customer, after all. This was the *third* time Grande had solicited his services, he repeated.

The first two times, Grande had paid the amount he had agreed to pay. No problem. He promptly spent the money on drugs. This time Grande tried to shortchange him. Wasn't right. He didn't know why he snapped. He was high. He was always high when he got violent. Crack always brought out that part of him, that nasty part deep inside, which couldn't help it. *Gotta kill.*

He grabbed a hammer in the bedroom, waited until Grande had his back turned, and smashed Grande's head until Grande got that faraway look; then Spahalski knew the job was done.

With Grande dead, his head bashed in, Spahalski thought like a crime scene investigator. He found a blanket and used it to cover up the body. He turned the thermostat all the way up to speed up the decomposition process, making it harder for police to figure out what happened.

Spahalski admitted that he rifled through the house,

finding and pocketing several hundreds of dollars in cash. Leaving the house, he stole Grande's car and left the scene.

He often thought of the stench that must have been created when he kept the furnace on in the house, allowing his victim to rot faster. (That was why he had moved Irizarry to the coolest, yet private, spot he could think of before he abandoned her corpse, he told his RPD interrogators. With Irizarry, he'd done the *opposite* of turning up the thermostat. He wanted to slow down the decomposition process. Irizarry was pretty, so he wanted to make sure she left a pretty corpse.)

After killing Grande, Spahalski stole his victim's car and cruised around. "I picked up a black hooker," he said, "and we smoked some crack."

He was stopped by police while driving Grande's car. Spahalski told his interrogators how he successfully identified himself as Grande, even though he was a good five inches taller than the description on Grande's driver's license. As Weather and Benjamin already knew, sheriff's deputies eventually got wise to his deception, but they couldn't make charges of criminal impersonation stick.

Thinking about his trial for criminal impersonation must've made Spahalski recall that occasion outside the courtroom when Grande's brother—an intense dude— got nasty with him.

Spahalski told the investigators that he felt terrible about killing Charles Grande. Perhaps recalling what he had been told about Grande's family praying for him, Spahalski added, "I pray for him every day. I'd like an opportunity to apologize to his family."

The interrogation again paused. Notes taken during his statement admitting to killing Charles Grande were transcribed and typed. The result was a four-page document. Spahalski was read its contents and insisted on two small changes before he signed.

With pen in hand, he said, "I knew that coming forward

was the best thing to do. I settled all of my past business today and want to put it all behind me."

Weather said, "Are you hungry?"

"Yes, I guess I am."

"What would you like?"

"Could I have a cheeseburger?"

"Sure," Weather said, and Spahalski was given something to eat.

Robert was hesitant to confess to anything more. He believed more than two kills would classify him as a serial killer, and he did not want to be put in that category.

During the break, the investigation into Robert's known victims was in high gear. Police learned that Irizarry had lived on Norton Street. At least that was the most recently listed address. Norton Street ran across the northeast portion of Rochester. That was where the old ballpark was, Silver Stadium, the one Chuck Grande frequented before they tore it down and built a new one downtown called Frontier Field, in 1996. Vivian was not an Edgerton local. She lived four or five miles away.

As the interrogation of Robert Bruce Spahalski continued in the PSB, investigators in the field discovered that Vivian Irizarry had worked for the Center for Disability Rights (CDR), an organization that helped take care of disabled people stranded in Rochester's inner city.

Why stop at two confessions? The investigators went for more. But the initially bold Spahalski was now antsy when it came to getting things off his chest. He hated that term "serial killer." He didn't want to be known as one of those. It didn't apply to him, he said.

Was he *absolutely sure*, however, that he'd only killed two people in his life? In his whole life? That's a lot of life.

He wasn't sure. He said he might have killed some people over the course of time. He was a fifty-year-old man. He'd been around for a while. But that still didn't mean he was a serial killer. He wasn't like one of those freaks on TV with signatures and MOs and stuff like that.

He *might* have killed; in fact, he might have killed *more than once*—but it sure as hell wasn't because he thought it was fun. He always felt like he had to. Something inside of him pulled taut, then snapped—and he lost all control of himself.

The situations were all different. Different things made him feel like he had to kill, and when he had to, he did. It was as simple as that. There was nothing "serial" about it. He wanted to make that clear.

He said to the police, "I don't want you to think I go around killing people."

The investigators explained that they understood he wasn't a serial killer. They weren't trying to pin that tag on him. They just had to clear some things up. Get as many cases as possible off the books. That was their job. Robert Spahalski said he understood.

They took another break. This time they prepared to ask him questions about Moraine Armstrong, the woman who lived across the street from him. That was the case during which Investigator Tony Campione found Robert Bruce Spahalski to be a neighbor who was just a little too curious.

Detective Weather began the next phase of the interrogation. "Tell me about Moraine Armstrong."

Spahalski gave an unexpected response: "Was that the woman who lived on Emerson Street?"

Weather took the cue and immediately shifted gears. "No, but tell me who you are talking about."

"Oh yeah, her name was Adrian," Spahalski said. He should have known her name. He had been described by Adrian's parents at one point as Adrian's "no-good" boyfriend.

For the first time, police knew for sure that Adrian

Berger had been murdered. She was the victim whose body, killed during a historic heat wave, was too far gone when discovered for the medical examiner to determine what had happened to her.

The interrogators took a quick break to look up any files they had on Berger. They discovered that they had talked to Spahalski in connection with the suspicious death, had brought him in and grilled him.

At the time, Robert steadfastly maintained that he didn't know what had happened to Adrian, so they had to cut him loose. Now the man was singing a different tune.

Weather and Benjamin had three confessions down, and they hadn't even had a chance to question him about Moraine Armstrong yet. The dialogue between the investigators and the suspect might *read* rapid-fire, but it was played out slowly, with Weather taking copious notes, getting as much of Spahalski's confession verbatim as possible.

"Tell us what happened with Adrian."

"We were having sex and I started choking her."

"Why?"

"I don't know. I snapped. We were on the couch in the living room. We began to mess around."

"Sexually?"

"Yeah. She took off her pants and her panties and I took off all of my clothes and I was rubbing my penis on her. I got a hard-on, and all of a sudden, I snapped."

"What made you snap?"

"I don't know what happened. It's a mental problem I have. I started choking Adrian. I put my hands around her neck and squoze her tightly."

"How long did you squeeze her neck?"

"A long time. Five minutes."

"She struggled?"

"She tried to, but I had her pinned down pretty good. She didn't want to die. I choked her until I noticed the yellow pinpricks in her eyes. Then I knew she was dead. Then I stole her car."

"For transportation?"

"No, just to make it look like she wasn't home," Spahalski explained.

"Do you get more sexually aroused when you are high on crack?"

"Yeah, I do."

"Did you ejaculate in Adrian?"

"Yes."

"Did you kill her before or after you ejaculated?"

"After."

"Did you use a condom?"

"No."

"Did you ever use a condom?"

"No."

That last question might seem extraneous, but it wasn't. An HIV-positive man who engaged in sex without a condom could be charged with reckless endangerment.

Spahalski told the investigators that after killing Adrian Berger, he made sure all of the windows were closed. It was summer, the dog days. He knew that her body was going to cook in there, grow bloated, and possibly explode into cat food.

Visions of this decomposition process had haunted his mind in the years since he killed Adrian Berger. He was haunted by the killer inside him. He became a living embodiment of the narrator of Poe's "The Tell-Tale Heart."

Killing Adrian was one thing—sometimes that happened when he lost it. However, causing such a despicable thing to happen to her corpse was something else.

It was the same thing with Vivian years later. He couldn't stand the idea of insect activity, of Vivian Irizarry's body decomposing that way.

That was the whole reason he was turning himself in. He couldn't stand the thought of his friend decaying.

e'd taken a lovely human being and turned her into a
ience project.

Spahalski needed to call a halt to the whole process so
at the medical examiner would rescue Vivian's body
d save her from the truly gross fate of Adrian's remains.

A third written statement was prepared by Weather
om the notes he'd taken during the interview. Spahal-
i confessed that sometime in June or July of 1991
hile he was living in an apartment building on Lake
venue he befriended a girl named Adrian Berger, who
ved not far away on Emerson Street. They were both
iends and sex partners. "I'm bisexual and I was dating
man at the time also. I saw Adrian almost every day and
e got along well," Spahalski confessed.

Then the whole thing went bad. One night, during
e especially hot summer of 1991, sometime around
ight or so, he went over to Adrian's house. They started
oling around in her living room.

She took off her pants and underwear, but she left her
irt on. Spahalski responded by getting buck naked. He
as in the mood to be nude. Adrian sat on the couch
d he sat on top of her, straddling her.

"I began to run my penis against her and became sex-
ally excited," Spahalski said.

And that was when it happened. *Snap!* He didn't know
hy. It just happened. It was a mental problem he had.
e was a split personality or some such.

"I started choking Adrian. I had my hands around her
eck and I squoze her tightly," he said.

Spahalski noted that this kill was not a physically chal-
nging one. Adrian didn't fight back. He had her arms
inned down to her sides with his legs. Not that it was a
uick kill, just not a tough one.

He controlled her quickly, but it still took maybe four
r five minutes before she suffocated. She stopped

breathing. Her eyes were open and dull-looking. The
was no light in those eyes.

When Spahalski realized what he had done, he pulle
Adrian from the couch and brought her to the bedroo
and laid her down on the floor in front of the bed.

Spahalski wasn't sure why he did that or what he w
thinking. He did recall taking the keys to Adrian's c
from atop her dresser, getting dressed, and then leavin
He drove her white Mercury to Ravine Avenue.

"I pulled over and wiped the car down with some t
sues Adrian had," he said.

Spahalski figured if he moved the car, people wou
think Adrian was not at home, and that would buy hi
some time to work his way back to the neighborhoc
and remove suspicion from himself.

The police eventually picked him up and questione
him. He knew the secret was to play dumb. Give them
big shrug of the shoulders, tell them he knew nothing

Getting back to the murder itself, Spahalski reiterate
that he was sorry about killing Adrian, that he'd ju
snapped. He knew what he did was wrong. He unde
stood his rights and wanted to confess. He didn't need
lawyer because he planned only to plead guilty and pa
his debt to society. He said he felt like a condemne
man, anyway, even when he was on the streets.

"I just want to get this off my chest," Spahalski conclude

The written version of his confession was read alou
Robert signed it; Weather and Benjamin witnessed it.
was 4:48 P.M.

At this point, Investigators Weather and Benjami
were relieved as interrogators by Investigators Tom Ca
sidy and Joseph Dominic, the same pair who had earlie
picked up and questioned Spahalski's girlfriend.

When the interrogation of Spahalski continued, th
new pair of investigators picked up where Weather an

Benjamin had left off, trying to get Spahalski to confess to killing Moraine Armstrong.

They figured him to be a good fit for that murder because of proximity alone. Armstrong had lived directly across the street from Spahalski, on the other side of Lake Avenue. Tony Campione had seen him there, nosing around.

But again Spahalski hesitated. It wasn't the family this time. It was his legacy. The body count was growing, and Spahalski still didn't want to be known as a serial killer.

In history, in prison, he feared that kind of notoriety.

As it turned out, his attempts to avoid the label were in vain. His murders might have seemed very different to him, but to observers, the connections seemed clear. Sex, crack, money. Common denominators.

Sex, crack, and money comprised Spahalski's entire life. Nothing else could have caused the murders because there *wasn't* anything else. Sex to make money, money to buy crack, repeat until fade.

Cassidy and Dominic again allowed Spahalski to sit alone for an hour or two to think about it before they resumed questioning. During the break, all four of the questioners put their heads together. Weather noted to the others that Spahalski had been in there for hours, had confessed to three murders, and still hadn't asked for a lawyer to be present. That was a good sign.

The interrogators spoke to Tony Campione, who had retired from the force to run a restaurant, and Campione filled them in on the details outside the Armstrong crime scene.

When they reentered the interrogation room, they tried a different tact. Spahalski's remorse seemed focused exclusively on the decomposition of the bodies of his victims. Still, the fact that he could feel remorse was encouraging. He was eager to apologize to the Grandes, but he was afraid of them. Maybe . . . probably it was an act—but maybe there was a conscience in there somewhere, and they decided to work on it. They told Spahalski to think about the families of his victims and how much they needed to know the truth, how much they needed closure.

They showed him a photo of Armstrong's corpse.

"We got a case at Lake Avenue, a woman strangled. It's a lot like the Vivian case, Robert. Here, take a look."

The investigators placed photos of the Moraine Armstrong crime scene in front of the suspect.

"You know that woman?"

"No," Spahalski said, but he kept looking at the photos. "Yup, that's how they look when they go out."

"What did you just say? Could you repeat that?"

"I said, this is what they look like when they go out."

"What do you mean by that?"

"I mean, that's the way they look when they been strangled."

"Did you do that, Robert?"

"If I did, I don't remember."

Still, he didn't look away. Spahalski put his finger on one of the photographs and left it there, tapping a couple of times. It was a photo of Moraine Armstrong taken at the morgue.

"This photo," he said.

"What about it?"

"It looks familiar. It looks very familiar."

They showed him another photo, this one of Moraine when she was alive, standing on the street with two other people. Again the suspect used his finger. "That's her right there," he said.

Spahalski was suddenly more nervous, and got up to pace around the conference room. "Is it all right if I do this?" Spahalski asked.

"Sure, Robert. Pace all you want. Whatever you need to do in order to do the *right thing*."

"Okay, thanks. I remember better when I pace."

"You got to admit, Robert—Vivian, Adrian, Moraine. They were pretty similar kills, huh?"

"Yeah," the suspect agreed. "Similar."

"Is there a chance you killed her?"

"Yes. I may have. I don't remember. I, you know, I lock away bad memories in my brain."

"How big of a chance you killed her?"

"About fifty percent."

"We were looking through the case files for Moraine and we noticed that police talked to you. You lived across the street and were hanging around, watching the police work. You remember that?"

"No."

While Dominic was asking questions, Cassidy placed on the table a composite drawing, drawn from information supplied by witnesses outside Moraine Armstrong's Lake Avenue apartment building. The investigators didn't need to ask the suspect about the drawing.

"Hey, that looks a lot like me, huh?" Spahalski said.

The resemblance, in fact, was not apparent, but the investigators didn't offer their actual opinion.

"Spittin' image," they said.

"You know, I'm trying to remember, but I'm having a hard time."

"What's the problem?"

"That was a long time ago. I was just getting heavily into drugs at that time."

"What else you remember about that time in your life?"

"I remember I did a bank robbery. At Westgate Plaza. Late 1990, early 1991, something like that. I can tell you about that. I know the statute of limitations has run out on that one. I need my medications."

"Okay, we'll get them for you."

Lieutenant Michael Wood requested that a search warrant be drawn up for the downstairs apartment on Spencer Street. City court judge Stephen K. Lindley reviewed the application and signed the warrant. Members of the Major

Crimes Unit and Technicians Unit executed the search warrant at 4:40 P.M. Before starting their search, the house was cleared to make sure there were no other people present. Photos were taken of every room, and Robert and Christine's apartment was thoroughly searched.

While the prisoner remained on the fourth floor of the PSB, investigators Cassidy and Dominic took a quick ride over to pick up the suspect's medication. While they were there, they decided to see what they could see.

It turned out that Spahalski had prescription medications spread out all over the apartment. Some were in the kitchen on top of the refrigerator, another in his top dresser drawer, and one on the nightstand next to the bed. All in all, seven vials of medication were found:

Gabapentin, 800 mg., one pill to be taken four times daily. This drug was originally developed to treat epilepsy, but it was also prescribed for neuropathic pain relief. Spahalski told police that he took this drug for his mental problems.

Ibuprofen, 400 mg., one or two pills to be taken four times daily. It is a common analgesic.

Crixivan, 400 mg., two pills to be taken every four hours. An anti-HIV medication, it decreases the amount of HIV in the body.

Zerit, 40 mg., one pill to be taken twice a day. It prevents HIV from mutating the body's healthy T cells.

Ziagen, 300 mg., one pill to be taken twice a day. It is similar in purpose to Zerit.

Gabapentin, 600 mg., one pill to be taken four times daily. It is the same as the prior Gabapentin, but in a smaller dosage.

Ibuprofen, 800 mg., one pill to be taken three times daily. It is a common analgesic in prescription-only strength. Spahalski had two versions.

Also found on top of the refrigerator was a bottle of multiple vitamins. The pills were gathered up by Dominic and Cassidy, who helped with the search momentarily.

The search of Spahalski's apartment yielded other results as well. On a shelf under a window in the living room were several pieces of mail. There was a written prescription, a bill from Rochester Gas & Electric, a bank statement from the U.S. Department of the Interior, and a pay stub from the Volunteers of America. These were all in the name of Christine Gonzalez, Spahalski's live-in girlfriend.

There was also a Time Warner Cable bill, a letter from Attica Correctional Facility from Robert's twin, Stephen, and a collections letter from the Mercantile Adjustment Bureau, all in Spahalski's name.

The district attorney's office would later want to introduce the letter from Stephen to his twin as evidence—as it was full of what they described as "bizarre ramblings"—but failed to prove its relevance.

According to the police report, signed by Sergeant Mark Mariano, these items were collected to *show ownership, dominion, and control of the apartment and were turned into the property clerk's office as evidence.*

There was blood evidence found in the apartment that Spahalski and Gonzalez shared, but it wasn't in the pantry, where Spahalski said it would be. It was in the hallway, where the body was dragged toward the basement stairs. That was just the initial eyeball search. Later when the technicians went over the place with their special lights and chemicals, further blood evidence would be discovered.

Dominic searched the bathroom hamper and found several items of clothing that he felt might be pertinent to the murder. He found a set of clothes for a male— a shirt, jeans, and socks—that appeared to have blood on them. There was also what appeared to be blood on the bedsheets.

Cassidy and Dominic didn't stay in the apartment long. Spahalski needed his pills, and his pills he would have. They returned to the PSB and rejoined the suspect on the fourth floor.

Before taking the pills, Spahalski ran through what each pill was and why he took it. Some of the pills were to treat his mental illness and others were because he was HIV positive. The investigators carefully monitored Spahalski's pill intake. They didn't want any spur-of-the-moment suicide attempts. Once the pills were taken in their proper quantity, Dominic and Cassidy got back to the crux of the matter: the Moraine Armstrong murder.

"Think about this woman's family. The heartache. You can help them heal now by telling us what happened. You can help give them closure."

Spahalski replied, "I might be able to help you better if you left me alone for a few minutes. You know, to meditate."

The detectives again left him alone, this time for a shorter break, fifteen minutes only. When they returned, Spahalski asked them if, by any chance, an electrical appliance had been involved in the killing.

They said yes, one had.

"I killed her. I killed Marissa," he said, getting Moraine's name wrong. Detectives asked how it had come down. Spahalski said, "She got stupid and I choked her out, that's all."

"Were you high?"

"Yes."

"How high?"

"I brought some crack and we smoked it together."

"How much?"

"One hundred dollars' worth. We got into an argument over money. She said I owed her money for sex."

He hadn't meant to kill her. He never meant to kill anyone. These things just happened. These things just kept happening. It was like a mental defect he had. A spot in his brain was messed up. The wiring had been put in wrong.

Spahalski's fourth confession was put in written form. He told the investigators about how, during the winter of 1990, he met this girl named Marissa, a black hooker. He was either living on Phelps Avenue or Lake Avenue at the time. He didn't remember. He befriended Marissa. They were crack-smoking buddies. She lived in the apartment building right across the street from him. She lived in the downstairs apartment. He usually went to her place, and they smoked crack sometimes.

That was their relationship that holiday season, with New Year's Day approaching. He could see her standing on the other side of the street, wearing a goldish brown African-type outfit. He went over to her and asked her if she wanted to get high and "trick" with him. She said all right and invited him into her apartment. They sat on her couch in the living-room area and smoked the crack.

"I had about ten bags, and it took us a couple of hours to get through it," Spahalski said.

After smoking all of the crack, Spahalski confessed, he and the girl went into her bedroom and had sex. After they finished, she demanded money for the sex. He told her they'd just smoked up about $100 worth of his dope. He wasn't about to give her any money.

With that, "she started getting really loud and stupid," and told him he couldn't leave until he'd forked over the cash. When he started to get up, she slapped him across the face. She told him again: he was going nowhere.

Getting slapped in the face was enough to tip Spahalski over the edge. "I grabbed her, threw her on the bed, and started choking her with my hands," Spahalski confessed.

He grabbed something with a cord—he didn't remember what—and started using that on her. He then grabbed an iron, with a long, dark cord attached to it, and wrapped that second cord around her neck.

Killing this girl had been a bit of a workout for Spahalski.

He had quite a size advantage on her, of course, but she realized that her life was on the line and she fought. She fought hard, and she didn't stop fighting until she couldn't anymore. It took him a couple of minutes to strangle her. When she stopped breathing, and her eyes stayed open, he knew she was dead. Spahalski got dressed and went home.

He wanted to make his motives clear. The reason this happened was because Marissa was threatening him and he wanted to leave. He was sorry that it had happened.

The written confession ended with a statement that Spahalski understood his rights, wanted to confess, and didn't want a lawyer. He wasn't interested in having this case brought to trial.

The written statement concluded: *I'm trying to "wipe the slate clean" with the things I have done in the past.*

It was 10:25 P.M. when he took a pen in a bony and scabby hand—the knuckles stained deep yellow, almost orange, by nicotine—and nervously scratched his signature at the bottom of the written confession.

Robert Bruce Spahalski was exhausted, and the throes of crack withdrawal were just about upon him. The investigators knew there were more murders to question him about. The Hortense Greatheart case was particularly intriguing.

They started in, but Robert waved them off. No more, he said. There would be no more confessing that day.

One last question: why was he coming forward now?

"I knew that coming forward is the best thing to do," he said. "I settled all of my past business today and want to put it all behind me."

Confession time was over.

Backing up a few hours, at about 6:30 P.M., on November 8, 2005, Sergeant Mariano, having completed his interview with Spahalski's landlord, returned to the Public

Safety Building, where he was informed of the progress in Spahalski's confession. It was a big day, with multiple murders being cleared off the books.

Mariano had only been there a few minutes when he was told that there was a guy named Miguel Pitre downstairs who said he was Vivian Irizarry's boyfriend. He said he wanted to speak to someone from homicide.

"I got him," Mariano said.

Mariano took the man's name and address, which was on Norton Street, the same as Vivian Irizarry's address. Pitre told Mariano that he was concerned about Vivian. She had not contacted him since Friday, when she went to visit her friend Christine on Spencer Street. Her son drove her over. Then Pitre saw on the news that there was a murder at that address, and he had a terrible feeling that something horrible had happened to his girlfriend.

Mariano confirmed his worst fears and told him Vivian Irizarry was dead. Pitre was distraught. He tried to offer the policeman background information on the victim, but he kept breaking down. Mariano gave the man his card and said that he should give him a call and be interviewed when he felt better. Pitre said that he wanted to be the one to tell Irizarry's family the bad news, so Mariano arranged for Officer Boily to drive Pitre to the house on Steko Street, where Irizarry's family lived.

Why had Robert Bruce Spahalski turned himself in? Was it really because Vivian Irizarry had touched his heart, as he claimed. Experts have said this was not likely, for the simple reason that Spahalski didn't have the capacity to feel sympathy.

Was it because he had lost his head and killed someone in his own home? He wasn't going to tap-dance around this one. He only had two choices. He could turn himself in or flee.

Why not flee? Well, for one thing, he was a sick man. HIV positive, he was going to need continued medical treatment, something he was not going to receive if he was on the lam.

Years later, Robert claimed he didn't remember much about his confession. "I was a slobbering psycho-mental mess," said Robert. He didn't recall telling police that he was suffering from post-traumatic stress disorder, but it wasn't a lie.

"When I was in prison, I was racially raped by three gang members that held me down and sodomized me while moving into my new cell. That is a lifelong traumatic experience, which never seems to go away," Robert explained.

Robert Bruce Spahalski was ordered held at the Monroe County Jail without bail. His shoes were confiscated as potential evidence. He complained of being chilly, without a jacket and in his stocking feet. Since Spahalski now needed something to put on his feet, Officer J. C. Hall was dispatched to Spencer Street to pick up a pair of boots. Hall spoke to Christine Gonzalez, who had been allowed back in the apartment, and she handed over the boots, along with a green jacket. Hall turned the jacket and boots over to Investigator Benjamin, who gave them to the suspect.

Spahalski's mug shot was snapped, capturing something vampiric, a ghost of a man—lids heavy, lips dry and parted. He was led into a cell, and the door slammed shut behind him. He would—initially, at least—be charged with only two murders, Irizarry and Grande. He wasn't going anywhere, and there was plenty of time to charge him with the Berger and Armstrong homicides after police, the DA's office, and a grand jury had an opportunity to investigate those cases more closely.

Initial press releases regarding the arrest said Spahalski had been charged with two murders and was "implicated" in two others. That led to newspaper headlines such as SPAHALSKI: HOW MANY VICTIMS?

One of the investigation's focal points had to be determining how many people Spahalski had murdered. They had plenty of victims to choose from, but Spahalski wasn't the only killer working that neighborhood, so they would have to be careful not to presume.

Which two victims were Spahalski's responsibility was an open question. At that time, there were four possibilities: Vicki Jobson, Adrian Berger, Moraine Armstrong, and Hortense Greatheart.

Greatheart was the best fit. She died in a building in which Spahalski had lived, her body was left in the spot where she had died, and—here was the clincher—the thermostat was turned all the way up, just as it had been in Charles Grande's house following his murder.

Following Robert Spahalski's confession, police told the public little. Privately, investigators were telling reporters that they were working to separate "fact from speculation" when it came to which crimes Robert did or didn't commit.

Investigator Glenn Weather later described the many hours he spent with Spahalski in the interrogation room. There was a chance, he said, that something about Vivian Irizarry had actually touched Robert's heart, if he indeed had a heart.

But that couldn't be said for the other three murders to which he had confessed.

Spahalski knew that he was supposed to feel sorry. But did he understand what sorry felt like? It wasn't clear. Perhaps he was mimicking the way others acted when they felt remorse.

He would, for example, say one moment how sorry he was that he'd killed Chuck Grande, and the next moment, he would debase his victim by claiming he tried to shortchange him after a sex act.

That was not the way genuine remorse worked, but

perhaps Spahalski was not a keen enough observer of human behavior to realize that. In his world, no doubt, being shortchanged after a sex act was a reasonable motive for murder. He was unaware that a person with a functioning conscience wouldn't see it that way.

He wanted the investigators to think that his victims were as bad as he, so that their deaths seemed like no great loss to society. It not only didn't work, it horrified Glenn Weather.

The guy was missing something that other human beings had. Weather tended to believe that the contrast between the killer and his victims, the contrast between evil and good, was much stronger than Spahalski was willing to admit. These were cold-blooded sex crimes. Spahalski mischaracterized his crimes, Weather was certain—but how? Maybe some of the deaths amounted to a pimp punishing women he saw as property. Maybe the Webster kill was a flat-out robbery.

The press sought in vain for Spahalski relatives who were willing to give them some insight into what made Robert tick. They found one brother, but he was openly hostile to the press. He not only wouldn't answer questions but screamed that reporters were making his life a "living hell."

Other than Robert's twin brother, Stephen, who resided in the Attica Correctional Facility, the only relative the press managed to get info from was a cousin named Stanley Spahalski, who lived in Erie, Pennsylvania, and had lost touch with the family. He said he thought one of the twins had died years before.

By the time Spahalski confessed, Tony Campione, Robert's archenemy from the Armstrong, Grande, and Berger cases, was retired. Since 2004, Campione was running a café with his fiancée, Evelyn Baez, also retired, the first female homicide investigator in RPD history, and the first Hispanic woman to become an investigator in any unit.

When they retire, some police officers get a job as a private investigator or in security or something like that. Not Campione. He was done. It was time to do something different before he really burned out.

Running a restaurant had been a dream of his for years. It was in his blood. His mom was a cook and had for years run the kitchens for the city school district. His dad was a caterer. As a kid, he'd worked at D'Andrea's Restaurant on Maple Street in the old Dutchtown neighborhood.

He'd always had it in the back of his head that he wanted to get back into cooking. When it came time to curtail his career as a cop, he kept his eyes and ears open for an opportunity. He was offered a job as an investigator with the DA's office and said thanks, but no thanks.

Campione didn't have to wait long for opportunity to knock. He and his old partner were having breakfast at a nice place off East Avenue, just the sort of place he'd always dreamed about. The place could maybe use a few extra square feet for seating, but it catered to the busy downtown lunch crowd, so the majority of the orders would be takeout, anyway.

His partner told him he knew the owner, Dan, and that he was looking to sell the place.

"You're shittin' me," Campione said with a grin.

And so, in 2004, twelve days before he retired as a cop, he and fiancée Baez bought the place, the Center Stage Café on Gibbs Street, inside the vee formed by East Main Street and East Avenue. It was a seamless transition into the next phase of his life.

Then came the day he got a call at the café from one of his old partners, who said, "Hear the news? Spahalski just walked in and confessed to killing some girl on Spencer Street."

Campione said make sure they ask him about the others: Armstrong, Berger, Grande, Greatheart.

Hours later the ex-partner called back. Spahalski had copped to three out of four. Not bad.

"I have no idea what tripped this guy to give himself up," Campione said in 2009. "I'd been with him on two extensive interviews, and we'd bantered back and forth on the street, and he seemed determined. What made him give up, I don't know."

With the initial interrogation of Spahalski complete, police did a background check on his final victim. Vivian Irizarry was born on October 3, 1951, as Vivian Rivera in Rochester, where she attended Benjamin Franklin High School on Norton Street.

She was in the Class of 1969 at the huge city high school, but she hadn't graduated. Instead, she left school and was married during what would have been her senior year.

With her new husband, Vivian moved to Cleveland to be near his family. She worked in Ohio as a home detention officer, supervising troubled teenagers.

The couple eventually divorced, and Vivian returned to Rochester. Keeping her married name, she made a living as a caretaker for her elderly uncle. She was also a home health aide for the Center for Disability Rights.

One of the persons Irizarry cared for was sixty-nine-year-old Helen Miller, who lived on Lake Avenue. She said that Irizarry came to visit twice a week to clean house, help cook, run errands, and helped her do her chores.

"She was a very pleasant person, very nice. Everyone liked her. My whole family liked her. She was so full of life," Miller recalled.

Irizarry still lived on Norton Street at the time she died, with her boyfriend, Miguel Pitre. She'd been close friends with her cousin Christine Gonzalez, who happened to be Spahalski's girlfriend.

According to Irizarry's youngest son, eighteen-year-old Carlos Rodriguez, his mom spent a lot of her leisure time, especially on weekends, with Gonzalez.

"She was always there," Carlos emphasized.

An older son, Harry Irizarry Jr., lived in Texas. A former marine, he said that he'd asked his mother to come south and live with him, but she said she preferred to stay put, that she was happy in Rochester.

Harry said that his mother was the peacekeeper in the family, and, like most families, a peacekeeper was regularly required. She was also the problem solver and arbiter of familial disputes.

"She would be the one to call when I had a problem. She wouldn't hurt anyone," Harry said. "She taught me at an early age how to behave, cook, and clean. When I was in the marines, my senior drill instructor at boot camp complimented my mother when she came to visit.

"He told my mother that she did a great job raising me," Harry said.

Vivian had another son, Samuel Santiago, of Rochester. And both of her parents, Carlos and Julia Rivera, of Rochester, were still living, as were all of her brothers and sisters.

The wake for Vivian Irizarry was held on Friday, November 11, 2005, at the Falvo Funeral Home on North Goodman Street, and she was buried the next day in Riverside Cemetery.

11

Another Name Added to the List of Possibles

Two days after the confession, the name of 1991 homicide victim Damita Gibson was added to the list of possibles when the victim's mother, Ethel Dix, came forward and identified Robert Bruce Spahalski as a man she had seen with her daughter shortly before Damita's disappearance.

"I recognized him when I saw his picture in the newspaper and on the TV news on Wednesday," Dix said to a *Democrat and Chronicle* reporter. "I saw that face and said, 'This man has been around before. I saw him talking to my daughter.'"

She said she'd called the cops a couple of days before about recognizing that man. She wanted to make sure they showed the guy a photo of Damita, to see what he had to say for himself.

"He seems to have a good memory of the people he killed," Ethel said.

He might not have known her as Damita, Ethel added. Her full name was Damita Jo Bunkley, and her friends called her "D.J."

Ethel recalled for police that she first noticed the man she believed to be Spahalski when she saw him talking to her daughter at a convenience store on West Main Street, not far from where they lived at the time. A few days later, he came by their house on King Street looking for a friend of Damita's. When Ethel asked Damita how she knew the man, her daughter said they had a mutual female friend. In a later interview, the mother said she'd seen Spahalski at her home "several times."

When they lived "in the alley" at the back of a house on King Street, Ethel's view out the window looked at the old FIGHT (Freedom, Independence, God, Honor, Today) Square Housing Project, just across West Main Street. The projects were built on the site of the old Rochester General Hospital, which was torn down in 1966. The projects, too, were eventually torn down. The hospital had been demolished because it was moving to a modern facility on Portland Avenue. The projects came down by popular demand for the simple reason that they were infested with everything vile—human and otherwise.

Ethel saw that man over there in the projects, too. He was picking up and dropping off prostitutes. One time, a few years back, Ethel remembered seeing one of the prostitutes running down the street, her clothes torn. When she asked the girl what was wrong, she screamed that one of her customers had tried to strangle her. Ethel told the newspapers she hoped some witnessesses might come forward and say that they knew this man Spahalski and he knew Damita, a little bit of confirmation so a mother could get some closure.

To make sure her memory wasn't playing tricks on her, Ethel went to visit Tina, the friend of Damita's that the man had been looking for when he came by the house on King Street. Ethel found Tina in the Monroe

County Jail, where she verified that the man had, indeed, been Spahalski. She'd seen him on the news and recognized him right away. So Tina was *sure*.

Tina said she didn't want to go to the police about it, though, because she was married and she didn't want her husband to know about men she knew.

This wasn't the first time Ethel Dix's name was in the newspaper. In 2003, twelve years after her daughter's murder, she began attending antiviolence meetings and demonstrations in Rochester. The protesters were seeking better gun control, more money for community youth centers, and an end to racial profiling.

There was so much violence at the time in Rochester—folks were being mistreated by each other and by the police—she wanted her voice to be heard.

Dix told a reporter at that time that she knew the meaning of tough love. One of Damita's sons, who was only four years old when his mother was murdered, was heading down a bad road, and the grandmother had worked hard to turn herself into a human roadblock.

"I took hold of this child when I saw the road he was on. I want parents to realize there is help for them," she said as she helped collect signatures on a petition asking that legislatures toughen up New York State gun laws.

Her grandson William was "running the streets," she said, getting in after dawn, wild-eyed, high on Lord-knows-what. So she made a tough decision and had a "Persons in Need of Supervision" warrant issued for the boy, thus getting the courts involved in getting him the help he needed, which ended up being counseling and an attentive probation officer.

Parents needed to look at the toughest decision of all, she said. How could they deny that it was better to see their sons and daughters in prison than to see them in the morgue?

* * *

Investigators were asked point-blank about a possible link between Robert Bruce Spahalski and Damita Gibson. "We're still looking into the information Spahalski gave to investigators. Major Crimes wants to make sure a thorough job is done on the investigations," Investigator Dominic said.

Not long after Robert Bruce Spahalski's confession, a press conference was held in Rochester's Public Safety Building. The man at the podium was Rochester police chief Cedric Alexander.

Alexander wasn't your typical police chief: an African-American scholar, with a doctorate in psychology from Wright State University, and a master's degree in marriage and family therapy. He was an expert in domestic disputes, a subject with which a cop had to deal frequently. He'd only been with the Rochester Police Department for a couple of years, joining as deputy chief, and soon moving up to the top spot. Before coming to Rochester, he was a cop for fifteen years in Florida.

Alexander told the press that Spahalski was under investigation for other murders, besides the two with which he'd been charged. The chief said, "There appears to be a long history of violence."

How many others?

"It could be two. It could be more," he said.

He couldn't be specific, but these were cases that had occurred in the city in the past "ten years or so." And the investigation was not limited to the city. "We are looking into homicides and suspicious deaths in Rochester and elsewhere," Chief Alexander said. "We are casting a wide net on this one. These families deserve closure."

Then it was Webster police chief Gerald Pickering's turn to talk. A bright-eyed and youthful-looking man,

Pickering had been chief since April 19, 2001, the eighth chief since Webster got its own police department in 1928. His early days as a cop, 1978 through 1984, were spent with the Ontario County Sheriff's Office (OCSO). He came to Webster in 1984.

At the press conference, Chief Pickering called Spahalski an "incredibly dangerous individual," and reassured his town that even though Grande's murder took place there, Spahalski was not a suspect in any other Webster slayings.

Pickering revealed that Spahalski might have been arrested soon, even if he hadn't turned himself in. Earlier in the year, Webster officials had contacted the New York State Police cold cases squad to look into Grande's murder.

State police did look into the case and gave the Webster police their recommendations. Among these was the suggestion that fingerprint and DNA evidence from the Grande murder scene be checked against a modern computer database. Two weeks before Vivian Irizarry's murder, DNA evidence gathered from the Webster crime scene had come up as a match with that of Robert Bruce Spahalski.

Preparations were under way to present evidence against Spahalski to a Town of Webster grand jury even as the accused walked into Rochester police headquarters.

The Webster police chief was asked if Spahalski might have turned himself in because he knew his days of freedom were rapidly dwindling.

Pickering said he didn't believe that to be the case. As far as Webster police could tell, Spahalski didn't know the case against him in the Grande murder was falling into place.

PART TWO

12

Elmira: Running Amok

Robert Bruce Spahalski was a serial killer. True—no matter how much the killer himself despised that label. That fact alone put him in a rare criminal category. Even among serial killers, he was rare—an anomaly. He killed both white and black people. Being bisexual, he killed both a man and women. He also killed in different ways. He strangled the women and bludgeoned the man. The variant methods were a matter of control, police figured. Charles Grande, after all, was stronger than the killer's female victims. He needed to be bludgeoned from behind. The killer couldn't control another man simply by throttling him and wrapping his hands tightly around his neck, as he had with his female victims.

But the thing that made Robert truly fascinating to criminologists—the thing that made him perhaps unique—was that Robert had a twin brother who had also killed. Robert Bruce Spahalski and Stephen Joseph Spahalski were identical killer twins. The Spahalski twins were born in Elmira, New York, on December 12, 1954. Stephen was the oldest by a few minutes.

Elmira, nestled atop the Pennsylvania border in the lush, rolling hills of the southern Finger Lakes region, about halfway between Rochester and New York City, had a population of about thirty-five thousand. The small city was in the northern Allegheny Plateau in the Southern Tier of New York State.

For a city of that size, Elmira produced more than its fair share of celebrities. Famous people who hailed from Elmira included NBC news anchor Brian Williams, space shuttle commander Eileen Collins, fashion mogul Tommy Hilfiger, tragic Heisman Trophy winner Ernie Davis, and Academy Award–winning animator John Canemaker.

It was a city with quite a history. Mark Twain had a summer home there, and it was there that Twain completed his most celebrated work, *Adventures of Huckleberry Finn.* Twain loved Elmira so much that he chose to spend eternity there, requesting to be buried in Elmira's Woodlawn Cemetery.

Robert Bruce Spahalski described his time growing up in Elmira as "some of the most fun and carefree years for me." For the first twelve years of their lives, the Spahalski twins lived two miles from the city of Elmira, just off Route 17, near Newtown Battlefield on Old Lowman Road.

"My parents owned a six-bedroom house with eighteen acres on both sides of the road. There were no other neighbors to be seen, and we enjoyed our privacy and social solitude," Robert said. He painted a word picture of domestic tranquility: "I was one of five brothers and two sisters. We all got along with each other, and loved and respected each other's individuality in the family brood." Mom's name was Anita. Dad was Bernard.

Robert verified that twins do, indeed, have special communication powers—their own language, if you wanted to call it that. It was just like being married for many years to a spouse, he imagined. You're around that person so much that you "just know" what the other is thinking.

Summers in Elmira, forty years ago, were times of simple pleasures. The town's young people, especially those from West Elmira, would gather at Fitch's Bridge and jump into the Chemung River. The river originated in the town of Painted Post, New York, and flowed southeast through Elmira on its meandering forty-five-mile journey to the Susquehanna River.

Back then, on Fitch's Bridge in West Elmira, there was a rope so that youngsters could swing Tarzan-style before dropping into the center of the river. A generation earlier, there had been carnival rides at Fitch's Bridge and a huge slide that deposited youngsters into the river. The bridge was named after Daniel Hollenbeck Fitch, a farmer who years before had donated $10,000 toward the original bridge's construction.

In 2009, there is still a bridge at that location, and it is still sometimes called Fitch's Bridge, but it is not the same bridge that existed during Spahalski's youth. The former bridge, along with all rope swinging, was washed out during the major flood of 1972.

Even as children, the twins were not much for following rules. According to Robert, Stephen's first "crime" came in about third grade, when he stole a roll of lunch tickets from his teacher's desk. The tickets were worth a total of $25, a quarter apiece. Stephen was selling them to classmates for a dime apiece to make some money for the penny-candy store. He got caught.

"Dad whipped his ass for that," Robert said. "I, on the other hand, thought it was very innovative at the time."

Robert was no angel, either. The Spahalskis were Roman Catholic, and on the day of his First Communion, Robert was caught going through his grandmother's purse, looking for money and candy. Their mom was embarrassed. As Robert got his ass whipped, Stephen laughed.

Even back then, in second or third grade, the twins

had strong antisocial tendencies and did not like authority figures telling them what to do.

The Spahalskis' dad, Bernard, along with their grandfather, owned a place called Allendale Dairy, on First Street. Robert's strongest memory of the dairy store was that many of the regular customers were guards from the Elmira Correctional Facility, a fact that he currently finds ironic.

Robert didn't recall a lot of quality time spent with his dad. Some, but not a lot. They went deer hunting a couple of times. "Nothing exceptional happened," Robert said. "He wasn't much of a talker, only a good provider."

They went fishing together sometimes in the Chemung River. There never seemed to be a lot of fish to catch. "I guess you could say he taught me patience," Robert concluded.

Robert shared other memories of those days: "My father, as a hobby, raised lots of chickens, rabbits, a pig, and a few delicious turkeys. I got in trouble with my father when I was twelve, because I took his twelve-gauge shotgun and shot his pig in the head."

It wasn't because he was pissed off at his old man or anything like that. As far as Robert recalled, he was never pissed off at his old man.

"It was because me and my brothers were in the mood for pork," Robert said. His brothers were afraid to shoot the pig, so Robert stepped up.

After the deed was accomplished—a single shot to the head—Robert and two of his brothers butchered the pig and put the meat in the freezer. After the carcass was dead, reducing its temperature was essential.

"We had plenty of pork chops and bacon, but my father was really pissed off at me," Robert said.

Bernard Spahalski was a deer hunter, and the boys were raised to be comfortable around guns: the shotgun or the .303 British rifle, or a .410 over/under.

"I used to get a big kick out of shooting and killing the

neighbors' pesky cats and dogs," Robert admitted. "They always knocked over our garbage cans and I felt justified."

When the twins were twelve, life drastically changed for the Spahalski family.

"My father fell in love with his secretary and they moved in together. My mother stuck by us kids and took on the responsibility of raising us," Robert said.

It was a task that eventually overwhelmed her, however. Not that Robert could blame her. She had a lot on her plate. She was a divorcée with seven kids and a mortgage to pay. She worked as a nurse's aide to make ends meet, and even if she wasn't much of a disciplinarian, Robert still saw her as a "pillar of strength" throughout his teenage years. No matter how much he messed up, she stuck with him. If he had to be in court, she was always there to lend her support.

Those were the days of social upheaval, the "generation gap," and hippiedom. It was all too much for this mother, who threw her hands up in surrender.

As Robert later put it, "Because of living in a dysfunctional family environment, I wasn't nurtured or cultivated in social direction. I was pretty much left alone to pursue my own devices of entertainment."

In addition to sharing the same facial features, the twins also shared an incredible athletic ability. The same was true of their brothers and sisters. They were exceptionally athletic.

Each realized when they were eight or nine years old that they had tumbling abilities head and shoulders above their classmates. By 1964, the twins were spending far more time on pommel horses, rings, and parallel bars than they were on reading, writing, or arithmetic.

During the 1960s, David, Stephen, and Robert Spahalski spent a whole week during the summer building a cabin in their woods. The cabin had a door, a window, and a wooden floor. There were three mattresses to sleep on. Dad was very proud of his boys. They'd done a good job. The day after it was built, Stephen came running into the house, screaming that the cabin was on fire.

"By the time we got out there, the entire cabin and about a half acre of trees were on fire," Robert said. Their father asked what had happened and Stephen explained that he'd just been playing with his shiny lighter, lighting loose strings on one of the canvas beds, when the situation got out of hand.

When they entered high school, at Elmira Free Academy, on the city's north side, the twins' commitment to their gymnastic skills grew even stronger.

According to Robert, "We focused our inner energies on being gymnasts in school. We excelled in this for six years of school, attaining a certain discipline of mind and body—a perfection."

Both twins boasted. Stephen bragged that there was talk of him earning a college scholarship because of his gymnastic abilities. Robert said he was offered a free ride at the United States Military Academy. West Point wanted him.

The young gymnasts worked hard. Perfection did not come easy. They trained between four and six hours a day, five days a week. The only trouble with gymnastics, there was no money in it.

After the divorce, the Spahalski clan moved from their farmhouse south of town to a small but well-kept house in a nice neighborhood up toward Harris Hill, right off Church Street in West Elmira. The Spahalski house was only a few hundred yards from the Elmira Country Club's golf course.

"It was a cozy house with four small bedrooms for the brood," Robert said.

Not long after the boys entered high school, they became what has been described by old classmates and law enforcement alike as "totally wild."

Part of that wildness might have been caused by the

lack of "social direction," as Robert put it. Part might have been the twins' age at the time that their parents split—puberty and adolescence are tough for everyone. And part of it might have been the era, as changing social mores and world events drove a wedge between parents and their children. Whatever it was, the twins developed a new set of priorities, one in which the straight and narrow lacked relevance.

According to Robert, going to Elmira Free Academy was a blast. Every day was an adventure. According to his memory, he was a B+ student—and he had lots of friends.

"I grew up in the Vietnam era," Robert said. "Being teenagers, our attitude was literally 'sex, drugs, and rock and roll.' F*** Vietnam and the pigs that represented the establishment. I guess I was antisocial."

One classmate from those years, who was no doubt more in tune with the establishment, and who was speaking under the comfort of anonymity, recalled, "Here's what I can tell you about the Spahalski twins—punks from the get-go. Anyone that knew them knew they would wind up in prison, and they did. From their early teens on, they had no respect for anyone. They found out in short order they weren't nearly as tough or as smart as they thought they were. They should have put them out of their misery long ago."

"These boys just ran amok," recalled one former member of local law enforcement. "They were totally out of control at a very early age. The mother had no control over them."

Robert described his teenage years as a time of wild drug experimentation.

"I went on over three hundred acid trips," Robert admitted years later. The LSD back then had colorful names like "yellow sunshine," "four-way windowpane," and "orange barrel." While on the drug, Robert recalled, he would experience "cartoon fantasies." Vivid images and clear thoughts came to life.

It was quite an admission. From a psychiatric point of view, unsupervised use of lysergic acid could change a person's behavior permanently. LSD rearranged the firing of the body's synapses to the brain. Along with the hallucinations and sense of euphoria, which made the drug popular, came some pretty frightening repercussions. To paraphrase the Amboy Dukes' classic single, you could journey to the center of the mind, but you couldn't necessarily return.

If Robert actually took LSD three hundred times, that's the equivalent of tripping every day for ten months—certainly long enough to redirect his stream of consciousness, just as one might purposefully alter the flow of the Chemung River. Like many youths of the time, he apparently saw that the greatest boundary was between the young and the old. His old man was old. Cops were old. Teachers were old. Young people were cool—some of them, anyway. But old people were squares, complete straights. What was old? Anyone over thirty.

And the generation gap was war, man. Old people were so full of crap. Why shouldn't they pay for his youth, for the big party that was Robert's brain? It was a party with nasty overtones, for sure—but still a party. When Robert wasn't dropping acid, he was further fooling his synapses with magic mushrooms and peyote.

Robert recalled thinking that he'd taken LSD too many times, that he could no longer enjoy the colors and cartoons in his head, images he could control by just thinking. Those days were through. Now the drug was in control and he had lost some of his ability to distinguish fantasy from reality.

And Robert didn't limit his drug intake to hallucinogens. The party had to go on forever. For that reason, sleep sucked and was to be avoided. Why sleep? You might miss something.

"I did crystal meth, 'black beauties,'" Robert said. Crystal meth was a distilled-in-a-lab condensation of the already-powerful drug methamphetamine. It kick-started the metabolism like a Hells Angel on his Harley. Crank, as the bikers called it, made a person feel like he was on top of the world, speedy as hell, and a little mean, too.

What followed was an endurance test. Rumor had it that Keith Richards, of the Rolling Stones, stayed up for eight days. That was akin to the Guinness World Record for speed freakdom. After taking speed, sleep seemed totally ridiculous. If a user wasn't big on empathy to begin with, hurting others didn't cause anxiety. It was just another thrill in a life that was otherwise so painfully boring. Victims were not other people who deserved respect, but a member of the enemy ranks, who was there only to be exploited or destroyed.

When it came time to finally crash, when Robert's nerves were shot, Robert took a Quaalude to add a touch of dreaminess to his reentry into the atmosphere.

Any other drugs?

"You name it," Robert said.

Sometimes, after Robert and his brothers would get high, they'd steal their distant neighbors' horses and ride them all day. Or sometimes on weekends, they'd all go to the "country swimming hole," drink beer, and work on their tanline-free suntans.

Boredom was the enemy, and boredom was extreme and painful. There were long hours of nothingness that had the Spahalski twins fidgeting out of their skins. They needed a rush.

To spice things up, Robert and Stephen became dangerously competitive. They'd alter their brains by using whatever drug or drugs they had and would then challenge each other to engage in risky behavior.

"We'd do crazy things," Robert said. "Like doing a handstand on a ledge with nothing but hundreds of feet of empty space down below."

With time, synapses burned out, glands depleted, and their adrenaline rushes were harder to come by. The twins' temerity metamorphosed.

The mischievous caterpillar spun its own drug-fueled cocoon and died. A noxious butterfly emerged. Robert preferred being known as Bruce.

"Only the authorities called me Robert. I was Robert for all legal transactions, but my family and close friends called me Bruce," Robert said.

Robert wasn't the only Spahalski twin to look back at those chaotic years through nostalgic eyes.

"I was doing good," Stephen Spahalski recalled wistfully during a 2006 newspaper interview, thinking of his teen years. "I went to the state gymnastic meets and stuff. I had a nice girlfriend."

That nice girlfriend was Sue Cunningham (pseudonym), and by "nice," Stephen must have meant diligent, and certainly more faithful than he deserved. Easy on the eyes, too. Stephen's twin remembered Cunningham as "really cute."

"Steve Spahalski was my first love. We dated in high school, right up to his arrest," Cunningham said. Even now, she was unwilling to say anything bad about Steve and Bruce Spahalski.

Cunningham just thought about the twins' nice side. That was the side of them she knew best. She didn't even know that there was a dark side until right before Steve was arrested. Despite what people might think these days, the Spahalski twins were *not* all rotten to the core. In fact, she still was scratching her head, wondering where they went wrong.

It was only after Stephen went to prison that Cunningham found out that her boyfriend was a drug addict. Heroin, she said. She still believed that his violence and his troubles were due to drug deals "gone very badly."

They hadn't known each other that long. They met when they were both sixteen years old. She remembered their meeting vividly.

She was walking along the side of the road with two of her girlfriends. The girls were all on her way home from a dance, when the twins, their older brother, and a friend stopped in their car and gave them a ride home. It was a tight squeeze getting everyone in the car, and some fast friendships were formed.

"The girls called themselves the 'Duquette Gang.' Their leader was Debbie Duquette (pseudonym), who later became my brother's wife," said Robert.

The reason the Spahalski brothers and the Duquette Gang didn't know each other already was that they didn't live that close to one another. The girls lived south of the Chemung River, and the boys lived in West Elmira, north of the river. The girls went to Southside High. The boys attended Elmira Free.

For Sue and Steve, it was love at first sight, and they were together from that night on. There was a lot of triple-dating, the three brothers and the three friends, all crammed into Anita Spahalski's station wagon.

"We'd park on a dark lonely road, drink beer, listen to music, and explore our teenage sexuality," said Robert. Nothing kinky. All-American good teenage fun.

"I was in awe of Stephen's athletic talents," Cunningham explained. "He was extremely good in gymnastics. The side horse was his favorite. He worked that apparatus as if he owned it."

She recalled one day when they were all stopped at a train crossing while a particularly long freight train lazily crossed the road. Steve and Bruce got out of the car and started walking around on their hands, to entertain the other people waiting for the train to pass.

"Steve and Bruce were show-offs. They loved to show off their skills," Cunningham recalled.

Along with walking upside down, the twins also had noteworthy diving skills. Cunningham remembered the two of them at Robert H. Treman State Park in the town of Ithaca, New York (the home of Cornell University), at the southern tip of Cayuga Lake, one of the largest of the Finger Lakes. The park was known for its gorgeous scenery—with picturesque gorges, waterfalls, and cliffs.

Sue could still picture the exhibition the twins put on there, flipping and twisting in midair while diving into a swimming hole.

Robert remembered diving, too, and recalled that Stephen was the better athlete of the two, both as a gymnast and a diver. Stephen could do double and triple flips into a perfect dive, full-twist dives, full back layout dives. Robert was limited to double front and backflips. Spectators were impressed with them both, nonetheless. The twins hadn't learned how to dive in the park, but rather at the Elmira public swimming pool, where they had three diving boards at different levels.

Robert said that Stephen was the more skilled gymnast. At six-two, two hundred pounds, they were both large for the sport. Robert specialized in two events, still rings and side horse. He didn't consider himself "world-class" but was enriched by the experience, spending four years of his life with a "profound team of gymnasts, both male and female."

Cunningham added with a sigh, "Steve held in the palm of his hands a scholarship promise with a great future ahead of him. If only, if only, if only. Such a waste of tremendous talent."

She had no sense that the twins were committing crimes. She knew they were mischievous and used their similitude to trick people—but crime? It never occurred to her.

"Not in my wildest dreams," she added. *Especially* not

to the extent that it happened. Small crimes? Maybe.
Murder? No way.

She kept going back to that night when the boys had
picked them up while they were walking home from the
dance. *This magic moment* . . . One second she was walking along the road, giggling with her girlfriends, and the
next—bingo—she'd found a boyfriend. One of the girlfriends she was with was Yvonne Williams (pseudonym).
Yvonne dated Robert Bruce Spahalski for a long while.

Cunningham never knew the Spahalskis' dad. He had
been gone for years by the time she showed up. She got
the impression from what the boys had said that he was
an extremely strict father, especially toward the twins.

Did the twins ever try to switch places and fool her?

"Yes," Cunningham said. "They both tried a switcheroo
with me and my other friend, but we were onto them
right away." They might have been physically identical,
but there were subtle differences in their vibes, Cunningham said. Bruce was dangerous, pernicious—rough
around the edges. Steve was seemingly benign, more of a
baby face. "But you had to be around with them a lot to
be able to tell that about them. Otherwise, it was difficult," Cunningham explained. Besides, if you knew them
well, there were physical differences. Stephen had a scar
in the middle of his forehead and was missing the tip of
one finger.

According to Robert, his attempt at the old switcheroo
was at least a little successful. They were all at a beer party
at a friend's house when Stephen fell asleep/passed out.
Seeing his opportunity, Robert started making out with
Sue Cunningham. According to Robert, Sue couldn't tell
the difference, and he was halfway to second base by the
time Stephen woke up, discovered what Robert was
doing, chased him for about a quarter mile, caught him,
and beat him up a little. "It was worth it, though. Sue was
a good kisser," Robert recalled. And the expression on

Stephen's face when he realized Robert was with Sue was priceless. It was Robert's favorite memory of his twin.

One fond memory Robert shared with Stephen was the night the three brothers, the twins and David, were triple-dating in their mother's station wagon. David and Stephen were with their usual girlfriends, but Robert was with a girl he'd just met, a "blond country girl" who was curious in the ways of physical love. Robert remembered he'd just about gotten to third base with her, which was quite an accomplishment back in those days, because, as he put it, "third base is tricky." As per the custom of the time, he'd given her a hickey on her neck. But, as all things must, the magical night came to an end and they dropped the blonde off at her "country house on a country road," and she was still stoned, drunk, and half-naked when she got out of the car. They drove off, and a quarter mile down the road, Robert announced he needed a "piss call." So David pulled over onto the shoulder and Robert staggered out to answer the call of nature. First, Robert stumbled and tumbled down an embankment. That got a laugh. "But I'm feeling happy," he said. "I pulled my dick out to piss and pissed on an electrified cow fence. My dick and balls got zapped real good." Cursing and suddenly sobered up, Robert climbed back up the embankment. As he did so, he could see that there was a truck parked next to the station wagon, and his brothers were screaming, "That's not Bruce! That's not Bruce!" He couldn't figure out what the hell they were talking about. When he got to the top of the embankment, the truck pulled up next to him and the guy driving said, "Are you Bruce?" Robert replied, "Hell yeah!" With that, Robert recalled, the huge hulk of a man "got out of his truck with a tire iron in his hand, and announced he was going to kill me for what I did to his daughter and getting her drunk." The truck driver swung the tire iron, but Robert caught his arm. Stephen and David poured out of the station wagon and grabbed the guy, lifted him up, and threw him down the embankment and into a tree. "We told you not to say you were Bruce, asshole," his brothers said. Two state troopers came to the Spahalski house the next day, and Robert never saw the blonde again.

In the meantime, Stephen and Robert, police knew, were doing more than cruising around Chemung County, practicing their gymnastics and picking up girls.

As for the Duquette Gang, Debbie went on to marry a Spahalski, Sue moved on with her life, but Yvonne's story was tragic. According to Robert, she died of complications during surgery. "She bled to death right there on the table," he said.

Robert recalled a prose poem he wrote when he was tripping all the time and everyone's hormones pumped like the Chemung in springtime. It was an attempt to get back the girl who had left him and was called "1970 Acid Trip by Robert Spahalski." He could recite it by heart: *"If you could only see through my magnificent disguise, and hear the gaiety of my laughter being drowned by the harsh moans of my painful heart as you said good-bye. . . . Soon I will face the mirror of my soul and the bitterness of my lies will choke me to the point of madness. I wish I could recite the words of love and set them afire."* Hot, molten, yet melodic, love poetry.

Robert remembered a time, after his dad left and his mom moved the kids to Bower Road, circa 1971, when he "dragged his butt home" after popping a Quaalude and smoking good weed with Cindy Bennett (pseudonym), his friendly and accommodating girlfriend at the time. He got home and was sprawled, "zonked out," on his bed when Stephen got home from Sue Cunningham's house. Robert was so stoned that he couldn't move, but he could open one eye a crack and he saw his twin, Stephen, take his wallet from his jeans pocket and steal a ten spot from it. Stephen further searched Robert's pants, and found his four-finger lid of pot. Stephen stole half of it and replaced the Baggie in Robert's jeans pocket. "Like I wasn't going to notice,"

Robert said with a laugh. "Then he's got the balls to light up, turn on the black light, the strobe light, put Oriental music on the stereo, and sit there, laughing at me. Ah, what are twins for?"

It was the twins' antisocial feelings, mixed with their steady intake of drugs, mixed with their competitive natures, that, according to Robert, first led them into lives of crime.

"I dare you to walk on the ledge on your hands" and "I dare you to jump off that high bridge into the turbulent waters below" evolved into "I dare you to break into that house and steal the jewelry."

The special communication skills that had always existed between Robert and Stephen grew stronger when the boys took drugs and fought the boredom. They would have ideas simultaneously. They'd see "competitive opportunities," as Robert called them.

"We'd compete at burglaries," Robert said. "Winner was the one who could steal the most money or jewelry or other items of interest."

It was kicks—more about the dare than the treasure. Breaking and entering (B&E) started out as a repeated unspoken dare between the twins, just a manifestation of their secret twin-communication skills. Then it became an addiction.

The early crimes were simple B&E jobs, poking around neighbors' houses, grooving on being where they didn't belong. When they got caught, at first, police just took them home, and the only people who really got mad were the twins' mom and dad.

Right from the beginning, and through the escalation of the crimes, the twins stole in competition with one another rather than as a team. That is, with one exception.

"The one time we did commit a burglary together, we messed up," Robert said. It was winter and the twins were walking home from school in West Elmira. They "observed a secluded house" near the corner of Church and Hoffman Streets. They pretended to have a snowball fight as they slowly approached the house. Eventually they knocked on the door, no answer, so they broke a window to get in. Inside the dwelling, Stephen rifled through an antique desk and found stacks of cash—$20's and $100's. Robert was in the bedroom discovering a fortune in jewels and gold when he heard a car pull into the driveway. He peeked out the window and saw three men getting out of a car. They must have seen the footprints in the snow. One of the men opened his coat and reached for a shoulder holster. "I told my twin we had to leave right now," and they had time to snatch a few $100 bills before escaping out a side door just as the men burst in through the front. The twins jumped over some tall bushes and were gone.

Robert still thought of that day. They could have been rich if they'd managed to take all of the money. On the other hand, they could have been dead. Instinct had kicked in, and Robert had no doubt that they were messing with the wrong people. A few months later, according to Robert, the twins hit that house again, but the money and jewels were long gone.

"We treated the world as our backyard and we did burglaries as a sport," Robert reminisced. "We didn't mean any harm, but to the local police, we must have seemed like a constant crime wave."

Elmira cops would have said that was a fair representation of the twins' behavior, with the exception of the "we didn't mean any harm" part. The twins might not have felt bad about it, but they knew their crimes had victims—and, police believed, they were picking their victims wisely.

Police had info that Robert and Stephen were perpetrating a well-thought-out criminal enterprise, an operation that exploited some of Elmira's most vulnerable and

least likely-to-talk citizens. The twins, police believed,
were enjoying the benefits of a steady income from tryst-
ing with, then shaking down, Elmira's small and subter-
ranean gay community.

In 1970 and 1971, gay guys in Elmira were an exploited
portion of the population, anyway, a retired police officer
recalled. Other than the twins, there was at least one other
teenage boy who was doing the same thing—that is, emp-
tying his victims' wallets either before, after, or instead of
illicit sexual activity.

"Homosexual men in Elmira tended to meet boys and
get rolled," the retired cop recalled.

The twins were young, but they were not small. Already at their full height, taller than six feet, and heavily
muscled, years of gymnastics had built them into powerful young men. They didn't need weapons to control the
men they robbed.

If the twins were trolling for men, the way police believed, their chances of being caught and punished were
between slim and none. Their victims were easy marks,
plus they didn't complain.

Coming out of the closet, even to report a crime to the
police, was out of the question in 1970. According to
police theory, as long as no one got hurt, the twins had
a profitable and risk-free thing going.

The police gathered intelligence from that subter-
ranean world through snitches and stoolies. When a gay
guy was busted, sometimes he was offered a deal: talk
and you walk.

Elmira cops had info. They just lacked complaints. According to their secret sources, Bruce was the dominant
twin, the more acrid of the two, the time bomb.

Informed years later of those police beliefs, Robert
Bruce Spahalski said that it was nonsense: choosing targets who would keep their mouths shut, shaking down

gay guys. It was unadulterated "bullshit." Robert was not saying anyone was lying. It was just that they were wrong. Someone tried to connect the dots, when the dots were too far apart.

Maybe he was bisexual. Robert would admit to that. But only on a part-time basis. And never in any kind of aggressive fashion. "I have *never* sought out men for sex. But ever since I can remember, men have been attracted to me. It's because of my aloofness," he said. And because of his physical skills. "I've always been a gymnast and a martial artist, so I move with the grace of a dancer. That attracts a lot of men, and it can be quite bothersome, if you know what I mean."

Why did police believe that he was targeting gays when doing crimes?

"In my teenage years, I did a lot of hitchhiking, which made me a target for gay perverts, so I got a lot of free blow jobs on the way home from school," he said.

It wasn't that he picked out gay people on purpose to prey on. It was just that, if you commit enough crimes, chances are good that some of the victims would be gay.

"It's just a fact of life that most gays are successful businesspeople," Robert said, adding that he was embarrassed by the police description of his MO.

On this one occasion—sometime after the family moved to Bower Road—Robert was alone and was picked up hitchhiking by a "big, burly" gay guy.

"He molested my crotch and bought me a twelve-pack of beer," Robert recalled. "While he was in the store, I searched his car. I found a wrench in his glove box. I thought he was a whacko and was going to do me some serious bodily harm. I ended up running him over with his own car and taking his wallet."

Eventually Robert ditched the crotch molester's car over by Fitch's Bridge and walked home.

"He refused to press charges. Maybe that's why the police had that opinion," Robert said.

* * *

It was funny, one of Robert's favorite memories of his mother, and his favorite memory of the house on Bower Road, involved a crime. Truth *is* stranger than fiction.

It started out innocently enough. He was walking down the street with his girlfriend Yvonne on the south side of Elmira. The pair watched as an unmarked cop car rolled up to the curb in front of a bar, apparently responding to a call that there was a fight inside.

The cop was in such a hurry to get inside the bar that he left the door unlocked and the engine running.

"So I stole it," Robert said, "so I wouldn't have to walk home." He said good-bye to Yvonne and was barely on the move when the cops were onto him and a chase around the south side streets ensued.

"Lights were flashing and sirens were wailing," Robert said. "Two cop cars were on my tail, chasing me to kingdom come." With the pedal to the metal, Robert led the chase northward, across the Chemung River, and headed for home. He turned onto Bower Road.

"I have two cop cars chasing me, and I see my mom sitting on the front stoop, drinking her coffee, as I zipped by. I honked the horn and waved to her. Then I got out of Dodge!"

A couple of miles up the road, Robert crashed the unmarked cop car, bailed out, and walked cross-country through mountainous woods to his grandmother's house.

"I cleaned up there and eventually wandered home. At first, my mother smiled, then she hung her head and told me I couldn't be doing that. What would the neighbors think? Then she went on to lecture me. She told me to be more positive and seek God's direction."

Despite the police belief that the twins were skating on their crimes against gays, Stephen and Robert still faced chronic troubles with the law as teenagers. Every cop in the county knew who they were, and knew to keep an eye on them.

When Robert was still only sixteen years old, during July of 1971, he was pulled over near the corner of Hoffman and West Clinton Streets in Elmira while driving a stolen car. He was charged with unauthorized use of a motor vehicle.

Less than a month later, a fire broke out in the Fassett Elementary School, located in Elmira. Someone had ignited the auditorium's stage curtain. Robert was arrested and charged with arson.

In October 1971, Robert pleaded guilty to the car theft charge and was sentenced to fifteen weekends in jail.

Robert's problems continued for the worse. In December, he was arrested again, this time for criminal trespassing when he returned to an Elmira business on South Main Street, after he had been kicked out and told never to come back.

Those three arrests were all reported in the local paper, the *Star-Gazette*.

The Spahalskis' crimes were escalating. The next known crime committed by one of the twins would be murder.

13

The Murder of Ronald Ripley

Ronald Ripley was born and raised—along with four brothers and one sister—in the Elmira, New York, area. He was the son of a master carpenter. His dad built homes and specialized in cabinets, fancy inlaid walnut coffee tables, and the like—some of the handiwork still resides in Ripley households.

Ronald met his wife, the former Edna Lucille Zeigler, at Southside High School in Elmira. After graduation Ron and Edna went to Bible college together in Houghton, New York, and studied for the ministry. They got married, had kids, and Ronald enjoyed spending as much time as possible with his family.

Ripley was an ordained minister with the Wesleyan denomination. For years he took his soul-saving mission on the road as a traveling evangelist. He was known alliteratively around Elmira as the Reverend Ron Ripley.

Despite his travels, he was the sort of father who would

announce, "Let's go to New York City," and the family would pile into their station wagon and off they would go to see the Rockettes at Radio City Music Hall, or whatever was going on.

On one trip to New York, he purposefully took his family off the beaten path, driving down the Bowery, which was at the time New York's skid row. So many impoverished bums all in one place. Ron wanted his children to see the horror of where they might end up if they didn't work hard in school and stick to the straight and narrow.

"This is what'll happen to you if you give in to the temptations of sin," he would say.

"We had a strict upbringing," David remembered. Utterances of even a euphemistic phrase like "goshdarnit" to "heck" would warrant Fels Naptha soap in the mouth.

The Ripley clan went to church almost every day. Movie theaters were where the Devil lived, and when the kids passed a cinema, they'd try to imagine what the Devil looked like in there.

When one of the Ripley children got to be five or six years old, he or she would join the rest of the family around the piano and be painstakingly taught how to harmonize vocally.

The Ripleys accompanied their dad from church to church for revival meetings and sang their hearts out. These were old-fashioned tent meetings with fire-and-brimstone sermons.

Being the oldest, David remembered when it was just he and his dad singing, traveling all over the country, singing and spreading the word. Later other siblings joined in.

Ronald was a talented musician, proficient at playing more than twenty instruments, including just about anything with a keyboard on it—piano, organ, accordion. David had a professional-quality singing voice. The pair of tenors made a couple of records together.

One, recorded when David was fourteen, was called

Gospel Light Recordings. It was released on Fine Records, a local Elmira record company. The back cover referred to David's father as an "internationally known evangelist."

At age eighteen, and already married, David traveled to Allentown, Pennsylvania, and auditioned for the Keystone Quartet, a gospel group that sometimes referred to itself as the Keystones, when they had more than four members. The Keystones offered David $100 a week to become a Keystone, but he had to turn them down.

"If I'd been single, I'd've joined up for free," David said. "I'm still kicking myself square in the ass for passing up the opportunity. A couple of those guys—Joey Bonsall, the tenor, and Richard Sterban, the bass singer— now sing with the Oak Ridge Boys."

The Reverend Ron Ripley's life had always been a lot more missionary than mercenary. Now, with so many mouths to feed at home, Ripley needed some extra scratch, so he decided to become entrepreneurial. He bought a store.

Beginning in the summer of 1971, at the same time that Robert Bruce Spahalski was first arrested for stealing a car, the reverend began selling pots and pans out of a storefront.

Ripley's store was on East Fourteenth Street in Elmira Heights, a small town just north of Elmira and south of Horseheads. The store was called Your Saladmaster Kitchen, and was an official franchise of the Saladmaster Corporation of Dallas, Texas.

For years the store, at the corner of Fourteenth Street and Prescott Avenue, had been Len's Bakery, operated by former Elmira Heights Village trustee Leonard J. Share.

The shop was not just a place to buy pots and pans, but also a place where customers could get one of those newfangled drip coffeemakers. The store, according to Reverend Ripley's family, was his "pride and joy."

* * *

Despite the wholesomeness and profound Christianity that enveloped the Ripley family, Ron Ripley was a man with a secret: during the 1960s, a few years before he bought the store, Ron was convicted of a sex crime.

As one of his sons sadly related in 2009, "My father did time in prison for it. Back then, it was illegal to be a homosexual."

Until his troubles with the law, no one in the straight world had the slightest inkling that Ronald Ripley was anything more than he seemed. And what he seemed to be was a highly religious married man with a loving family.

His oldest son, David, was the child with whom Ronald was closest. According to David, it wasn't an act. Ronald's pious and wholesome persona was real.

David had no clue that his father had a secret life until his dad's arrest. "He told me he had a problem. That was quite a moment. Quite a moment," David recalled.

But David didn't believe his father's secret had anything to do with what happened next.

Sometime during the late evening of Tuesday, November 23, 1971, two days before Thanksgiving, Ronald Ripley, forty-eight years old, was murdered in the basement of his store.

According to police, who based their theory exclusively on the reverend's criminal history, Ronald Ripley was living a double life on the down-low. They said he had fixed up the basement of his store with a bar, a desk, a pool table, and a covered chaise longue. It was, the police theory went, his underground den—secluded and windowless—suitable for illicit and clandestine liaisons. His wife said he sometimes slept there.

Photos of the crime scene, however, revealed no evidence of a nightclub ambiance. It looked like a cellar. Sure, it had a pool table and a chaise longue, but it could have as easily been for napping as for romping. One thing was for sure: now it was the scene of his death.

Ronald Ripley's body was found the morning after his murder by his seventy-five-year-old mother-in-law, Ida Zeigler, who was in the neighborhood because she and her driver were dropping off repent pamphlets at the stores of Elmira Heights.

(Ida was wearing her Salvation Army uniform, she wasn't shy, and she knew enough about her son-in-law to know his soul also might need a little saving every once in a while. She had spent years saving souls. She delivered the "war cries" to the bars, standing outside taverns at night to preach about the dangers of demon alcohol to the boozehounds who needed it most.)

The family had been worried all night, but also a little irritated with Ronald. It was not a good night for him to disappear. He was expected home with the Thanksgiving turkey, which needed to be defrosted.

The Ripleys were planning a Thanksgiving celebration. Company was expected—and Ronald didn't come home. The family had been wondering if he'd been in an accident.

Edna had phoned the store every few minutes all night, but the phone just rang and rang. Maybe he'd left and something had happened to him on the way home.

Or maybe he was okay, but he was just being a bastard. This wasn't the first time he hadn't come home, Edna thought, and he'd always turned up safe and sound before.

At 10:45 A.M., Ron Ripley's mother-in-law, Ida Zeigler, and her driver had pulled up in front of Ripley's store. Ida looked around and didn't see Ron's car. "I'll just leave a pamphlet in his door," she said. As she got out of the car, she noticed something was wrong.

The store's front door was open a wee bit, and through

the large front windows, she could see the store was in disarray—ransacked, papers scattered, drawers pulled out.

She entered the store hesitantly and called out her son-in-law's name. No response. She walked through the store and into a back room. She called again. Nothing.

Maybe he fell asleep in the basement, Ida figured. At that point, a cold chill ran up and down her spine, and she left the store and returned to the car.

"You'd better come inside with me," she said to her driver, and he accompanied her. They entered the store, and along the right wall, the driver opened the door to the downstairs staircase. The driver flipped on the light and Ida looked down the cellar stairs.

She could see a small portion of the cellar floor and—to her horror—Ron Ripley's prone legs, motionless.

Somehow the old woman gathered the strength to make a phone call. She called the Elmira Heights Fire Department, its number was on a red sticker on the phone. Dispatch asked if they should bring the resuscitation equipment and Edna said yes.

The first responders were firemen, who pulled up in front of the store in their emergency truck. Elmira Heights police quickly followed. The village's fire and police departments shared a small building only a block away and they were there in minutes—maybe seconds. They could have walked to the scene and been there in under a minute. The firemen clomped down the wooden staircase in their boots and surrounded the body. Several of them made efforts to determine if there was any life left. They were pretty sure he was dead, and would have checked to see if there was a pulse at his neck, except the side of his neck was bloody with what appeared to be multiple stab wounds. At least one fireman decided to give the cellar a once-over, just to make sure there wasn't more than one body. Maybe a witness was hiding. Maybe the perp was still there. At least one fireman did this after getting the victim's blood on his boots.

Although sincere in their efforts, the police and firefighters of Elmira Heights were neophytes, when it came to major crime scenes. When they should have withdrawn, they charged forward. Instead of sealing off the crime scene area and waiting for experts to arrive, they looked around, trying to be helpful.

Turned out they weren't much help. No one had a clue—or found a clue. There hadn't been a murder in Elmira Heights in more than forty years. No one remembered exactly how long.

The Elmira Heights Police Department (EHPD) was a ten-man squad. None had seen a murder scene before. Elmira Heights didn't even have criminal investigators.

Bottom line: none of the first responders knew what to do. They contaminated the crime scene and came away thinking that the man's wife must have done it. Maybe she caught him fooling around or something. (The 2009 Elmira Heights Police Department would be quick to point out that, though still small in numbers, they were now all modern, well-trained peace officers, devoid of their predecessors' naïveté.)

Luckily, help was quickly summoned, but not before, as investigators later put it, the firefighters had "stomped all over the crime scene."

Within ten minutes of the body's discovery, Elmira Heights police chief Lloyd D. Roberts was at the scene and in command. Roberts took one look at the body and said, "Call the coroner."

Deputy coroner Dr. Robert K. Worman pronounced the body dead and ordered that no one touch it until the DA's office had a chance to get there. Assistant District Attorney (ADA) Paul Corradini answered the call. Worman ordered that after Corradini and his people were done with the body, it was to be taken to Arnot-Ogden Hospital via Erway Ambulance. Worman left the scene and went to the hospital to await the body's arrival.

Four well-trained investigators got the call. Good-bye

Thanksgiving with the family, they each thought. A couple of them arrived in the same car as the ADA.

Chief Roberts watched as the crowds of officials inside and the onlookers outside grew. He was pleased that investigative help had arrived, but that didn't mean he wanted to give up his command in the case.

In his report, Chief Roberts wrote, *I informed them* (investigators from other departments) *that the case was being handled by the Heights Police Department, with all the assistance the other departments could give me, and they all said they would help in any way I wanted.*

As this was going on, the victim's wife, Edna, drove to the store herself. By the time she got there, she recalled, "There were police cars parked out front and a crowd of people."

She was interviewed even before she was informed that her husband was dead. Heights officer Mike Perovich (pseudonym) took her statement on the sidewalk outside the store. She thought at first it was only a robbery, but this chaos at the store, coupled with the fact that Ron hadn't come home, gave her a dire feeling. She answered all of the policeman's questions. She said she was Edna Ripley and she was forty-six years old. She gave her address.

"Why are you here?"

"I am looking for my husband. I called him a few times during the night. I let the phone ring and ring, a hundred times, before hanging up. After a while, I stopped calling. I figured he slept in the store . . . like he does sometimes," she explained.

Edna said Ron's car was gone, and she gave the officer full info regarding the station wagon. She apologized if she got the plate number wrong, she was a little confused at the moment.

"Why didn't you call the police last night?"

"I thought about it, but decided not to."

"Why not?"

Edna did not answer. The cop raised an eyebrow. What he had here was a jealous wife out looking for a husband who sometimes didn't come home when he was supposed to.

Edna was told she was a widow by Officer Wayne Hartzel. She staggered in a daze inside the store to see Ron. She was stopped at the top of the cellar stairs by someone big, so she stepped back from the activity between the front door and the cellar door. She just so happened to be standing next to the phone when it rang. She answered and it was Leo Hoodak, a young-sounding man who said he was a friend of Ron's, and that Ron had given him a ride home the previous night at eleven-thirty.

Edna was led by the arm down the narrow stairs.

"Is this the body of your husband, Ronald Jay Ripley?" a voice asked.

"Yes," she said.

"Take her back upstairs," the voice said.

Edna didn't recall going back up the stairs, the next thing she knew she was again outside and talking to Officer Perovich. She told him about the call inside the store from the man named Hoodak.

Both Ida and Edna were taken to Heights Police headquarters, where they waited and waited, and then were eventually questioned further by a member of the New York State Police (NYSP) Bureau of Criminal Investigation.

Later that afternoon, Perovich went to Hoodak's home. Leo wasn't around, so the policeman talked to Leo's parents. They said that Leo—who was a teenager—got home at eleven-thirty the previous night. He came into his parents' bedroom, announced that he'd "made a dollar," placed the $1 bill on his parents' dresser, and then, as far as they knew, went to bed and went to sleep. Neither

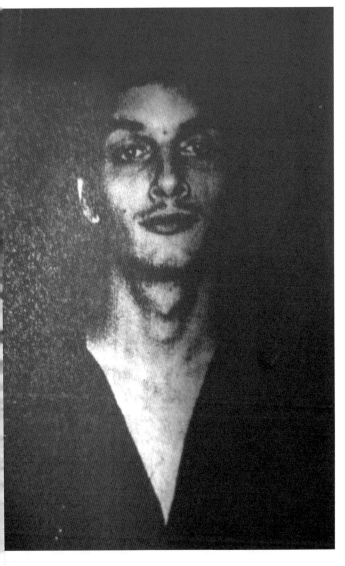

Mug shot of a teenaged Robert Bruce Spahalski following one of his many arrests. *(Photo courtesy of the Elmira Police Department Records Bureau)*

Stephen Spahalski, just arrested for the murder of Ronald Ripley, is led to his arraignment by Elmira Heights Police Chief Lloyd Roberts.
(Photo courtesy of the Star-Gazette)

Stephen Spahalski in 1971 with the Elmira Free Academy track team.

As teenagers, the Spahalski twins lived in this lovely West Elmira home.
(Author photo)

The store on the right was once Your Saladmaster Kitchen, where Ronald Ripley was murdered. *(Author photo)*

The Reverend Ron Ripley was a devoted family man and a talented musician. *(Courtesy of David Ripley)*

Ripley's body was discovered at the bottom of the cellar stairs.
(Crime scene photo by Pat Patterson)

Chemung County Sheriff's Investigator Pat Patterson observed that the victim had been bludgeoned from behind while coming down the stairs.
(Crime scene photo by Pat Patterson)

Ripley was repeatedly stabbed by someone who wanted to make sure he was dead. *(Crime scene photo by Pat Patterson)*

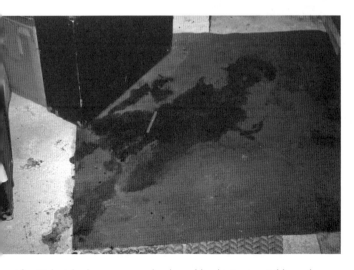

After Ripley's body was removed, a large bloodstain was visible on the basement rug and linoleum floor. *(Crime scene photo by Pat Patterson)*

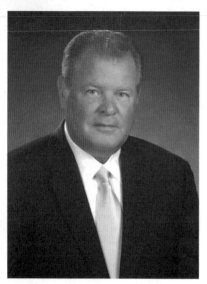

Following stints as an investigator for the Chemung County District Attorney, and as Sheriff of that county, Pat Patterson served for more than twenty years as a special agent with the FBI before retiring from law enforcement. Today he is the sole surviving investigator of the 1971 Ronald Ripley case. *(Photo by Pat Patterson)*

Edgerton Park, at one time a major hub of activity in Rochester— home of the circus, rodeo, museum, and pro basketball and football games—was by 1990 just a playground in a desolate neighborhood. *(Photo by R. Jerome Warren)*

During 1991, Cassandra Carlton and Katrina Myers were found murdered near an abandoned spur of tracks along Ferrano Street. The trestle visible in the distance crossed the Erie Canal at the city line. Follow those tracks southward a few city blocks and you encountered the dump sites of Vicki Jobson and Damita Gibson. *(Photo by R. Jerome Warren)*

At left, Damita Gibson, a young woman with a promising future. At right, Damita's mother, Ethel Dix, stands sadly at the spot near the railroad tracks off Jay Street where her daughter's body was found. *(Photo of Damita Gibson courtesy of Ethel Dix; photo of Ethel Dix by R. Jerome Warren)*

Chuck Grande as a young boy at a petting zoo, with his mom and sister Rose. *(Courtesy of Rosemary Van Dusen)*

Chuck and Rose on a visit to New York City during the spring of 1983, playing dress-up at the top of the Empire State Building. *(Courtesy of Rosemary Van Dusen)*

Vicki Jobson's life was going great until she fell into depression and tried to self-medicate using a crack pipe.

Sometime during October 1992, Vicki Jobson disappeared from her apartment. Her home was directly across the street from the apartment of 1990 victim Moraine Armstrong. *(Photo by R. Jerome Warren)*

On December 7, 1992 Vicki Jobson's body was found nude and stabbed to death in a corner of J.M. Wilson Park near railroad tracks.
(Photo by R. Jerome Warren)

Sergeant Mark Mariano, who was among those at the Moraine Armstrong crime scene, has worked past retirement to solve the murder of Vicki Jobson.
(Photo ourtesy of Jayne Dehm)

The building in which Hortense Greatheart died on January 3, 2003.
(Photo by R. Jerome Warren)

The house on Spencer Street where Robert Bruce Spahalski murdered Vivian Irizarry. *(Photo by R. Jerome Warren)*

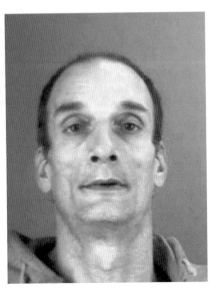

Robert Bruce Spahalski, street name Bruce, was convicted of four murders. *(Photo courtesy of the Webster Police Department)*

NYS DOCS

06B3454
SPAHALSKI, ROBERT
6'2"   180lbs
DATE 2/23/07

Sex - MALE   Race - WHITE   Hair - BROWN   Eyes - BROWN   DOB - 12/12/54

TAT LA

NYSID # -   ID CARD #

Robert as he appeared in his most recent available prison mug shot.
(Photo courtesy of the New York Department of Correctional Services)

Steven in his most recent available prison mug shot. *(Photo courtesy of the New York Department of Correctional Services)*

parent recalled hearing a car drive up, or a car door slam, before Leo entered the house.

"Did Leo ever mention a Ron Ripley?" Officer Perovich asked.

Yes, their son had mentioned him. Leo told them Mr. Ripley liked to flash big rolls of money. Ripley once showed Leo $5,000 in cash.

The four Ripley investigators called in on Thanksgiving eve were two investigators each from the Elmira Heights Police Department and the Chemung County Sheriff's Office (CCSO).

One of those was sheriff's investigator Pat Patterson. Today, of the four, he is the only survivor. Patterson joined the CCSO in 1968, right out of high school, worked for a time at the jail, and eventually became a sheriff's deputy. He demonstrated an aptitude for detail and worked his way up to investigator, which is what he was when Ronald Ripley died.

Patterson parked his car in front of Your Saladmaster Kitchen and went inside. He was told that the body was downstairs. Wooden steps led underground. The body was visible as soon as he got to the top of the stairs.

Patterson was also the crime scene photographer. He memorialized the scene by using two types of film, one for color slides, the other for large-format, fine-grain, black-and-white prints.

He observed that the body was that of a middle-aged white man who had longish white hair. He wore a black-and-blue sweater, beige slacks, and freshly polished brown boots. It appeared the victim had been slugged from behind while coming down the stairs.

The body was stretched out on its back. The back of his head was bludgeoned. The front of Ripley's body was marked by what appeared to be multiple stab wounds, to the chest, stomach, and neck.

The investigator noted that whoever had wielded the knife, he or she had gotten the job done efficiently. There wasn't the sloppiness that crime scene investigators associated with rage. The killer had lethal targets and the stab wounds were tightly grouped.

Patterson determined that the victim had been on his face at one point because of corresponding blood patterns on his sweater and the floor. There was material from the rug embedded in the victim's face.

At some point, the victim was rolled over, perhaps so the stabbing could be accomplished in a more personal way, or perhaps to get at his front pockets, which were pulled inside out and empty. There was some evidence of tearing on one of the pocket buttons. Despite the contamination of the scene, the firemen denied rolling the body over.

Patterson couldn't tell how many times Ripley had been stabbed, but there were at least four stab wounds on the neck. He first photographed the body in the position it was found; then he rolled the body over onto its side, face toward the wall, to photograph the bludgeoning wound at the back of the victim's head.

It appeared that the victim was struck from behind, thus rendering him unconscious, most likely while both he and his attacker were descending the stairs. He probably toppled forward onto his face, was rolled over, and then was stabbed on the floor.

There was no evidence of a struggle from the victim, another indication that he was, in all likelihood, unconscious after the first blow and throughout the stabbing. There were no defensive wounds. If the victim was unconscious when stabbed, that was telling. It meant that the killer did not want to leave any witnesses.

The assailant who did the bludgeoning had used a weapon of convenience, probably a hammer. He hadn't brought it with him. The hammer had been there, somewhere in the building, and had been picked up because it looked potentially deadly and was within arm's reach.

(Decades later, Patterson learned that one of Robert Bruce Spahalski's victims was also bashed over the head from behind with a hammer.)

The corpse did not show a significant amount of bleeding. This told the investigator that the victim had died quickly. The victim was wearing a shirt and sweater that could absorb large amounts of blood. However, if the deceased had survived for any period of time, Patterson would have expected to see more evidence of blood on the floor from chest wounds.

Robbery was an obvious motive. The victim's pockets had been searched, pulled inside out. Car and wallet were missing.

Elmira might have been urban compared to the rest of the region, but it was still a small world. Not long after the body was ID'd as that of forty-eight-year-old Ronald Jay Ripley, of Southport, just south of Elmira, Patterson recalled that he had gone to school, and had been good friends, with the victim's oldest son, David.

Ripley's basement walls were unfinished and showed the stones of the house's foundation. The floor was scattered with small rugs. The rug upon which the body had bled had already been red, but the bloodstains still showed up dark against the faded and worn material.

When investigators searched for footprints in blood that might have been a clue as to the murderer's identity, they first had to eliminate a firefighter's boot prints.

Your Saladmaster Kitchen was only five doors away from a twenty-four-hour joint called Wright's Restaurant. Heights officer David Padgett, who was assigned canvassing duty, asked the restaurant's proprietor, Frank Wright, if he had seen or heard anything unusual the night before. He shook his head no.

The victim's car, a 1971 green Plymouth station wagon, with a chrome rack on top, was missing, but it was quickly found. Police had received a call from a nearby resident, who said there was a car abandoned in a field near Fitch's

Bridge, where Hendy Creek Road crossed the Chemung River in West Elmira.

Police motored to that scene and identified the Ripley family station wagon. The area around the car was taped off, and a guard was posted, keeping curiosity seekers away until the car could be processed.

The station wagon was found with the Ripley family's Thanksgiving turkey and a smashed carrot cake still sitting on the front seat. An examination of the car's interior led police to believe that it had been occupied by two people not long before its abandonment.

In 1971, West Elmira was the neighborhood where the Spahalski twins lived.

Of course, in those days, the twins were suspects in just about any local crime that involved robbery, but the connection was a bit stronger in this case. Robert had ditched stolen motor vehicles in the Fitch's Bridge area before. From there it was an easy walk home to Bower Road.

As the first day of the murder investigation proceeded, a cooperative multidepartment force was put together, supervised by Chemung County district attorney John F. O'Mara, and consisting of Elmira Heights police chief Lloyd D. Roberts, Captain Richard E. Boland, of the NYSP Bureau of Criminal Investigations at Canandaigua, and Undersheriff Carl F. Draxler, of the Chemung County Sheriff's Office. A crime scene unit from state police HQ in Canandaigua was helicoptered in. State troopers from the Horseheads substation were also on the case.

Officer Hartzel, the Heights policeman who notified Edna of Ron Ripley's death, was now put in charge of finding a safe place for a helicopter to land. He asked what comprised a safe place and was told there couldn't be any wires around for two hundred feet in any direction. Hartzel figured the airport was a safe bet. He called nearby Mary Thurston Field and was told that they could

accommodate helicopters, no sweat. Hartzel notified the
state police and then drove to the field himself to pick
up the state's crime scene people.

After Patterson and the other homicide investigators,
including the men who flew in from Canandaigua, were
through inspecting and photographing the body,
Ronald Ripley's remains were placed on a stretcher,
strapped into place, covered with a blanket—except for
his square-toed boots, which stuck out—and were carried up the basement stairs and out of the store into an
ambulance. The bloody rugs that lay beneath were taken
along with the body, because of their strong forensics
value. It was about 2:30 P.M.

A photo of the covered body as it was removed on a
stretcher—boots visible, poking out from under the
sheet—appeared in the next day's paper. The carriers were
a state trooper from the Horseheads substation and an at-
tendant with Erway Ambulance.

At Arnot-Ogden Hospital, the autopsy was performed
by Dr. Charles Kuonen, with Chemung County coroner
Dr. M. Eugene Pittman assisting and advising every step
of the way.

Observing the autopsy were Officer Hartzel, Sergeant
Phil Shea, and ADA Ransom P. "Rance" Reynolds. The
procedure commenced at 3:10 P.M. After the victim's
clothes were removed, the surgeons counted the wounds
and came up with thirteen.

They started with the head. There was a three-inch laceration of the scalp on the left rear of the skull. It penetrated to the bone, was a clean cut, and had bled very
little. "This wound apparently occurred after death," Dr.
Pittman said.

A horizontal and jagged laceration and puncture were
examined behind the victim's right ear. This wound had
bled much more, and had probably been inflicted while
the victim was still alive, Dr. Pittman concluded.

When the scalp was pulled back, it was revealed that

behind this wound was a circular fracture of the skull, about one inch in diameter, and not pushed in far enough to have caused damage to the brain. The wound, the surgeons observed, appeared to have been caused by a small blunt instrument, most likely a hammer.

The surgeons moved their attention to the neck, where there were five wounds on the left side, all close together. From the amount of bleeding, Dr. Pittman determined that they were inflicted either postmortem or shortly before the victim expired.

On the victim's torso were six lacerations on the right chest, inflicted with a sharp instrument, probably a knife, and all were three-quarters to an inch in length. There was one next to the nipple, which had not affected any vital organs, and five more below the nipple, all of which entered the chest cavity and penetrated vital organs. These five blows were forceful, and perhaps their delivery was responsible for the fractures found in three ribs on the right side. There were five penetrations of the victim's diaphragm and six of the liver. This indicated that the killer did not pull the knife all the way out, but removed it only partially before shoving it back in at a different angle, so there were two internal wounds, but only one entrance. This happened sometimes when the killer was grappling with the victim and the fighting was close in. The deepest wound pierced the diaphragm, liver, and aorta. Dr. Kuonen stated that this deep wound would have caused immediately unconsciousness and was the one most likely responsible for the victim's death.

On the left side, ribs two through eight were broken. Best guess here was that the victim was brutally stomped on the left side soon after he fell.

Also noted was a discoloration around the right eye and a jaw injury. The victim had been struck at least twice in the face. Observing, Officer Hartzel concluded, "The victim had been stomped, stabbed, and beaten." As Pat

Patterson had observed at the murder scene, there were no defensive wounds.

When the body was opened up, it was discovered that there had been a great deal of internal bleeding. When the autopsy was over, items of evidence were turned over to the state police. These included the victim's clothing, blood samples, fingernail scrapings, material on the victim's face that was apparently picked up from landing facedown on the rug, a knife and hammer (which turned out not to be the murder weapons), the rugs, a hair sample found on a rug, the contents of the victim's stomach, and the victim's vital organs.

On Thanksgiving Day, police went to Ripley's home on Pennsylvania Avenue, southwest of Elmira. They questioned Edna again—this time far more intensely and aggressively. (Almost forty years later, the Ripley family was still bitter about the accusatory tone the police took with the grieving widow, who was visibly incapacitated by grief and shock.) Police did learn the highlights of Ron Ripley's bio, but they came up empty when it came to whodunit.

The victim's birthday, police learned, was August 20, 1923. He was a descendant of William Ripley, who had arrived in America on the *Mayflower* eleven generations prior. Ronald and Edna had five children. David was twenty-four, married, and had his own place in Elmira. Priscilla was twenty-one, and had recently married James Bourdette and moved out of state. Then came Joel Stephen, sixteen, who was residing at Fort Jackson, South Carolina. The two youngest boys, Ronjay Michael, eleven, and Jeffrey Lynn, eight, still lived at home with their parents. The victim's parents, Mr. and Mrs. Jay Ripley, still lived in Elmira. Ron had a sister Eleanor who married Elden Young and lived in Pine City, and another sister, Sharon, married name Oliver, who lived in nearby

Horseheads. He had brothers Allen, in Elmira, Carroll, in Wellsburg, and Thurman, of Elmira. The victim also had two grandchildren at the time of his death.

Police learned that the former traveling evangelist attended the Pentecostal Tabernacle in Elmira. The church's raison d'tre was to restore people's lives, lives broken by the "consequences of sin," by urging those individuals to be reborn and become devout Christians.

Ronald Ripley had not been the type to preach to the choir, as they say. He was a true evangelist, the sort of person who sought out sinners as part of his faith. The Pentecostal Tabernacle also heavily recruited young people, both to save their souls and to transform them into Change Agents, young people who would, in turn, become recruiters themselves.

In the antiestablishment world of the counterculturists—that is, the world occupied by Robert and Stephen Spahalski—these Change Agents were known as Jesus Freaks.

So, despite the flying gossip, there were legitimate reasons why the victim might have found himself with one or more male teenagers.

Even in 2009, the effect of the murder on the Ripley family remains sharply painful. A day doesn't go by when Ronald's wife and children don't think about that horrible time.

"I remember very well how I learned the bad news," David Ripley said. "I can't even put into words how horrible it was. I was at work, and my wife and my sister rolled up into the driveway. At first, I thought something had happened to my brother."

He could still see it vividly, despite the passing years: the car pulling up and stopping with an atypical jerk. Then the expressions on their faces. He looked at their faces and knew. *He knew.* Somebody was dead.

David's mom was crying. His sister was banging her

head against the window. His mom told him, "Your dad's just been murdered."

"I just lost it," David recalled. His legs turned to rubber. They couldn't support his weight anymore and folded beneath him, causing him to come down hard on his knees.

"It put unbelievable stress on us as a family. It blew us apart. We were a very close-knit family, and my father was a good family man, and now we're spread out from Florida to California. But spread out or not, this family is a great family and we miss our father dearly.

"It's tough. It remains tough," he said. Thanksgiving, a holiday known for bringing families together, is the last day the Ripleys want to celebrate.

In 2009, Ronald's wife was eighty-three years old and ill. She wouldn't talk about it. Even with her family, the subject of Ronald's death had been taboo for years. Her pain had been immeasurable, compounded beyond any human understanding by the inexperienced Elmira Heights police that had bullied when they should have comforted.

Policemen got in Mrs. Ripley's face, put the poor woman through hell, screaming, "You killed your husband, didn't you?"

"My mother about near had a nervous breakdown," David said. "Naturally, they interview the family," David recalled. But it was the way they went about it. "I was drug up to Canandaigua and hooked up to a lie detector test. I was treated pretty rough, too. It was a different time. Back then, they could do things they can't do today."

Lloyd Roberts, the Elmira Heights police chief, had held that position for forty-two years, and this was the first homicide on his watch, although he did know of at least one other Elmira Heights murder before he took office, which would have been in the 1920s.

News of Ripley's demise had to compete with a national news story, one of the largest of the year. It was also on November 24, 1971, that hijacker D. B. Cooper disappeared forever from a Northwest Airlines flight with $200,000 and a parachute.

As Ripley was last seen alive in Elmira Heights at around 11:30 P.M., a call went out to the public: anyone who had seen Ripley or his vehicle after that time should immediately get in touch with authorities.

On that last night, Ronald Ripley held a sales recruiting meeting on the second floor of his store. Ripley was thinking big, thinking expansion. So far, he'd handled the Your Saladmaster franchise by himself. Now he was looking to put together a sales staff to enlarge the operation and take some of the workload off his shoulders. After the meeting broke up, he might have given one of his prospective salesmen, Leo Hoodak, a ride home. After that, Ripley could have been on his way home when something or someone caused him to turn around and return to his store.

Hoodak and the others who'd attended the meeting were interviewed by police. All that police had learned was that Ripley sometimes flashed a potentially tantalizing roll of cash.

Not all of the press coverage of the crime was hard news giving new details of the murder. There were feature stories as well. Who was this man Ronald Ripley? A photo ran in the paper of Ronald and Edna standing in front of a painting of Jesus. He held an accordion, she posed with a trumpet.

The feature writer interviewed friends of the family. One quoteworthy friend was the Reverend L. C. Voorhees, of nearby Millerton, who'd been friends with the victim for thirty years. Voorhees called Ripley energetic, open-hearted, warm, and talented. Voorhees said his wife was first cousins with Ripley, and he was the one who had introduced Ripley to the career possibilities of selling Your Saladmaster merchandise. They were friends also. He was with Ronald Ripley at the sales recruiting meeting on Tuesday night, and thus had been among the last to see him alive. Voorhees described Ronald that night as being in very high spirits, eager to recruit a staff that would allow him to spend more time with his family. Voorhees also described Reverend Ripley as the most talented musician he had ever known.

Nowhere in print was there a breath of scandal.

The crime scene people, once done with Ripley's store, moved to the scene where his car was abandoned. The keys were missing. The car was completely dusted for fingerprints. Once processed, there came the laborious job of eliminating the prints that belonged to Ripley himself, his family, and other people who had occasion to legitimately ride in the car.

The murder weapons were never found. At the time, police didn't know if the knife belonged to the killer or came from the store. There was a wide variety of knives for sale, of course. Wherever it came from, the killer took it with him and disposed of it. The car keys, as it turned out, would be found. The murder weapons, both sharp and blunt, were lost forever.

By Thanksgiving night, Ripley's body had already been released by the medical examiner, and the family was holding a wake at Olthof Funeral Home, a huge mansion of a facility on Pennsylvania Avenue, which is what Route 328 was called when it ran through Elmira.

David Ripley said his dad's funeral was the biggest Olthof ever had. The viewing hours had to be extended to accommodate all the visitors.

"Thousands of people came from different states," David said. "My father was a well-known man. If God is real—and I have my doubts because of some of the things that have happened—there are a lot of people who are in Heaven today because of my father. That's the good that I see."

Ronald Ripley was buried in Woodlawn Cemetery. Not long after, someone defaced his gravestone, writing on it in lipstick a single word: *PUSHER.*

The public call for anyone who had seen Ripley between the time his sales meeting let out and his death generated a single witness. The anonymous caller told police that he'd seen Ripley alone in his car at about 11:45 P.M. on Tuesday, driving his station wagon westbound on West Church Street and turning onto Glen Avenue.

Because Glen Avenue came to an end at Water Street, just one block farther south, and Water Street was a one-way thoroughfare, heading east, police assumed that Ripley had turned east on Water Street soon after he was last seen. That location was also very close to where Ripley's car was found abandoned.

Since Ripley was last seen driving his car in West Elmira, he was killed in Elmira Heights, and the car was later found abandoned back in West Elmira, a geographic picture developed. There was a strong chance, investigators believed, that the killer or killers lived in West Elmira. That, and the fact that the crime included a car theft, put Robert B. and Stephen J. Spahalski at the top of the suspect list.

Again investigators used the press to ask the public for information, this time specifically witnesses who might have seen any hitchhikers trying to thumb a ride in the vicinity of Water Street and Glen Avenue.

In Chief Roberts's contemporaneous written report,

he recalled that there had been another witness, a highwayman, who, at seven in the morning on November 24, saw what appeared to be Ripley's station wagon driving at the top of Coleman Avenue.

Roberts wrote, *A short time later he seen two male persons walking east on Hendy Creek Road. Both were tall blondes, both with long, shaggy hair.*

The local newspaper continued to print the police plea for help for a week following the murder, but each day the story got smaller, until, by November 29, it consisted merely of a two-inch item in the bottom corner of a back page.

According to Ransom P. Reynolds, the assistant district attorney who prosecuted the Ripley case, the murder investigation's initial focus was on Robert—not Stephen—Spahalski. From dealing with the juvenile delinquents over the past few years, cops saw Robert as a better fit for a crime this violent.

The Spahalskis' home on Bower Road was only four blocks from the intersection (Church and Glen) where Ronald Ripley was spotted by one witness, and only two blocks away from Coleman Avenue, where Ripley's car was seen at dawn by the "highwayman."

"We were working on the Spahalski twins for a long time," Pat Patterson recalled. Like ADA Reynolds, Patterson was focusing on the edgier twin. "Our thinking was that it was Robert, because our information had always been that he was more violent."

Patterson recalled that taking an interest in Robert's whereabouts and activities was nothing new for himself and his partner, Edmund "Eddie" Wilkins, another investigator on the Ripley case, who was now deceased.

"I remember even before the Ripley murder, we would follow them if we saw them. Just for a little while, just to let them know how interesting we found them. One day

Eddie and I found ourselves cruising right behind the Spa-halski brothers in a car. I remember one of them pulled down the sunshade above them and used the mirror on the back of it to watch us. We thought that was funny."

The investigators visited the boys at their home in West Elmira. They stopped and said hi, whenever and wherever they saw them. The Spahalskis found this irritating, which was okay with investigators.

Police, it seemed, were *always* investigating one or the other of the twins for some crime or another. But—despite the theories of Pat Patterson and David Ripley—there was little evidence that Robert and Stephen worked as a criminal team.

According to Robert, crime was a competition between the twins, not a cooperative effort, and police records bear this out. Even when both were free, they only got in trouble separately.

Following the Ripley murder, the next mention in a police report of one of the Spahalski twins came less than three weeks later, on December 10, 1971, when Bob Spahalski was one of three teenage boys who had helped a teenage girl get so intoxicated that her mother called the cops.

The girl in question, Janet Wilson (pseudonym), later said she had been hanging out with three guys she knew from the SOS School at Grace Church, a group for kids who'd dropped out of high school. Cutting school, they tried unsuccessfully to buy a six-pack of beer at a couple of places, and one of Bob's friends gave her eight pills, which she took. Three of the pills were blue and white, one was small and yellow, and four were yellow and green.

After she took the pills, the boys brought her to a bar at the corner of Baldwin and East Market Streets. Sitting at the bar when they entered was Bob Spahalski, a friend of the other boys, who was drinking 7&7's and shooting pool. The boys bought Janet drinks: Rolling Rocks and a 7&7. It was about 1:30 P.M.

When Janet was really buzzed, she left the bar with Bob, who took her by taxi to a house on Columbia Street.

Wilson refused to say what she did at the house, but she did admit she saw evidence that the boys were taking drugs with needles. She remembered throwing up and was on her way back to school to pick up her books when her sister picked her up in a car.

In response to the complaint from the mother, the cops dressed down the bar for serving minors.

Despite the implications of this story, and the admitted addiction of his twin, Robert said that he was never a heroin addict.

"I tried it once," he recalled, "and I couldn't function on it. It brought me down, and I like to be up and aware."

On January 28, 1972, Robert was arrested for stealing basketball shirts, and received six months in the Chemung County Jail for breaking the terms of his probation. That's where he was when the great flood hit.

In the early afternoon of March 26, 1972, four months after the Ripley murder, Stephen and girlfriend Sue got into some mischief. They were walking past a vacant house on Kinyon Street, about two blocks from Southside High School, where Cunningham went to school, when Steve saw what he thought was a loose window. He went up to the house and pulled the window out. He and Sue then crawled into the house, looked around, didn't see anything interesting, and came right back out. They ran around the corner into the Cunningham family home. Unfortunately for the teens, children playing outside saw them remove the window and enter the abandoned house. The kids told their parents, and the police were called. The teens were brought to headquarters. Sue's mom accompanied her to the police station.

Spahalski and Cunningham admitted to entering the house, but they added they were just curious and didn't take anything. They were released with a warning, and the owner of the abandoned home, who lived in Jamestown, was asked to board up the broken window so as not to tempt other potential trespassers.

During that stretch, the Ripley investigation was yielding little new information. Beyond the eyewitness who saw Ripley driving his car on Glen Avenue, and the other who saw his car on Coleman, there was nothing.

District Attorney John O'Mara scheduled regular meetings with all of the investigation's supervising personnel. Everyone needed to be on the same page, and the left hand had to know what the right hand was doing. "We may not have anything new, as a result of the meeting, but we want to make sure we all know what we've got," O'Mara said at the time.

On January 12, 1972, the New York State Police Crime Lab released their report on the materials that had been turned over following autopsy. The results were not helpful. The lab technicians had been unable to even type the blood found on the rugs or Ripley's clothes because of "contaminating substances in the material." The holes on the victim's shirt and sweater corresponded with the holes in his body. A bloodstain on the left-side waistband of the victim's jockey shorts proved to be too small to be tested, and the shorts tested positive for semen, with intact human spermatozoan present. Tests on the fingernail scrapings were inconclusive. Hairs found on the rug and on the victim's clothes were determined to belong to the victim himself. An analysis of the victim's stomach contents revealed that Ripley's last meal had consisted of Chinese food. The remains of the squashed cake found in the victim's car turned out to be made of rice, carrots, and ginger.

* * *

Investigator Pat Patterson picked up Robert Bruce Spahalski at one point during the investigation and drove him up to Canandaigua, New York. It was a small town, south of Rochester, built alongside the Finger Lake of the same name.

Canandaigua was also home to the nearest polygraph machine and licensed polygraph administrator. Robert had agreed to take a lie detector test.

"Robert was in the polygraph room all by himself for a time and I was observing him from an adjacent room through a one-way mirror. We weren't fooling him. He knew he was being watched," Patterson said.

He began to behave peculiarly. He showed off for his audience, doing a handstand, walking around on his hands. Shifting his weight from his hands to his feet with one smooth move. At one point, Robert took a small piece of paper from the table and stuck it in his shoe.

"He was just being a jerk," Patterson said.

The polygrapher entered the room, explained to Robert what was going to happen, hooked him up to the machine, and asked his questions. The first few were control questions, to get a measure of a "normal" response, one in which Robert was obviously telling the truth. Then he got down to the crux of the matter and asked questions about the murder of Ronald Ripley.

When the question-and-answer session was through, the polygrapher unhooked Robert and removed the paper tape from the machine so the results could be analyzed.

Investigators waited anxiously for the polygrapher's interpretation of the exam. After a moment, the polygrapher reported that Robert did not kill Ronald Ripley, but he knew who did.

It was with a heavy heart that Patterson drove Robert back to Elmira. Robert was taken into the sheriff's office and interrogated briefly. Robert didn't want to talk about his friends or his brother any more than he wanted to talk about himself.

"We were just about to release him, when I said, 'Before you go, Robert, take out that piece of paper you stuck in your shoe.' He thought he had really conned us, smuggled a piece of paper out of the polygraph room. I could see it in his face that he was disappointed that we hadn't been confused by his activities."

Patterson recalled telling Robert, "'Do you really think if we thought you had evidence in your shoe that we'd let you keep it in there so long?' You could see it in his face. He was disappointed."

Months passed.

The Ripley family lived in fear, believing that whoever killed Ronald was going to come after them next.

"I went to sleep with a knife under my pillow," David Ripley recalled.

Only forty-eight hours before the case broke, the *Star-Gazette* ran an article entitled UNSOLVED MURDERS STILL HAUNT INVESTIGATORS. One of the cases discussed was the Ripley murder.

The piece quoted DA O'Mara as saying, *"We're still actively engaged in that case. Leads still come in, although not as often. We've interviewed hundreds of people."*

As an example, O'Mara spoke of Elmira Heights patrolman Mike Perovich, who recently traveled "out of state" to follow up a lead that turned out to be a dead end.

Following up a lead didn't necessarily mean they would find the suspect. Maybe they would only find someone with pertinent information on the case. O'Mara gave no indication that law enforcement was two days away from making an arrest.

Frustrated by Robert's unwillingness to admit anything about anything, investigators took a closer look at his twin. During the spring of 1972, the investigation shifted its focus to Stephen after phones were tapped, and Stephen quickly incriminated himself.

Police listened in to a phone call Stephen made in which he discussed Ronald Ripley's murder. "You better do as I say or you'll get the same thing Ripley got," or words to that effect.

Because of that, police were able to obtain a search warrant for the Bower Street house. In the Spahalskis' plumbing system, investigators found the keys to the Ripley station wagon.

On May 4, 1972, Captain R. E. Boland, of the state police, located Stephen and apprehended him peacefully at the home of a friend. A sheriff's lieutenant, Edmund C. Wilkins (Pat Patterson's partner), and Senior Investigator Michael C. Capozzi, of the state police's Horseheads substation, were with Boland. Stephen was advised of his rights and taken in.

The interrogation took place at the Horseheads state police barracks. Upon arrival Stephen was advised of his Miranda rights a second time, and for a second time, he waived those rights.

Stephen was taken to a room where he was interrogated by Capozzi, with Wilkins observing. The interview began with Capozzi asking the suspect his name, age, school, and home address. Stephen provided this info. "Junior, Elmira Free," he said. Capozzi sat at a typewriter and typed the answers down as Stephen gave them.

In response to questions, the suspect told Capozzi that he would answer the questions truthfully, that he was unmarried and that he was in good physical health.

"Steve, do you recall the Ronald Ripley case in Elmira Heights, New York, where he was found murdered?"

"Yes." (Capozzi originally typed "Yeah," but Stephen changed this to "Yes" and initialed the change when reviewing the written statement.)

"How and why do you recall it?"

"Because I was responsible for his death."

"Are you telling me that you killed Ronald Ripley?"

"Yes." (Again, changed and initialed.)

"Steve, do you know what night you killed Ronald Ripley?"

"I'm not sure of the night," Stephen said. "But I went to a party at Sue Copp's house that same night. I was with my girlfriend, Sue Cunningham, and Copp lived about a block from Delaware Avenue. I'm not sure of the street. It was on the south side."

Capozzi asked for details regarding Stephen's activities that night. Stephen said he left home at 6:00 P.M. and hitchhiked to his girlfriend's house. They went to the party and stayed until about eleven.

"My twin brother, Bruce, was also at the party. At eleven o'clock, I told Bruce I was leaving and I left my girl at the party. I was alone and walked from Sue Copp's house to South Main Street, to the Laundromat, near the Red Barn, on the south side. About a week before this, I had made an appointment with Ronald Ripley to meet him near the Red Barn, around eleven o'clock," Stephen said.

The suspect said he remained in the Laundromat until approximately 11:55 P.M., when he saw Ripley's car pull up to the curb outside.

"He honked the horn and I came out," Stephen said. He got in the car. First thing, he said, Ripley asked him if he had the money he owed him. "I didn't answer and he said, 'Okay, we will do business where we usually go.' He then drove to the Saladmaster Kitchen in Elmira Heights."

Steven said Ripley parked across the street from the store, in a small parking lot. They went in through the front door. "Ripley said, 'Okay, we might as well go right downstairs.' He asked me again if I had the money I owed him. I told him no. We were both standing up in the cellar, near the steps. He made a remark like, 'What are we going to do about this?' I said, 'I don't know.'"

Stephen said that Ripley put his hand "inside his clothing," near his breast, and came out with a gun in his hand. He said something, but Stephen didn't remember what it was.

"When he slipped the gun out of his shirt, or whatever, I got scared. When you see a gun pointed at you, you know it's either him or you."

"So you attacked him?"

"Yes. I grabbed a piece of metal off a suitcase nearby. I don't even know what it was, a wrench or something. It was sort of heavy, like a bar."

Stephen said he was facing Ripley and hit him in the side of the head with the heavy object. Ripley fell down right away, and Stephen said he immediately jumped on top of him.

"He started struggling, and I held him and took out a knife I had in my jacket pocket. He rolled on me. We were on our sides. I had my feet wrapped around him. I started stabbing. I didn't mean to stab him that many times. I was fighting for my life. It was self-defense, so help me."

He didn't know how many times he stabbed Ripley. He stabbed until "he just laid there." When he stopped, Stephen's hands were shaking uncontrollably.

"Why were you shaking?" Capozzi asked.

"I just stabbed a guy," Stephen replied. "You don't just stab a guy and then relax."

Stephen said that his mind immediately turned to covering his ass. He stood up and looked around the cellar. Other people might be showing up. He ran up the stairs.

"His briefcase or something was on a table. His keys and gloves were in the case. I put his gloves on."

"What type of gloves were they?"

"They were brown and really thin."

"What did you do next?"

"I thought I would make it look like a robbery, so I started throwing stuff all over the place. I knew that other people who came there used the back door, so I opened the back door and left it open."

Stephen said he returned to the cellar, where he picked up the heavy object he had used to first strike the man. He turned off the cellar light and closed the cellar door behind him. He recalled that a big tractor-trailer was parked out front, so big that it blocked the store's huge front window. He went out the front door and around the truck, crossed the street, and threw the heavy object and his knife into a field, where there were thick trees and shrubbery. He still had Ripley's gloves on. He unlocked the car and drove away. Because he was an inexperienced driver, he almost had an accident. He added that a few weeks later, he returned to the scene to see if he could find and better hide the weapons, but he found that the field with its trees and shrubbery had been leveled.

"Where did you drive the car to, and where did you almost have an accident?" Capozzi asked.

"Okay, I drove over the railroad tracks and turned on Grand Central Avenue," Stephen said. He said he wasn't sure of some of the street names. He just kept making turns until he saw a landmark he recognized. "I came out near the reformatory. Then I drove down Hoffman Street, to Church Street, and out West Church toward my home. It was on the way down Church Street that I almost had an accident. It was raining and I was near Underwood Avenue. The car started to slide back and forth. I whipped the wheel around and slid right up into a driveway. I backed up, straightened her out, and drove behind Jim's Car Wash, where I dumped the car."

"Did you stop directly behind the car wash?"

"Well, as far into a field as I could get it in."

Capozzi asked what he did next. Stephen claimed he left the gloves on, turned off the car lights, and walked to his house. Everyone was asleep. He went into the bathroom and sat on the toilet to think. There was some gunk on his pants, which, after he examined it, turned out to be cake. There had been a cake on the front seat of the car and he must have sat in it. He cleaned up and then went upstairs. He woke up Bruce.

"I told him I did something bad," Stephen said. "He was half-asleep and said, 'Yeah, yeah, tomorrow,' or something like that."

Stephen said he hid the car keys and the gloves under his bed. He took off his clothes, rolled them up, and shoved them into a dresser drawer. He tried to go to sleep, but there was no way. He still had way too much adrenaline pumping. He lay awake all night, and in the morning, the first thing he did was turn on the radio to see if there was anything about it on the news.

"I didn't hear anything right away. Then my twin brother, Bruce, woke up and I told him what I did," Stephen said. After that, they heard on the radio that a body had been found. He thought about turning himself in. The twins talked it over. Stephen ripped the gloves into small pieces and flushed them down the toilet. Then he flushed the car keys. "I was thinking to myself, 'I may have made a mistake dumping the car where I did,' because Bruce stole a car before and dumped it in the same place."

"What kind of car did Ripley have?" Capozzi asked.

"Station wagon. Maybe green. Maybe a Chrysler."

"What do you recall being in the car that night?"

"There was a jacket or coat on the front seat, a one-layer brown cake, and some other stuff that I don't recall exactly." He did not mention seeing a frozen turkey. "In the rear of the station wagon was a lot of pot ware."

"Can you describe the car keys to me?"

"There were several keys, some were colored. I can't recall exactly how they were held together. I do recall there was a cross. I think it was gold and possibly red. It was pretty."

"Describe everything you were wearing that night, including your socks and underwear."

"Desert boots, no socks. Fruit of the Loom white shorts, no T-shirt. Blue jeans and a football jersey. It had a number on it, but I don't recall what. Blue windbreaker, no hat. That's it."

"Where is that clothing now?"

"It's hard to say. I continued washing and wearing them. I'm wearing the boots now. My brother Dave has the jacket."

"When did you wash the blood off the clothing?"

"The next day in my basement."

"Could you describe the knife you used to stab Ronald Ripley?"

"It had a gold handle on it. The blade was about seven inches. Altogether it was a good ten inches or a foot."

"What kind of a blade did it have?"

"Very pointed. Just before the tip, it curved a little, like a machete. The blade folded back into the handle."

"Where did you get the knife in the first place, and how long had you had it?"

"I picked it up during the summer. I don't know exactly where—might have been in somebody's house. I had it for a long time—since summer, that is."

"What did you use it for?"

"Just messing around."

"Steve, who else have you told this to? Who else have you told you killed Ronald Ripley?"

Stephen listed a close circle of confidants.

"What did they say?"

"They were just shocked."

"Is there anything else you want to tell me about this?"

"There's nothing else to say. That's everything." Stephen added that everything he'd said was the truth, to the best of his recollection.

He read the seven pages that Capozzi had typed, made a few corrections, and then—before Chemung County attorney William A. Danaher, who was also a notary public—signed, *Stephen Joseph Spahalski.*

The statement was flawed, no doubt about it. The most obvious problem was that Stephen claimed Ripley pulled a gun on him, and then never mentioned the gun again. Although he had talked in detail about hiding the knife and the "heavy object," the gun was forgotten. Of course, no gun was found at the murder scene, and there was no evidence whatsoever that Ronald Ripley had ever owned or been in the possession of a firearm.

Also, Stephen's memory of the knife was far more precise than his memory of the blunt object. Was it possible that Stephen grabbed a metal object, used it in part to kill a guy, then hid it across the street without ever specifically identifying in his own mind what it was? Was it a wrench, a bar, or the tool that best fit the evidence, a hammer? Stephen said he didn't know.

Along with their belief that Ronald Ripley's gun was imaginary, some investigators felt an accomplice had used, and then hid, the blunt object, thus explaining why Stephen wasn't sure what it was.

Forty years later, Pat Patterson's theory remained that both Spahalski twins were with Ripley, that Robert had bludgeoned him from behind with a hammer and knocked him out, and Stephen had then rolled the man over and stabbed him. The theory went that it was the twins that the highwayman saw, a pair of tall teenage boys walking at dawn, eastward along Hendy Creek Road— indicating that Robert might have had a larger role in the cover-up than Stephen was giving him credit for in his confession.

It looked like the work of two killers, one with the blunt object, one with a sharp object, one from the back and one from the front. Police would never be able to prove that was the case, however. If Robert had been involved, both twins were keeping their mouths shut about it.

If they had done it together, then Stephen, for some reason, was cool with taking the rap solo.

Robert looked back with great sadness at the day his twin was arrested. Their fraternal rivalry of crime—to see who could break into the biggest house and steal the most stuff—had been a lot of fun. According to Robert, the crimes were just part of the big party—but the party was over when Stephen got busted.

"After he got locked up for that murder, we were never to walk the streets together again," Robert said thirty-seven years later. "I was left without my best friend and cohort." From a guy like Robert, who, for the most part, correctly used a surprisingly large vocabulary, the use of the word "cohort" was purposeful.

Stephen's arraignment was held during that same evening, May 4, before Elmira Heights justice Charles F. Dickinson, at the Heights Village Hall, only a block away from the murder scene. It was a rainy evening, and Stephen was transported from the state police substation in Horseheads to the Heights Village Hall on Scottwood Avenue via a brown unmarked Fury, the last in a twenty-car convoy.

Photographers were already there, waiting for a photo op. The instant Stephen stepped out of the back of the police car, bright lights went on and cameras clicked. The accused was wearing a green plaid jacket, white boat-necked shirt, lavender-colored slacks, and brown boots. He walked, eyes facing front, into the building, escorted by the new Chemung County sheriff Carl F. Draxler, Undersheriff Sherwood O'Dell, and Elmira Heights police chief Lloyd Roberts.

Once in the building, reporters tried to follow, but they found the accommodations cramped. Stephen was led past the offices of the Heights Fire Department and Police Department, the village clerk, and then up a narrow staircase to Justice Dickinson's tiny office. Only the first few reporters even made it to the top of the stairs before gridlock put a halt to the parade.

Dickinson hadn't anticipated the crowd and ordered that the proceedings be moved down the hall to a courtroom so that everyone would be able to see and hear what was going on. It was 8:55 P.M.

"You folks with cameras, be aware that there are to be no photographs taken in this courtroom. Outside you may take all the photos you want—but in here, no," Dickinson said.

Stephen was placed on a metal folding chair. Among those in the courtroom was his mother, Anita, whose face hung with long suffering. A son being charged with murder—her worst nightmare had come true.

Dickinson conducted the arraignment from behind a chest-high paneled enclosure, so he resembled a bust sitting upon a shelf. The accused was smoking a cigarette.

The justice read the complaint form, which included the statement by Lieutenant Wilkins that Spahalski had admitted in his presence that he had inflicted the fatal wounds.

As Dickinson was reading—in even, measured tones—Stephen coolly gestured with his cigarette hand that he needed to flick his ashes. A nearby plainclothesman handed him an ashtray.

"Stephen, you are charged with murder, a Class A felony," Dickinson said. Following the reading of the complaint, Dickinson said, "Stephen, you are entitled to counsel. If you are financially unable to obtain one, you can have a court-appointed lawyer."

"Can I talk to my mother about that?" Stephen asked.

"Yes, you may," Dickinson replied.

Stephen set down his ashtray and was escorted, along with his mother, into Dickinson's office, where the mother and son conferred in private for nine minutes.

Stephen was escorted back into the courtroom alone.

Anita stayed in Dickinson's office. Stephen took his seat and said, "We will get one."

Later, however, perhaps after being informed of how much legal representation on a murder charge would cost, the Spahalskis changed their mind, and Dickinson appointed public defender Samuel J. Castellino to handle Stephen's case.

Dickinson adjourned the proceedings, and Lieutenant Wilkins approached the accused. Stephen stood up and looked up at the ceiling, his cuffed wrists in front of him, a fresh cigarette in his right hand.

Dickinson said, "You are committed to the Chemung County Jail without bail."

Stephen was escorted out of the courtroom, and the building, and back into the rain.

After the arraignment, a reporter asked DA O'Mara if Stephen Spahalski and Ronald Ripley had been acquaintances. O'Mara declined to answer.

Wilkins told reporters that the suspect had been interviewed soon after the murder, but he had not become the prime suspect until about two weeks before his arrest when new evidence was uncovered.

The parade of cars, with the brown Fury again bringing up the rear, left the Heights Village Hall and headed east on Fourteenth Street, right past Your Saladmaster Kitchen, which now had a FOR RENT sign in the front window.

Robert was already behind bars for stealing shirts and breaking probation. So, on the evening of May 4, 1972, Anita Spahalski's twin boys were, for the first time, both in jail at the same time.

At one time, the case had remained motionless for months and months; then there had been a slow, encouraging movement. When it broke, it broke quick. Stephen was picked up, questioned, induced to confess, arrested, and arraigned, all on the same day.

* * *

Soon thereafter, Stephen met for the first time with Castellino, his lawyer, who recommended they opt for a preliminary hearing rather than wait for grand jury action.

That hearing was held on Saturday morning, May 13. The prosecution established that a crime had been committed, that Stephen had confessed to doing it, and that the victim's car keys were found lodged in the pipes beneath the Spahalski toilet. Dickinson ruled that the prosecution had more than enough evidence against Stephen to hold him over for grand jury action.

On Monday, May 22, 1972, Stephen was formally indicted by a Chemung County grand jury on charges of murder and second-degree grand larceny (for stealing Ripley's station wagon).

A second arraignment was held, this time in a Chemung County court before Judge Donald H. Monroe, who'd been a county judge since 1956, and was a stickler for schedule. The charges were officially upgraded from village to county. Castellino tried to get Judge Monroe to set bail for Stephen, but the judge would have none of it.

Elmira is built almost entirely in the floodplain of the Chemung River, and a month after Stephen's indictment, in the aftermath of Hurricane Agnes, the city recorded the worst flood in its history. The city suffered twenty-three deaths and almost $300 million in damage. About half of the city's buildings were affected in one way or another.

Robert remembered the flood well: "I was finishing up a six-month stint in the county jail, and I remember looking out the window, watching the water carry away a lot of valuables from local businesses." Hurricane Agnes: a better thief than he'd ever be.

He saw even more devastation, a lot of property damage, when his jail was evacuated and he was moved by paddy wagon to the Watkins Glen Jail.

"When I did get out of jail, I made a lot of money on the cleanup of domestic and business basements. I cleaned up a lot of mud and debris," Robert said.

On Thursday, October 19, 1972, Stephen again appeared in Chemung County court before Judge Monroe. The judge believed that court should begin at 9:30 A.M. on the dot, lunch breaks should be kept short, and evening recess shouldn't be called until 5:00 P.M.

Judge Monroe had gone to New York a few times as a visiting judge in Queens and Nassau County courts. He was appalled at the lackadaisical manner in which trials were held there. He saw to it that trials were handled efficiently in Elmira. But in this case, it was starting to look as if there would be no trial. A deal was in the works.

Stephen pleaded guilty to a reduced charge of first-degree manslaughter. Ronald Ripley's family was furious, but there was nothing they could do.

Stephen's sentencing hearing was held on November 28, 1972, just a little over a year after the murder. At the hearing, Samuel Castellino called for leniency.

Because of the case's homosexual angle, everyone spoke and wrote about it in euphemisms. Castellino reminded the judge that robbery was *not* the motive in this case, that items present at the scene, such as jewelry and cash, were not taken. The details, as understood by the prosecution, had been hashed out with the judge in the privacy of chambers.

"The act was effected in a state of extreme emotional disturbance," Castellino said, taking at face value Stephen's scenario of how the crime occurred.

Assistant District Attorney Ransom Reynolds didn't exactly ask the judge to throw away the key, either: "The county is aware of the nature of the act, and mindful of circumstances involved," Reynolds said.

For causing the death of the Reverend Ronald Ripley,

Judge Monroe sentenced Stephen Spahalski to an "indeterminate sentence of up to twelve years in prison."

Stephen was received into the custody of the New York State Department of Correctional Services on November 29, 1972. He was assigned a Department Identification Number.

When Robert Bruce Spahalski's version of the Ripley murder is chronicled, an insight is gained into the story that caused O'Mara to lighten the charge against Stephen, and, separately, into why Ronald Ripley's tombstone was desecrated in lipstick.

"Somewhere along the way, my twin met a homosexual minister who got him addicted to heroin," Robert said in 2009. "After this creep got him addicted, he extorted my twin for sex in order to get a fix. With the sexual extortion going on, the minister told Stephen that he'd tell all my brother's friends that he was homosexual. So out of desperation, my twin murdered the man to erase the threat. He stabbed the guy forty-eight times. It was a simple story, with a simple teenage solution."

In 2009, Pat Patterson remained frustrated that Robert was never brought up on charges for the Ripley kill, but that's the way it went. There simply wasn't enough evidence—no way for investigators to demonstrate to a jury's satisfaction that there was more than one killer. Even if they could, there was no evidence that Robert was the other killer. Robert had passed the polygraph. Stephen confessed to doing it alone. Case closed.

If Robert really did have something to do with the Ripley murder, how did Patterson explain Robert's ability to fool the polygrapher?

"A psychopath doesn't feel any guilt when he thinks about killing someone. He doesn't feel any anxiety at all.

He remains calm, contemplative. People like that don't have the subtle changes in body chemistry that indicate lying. They simply lack the physiological changes that occur in you and I. He not only could fool the lie detector, but he had the confidence to know he could fool it when he volunteered to take the test in the first place."

The only time Robert's polygraph exam indicated deception came when he was asked, "Do you know who did it?" He said no, and the needle wiggled.

"Polygraphs can be wrong, but the polygrapher in this case was very good, a state police polygrapher who knew what he was doing," Patterson noted.

Robert was specifically asked if he was there when Ronald Ripley was killed. He said no; the needle stayed rock steady. No signs of deception.

Maybe Chemung County got it right and Stephen Spahalski did kill Ripley alone. Or maybe Stephen's accomplice was not his twin.

Even after Steve went to prison, Sue Cunningham didn't break up with him.

"I continued to visit him at prison every Wednesday for a long time, then I finally came to my senses and moved on with my life," she recalled.

Today she is married, and her experiences with the Spahalski twins seem like ancient history. Cunningham, however, remains protective of her friend and the Spahalski twins' siblings.

"When Bruce was arrested for those murders in 2005, the press was unrelenting in trying to find out any information about his family back here in Elmira. My friend and his brother, who are married, did not want anything to do with cooperating. They're good people, and I'm sure [they] didn't want to be reminded all over again [of] the hell those two put their family through," Cunningham said.

* * *

Years later, Ronald Ripley's oldest son, David, was interviewed for this book. By 2009, David had been a New York State corrections officer (CO) for twenty-three years, and retirement was only a year away. He recalled fondly his old high-school friend Pat Patterson, who went on to be an investigator into his father's murder.

David Ripley and Pat Patterson might have been schoolmates and friends, but they had widely variant views on the death of Ronald Ripley.

"I believe that my father's murder had nothing to do with homosexuality," David said. "They (the Spahalski twins) were criminals long before they killed my father. They were robbers. They had robbed a couple stores in Elmira, and my father's store was doing really well. I think they were there to rob my father that night."

But David and Pat agreed on another point involving the crime.

"I believe that Robert and Stephen Spahalski killed my father together," David said.

He noted that during the early stages of the investigation, there was no mention of homosexuality. He said the murder trial was about to start when the subject first came up.

"At first, Stephen Spahalski was charged with first-degree murder and he signed a statement admitting it. His lawyer must have gotten wind of my father's past record, and the charge went to manslaughter second. Stephen Spahalski is an animal—and he ended up serving less than three years for killing my father."

During the 1972 to 1973 school year at Elmira Free, perhaps during his twin's murder trial, Robert was kicked out of high school for punching a teacher in the face. With nothing to do, and more bored than ever, the frequency of Robert's crimes increased.

On May 20, 1973, Robert was investigated for possible involvement in a car theft. A car was stolen on West Water Street early in the morning, then recovered on Fifth Street in an Elmira College parking lot, at 5:45 P.M. Only the keys were missing. The odometer had advanced 120 miles. The owner was concerned that the thief had kept the keys and planned to use the car again, so police removed the ignition. Robert was an immediate suspect because, according to Patrolman R. Moran, of the West Elmira Police Department, he was a known car thief who always dropped off the cars near his home, so he wouldn't have far to walk. Robert no longer lived in West Elmira. He had moved out of the family house and had his own place, south of the college, so this theft fit the pattern. Robert denied stealing the car, and that was that.

An interesting sidenote in history. Robert moved out of his mother's house and into his own apartment on Gray Street in 1972 or 1973. "That was my first apartment," Robert said nostalgically. "I dealt drugs out of it." Robert's mother had tolerated him smoking weed. She was relatively cool with that. But she hated for him to take acid, meth, or any harder drugs. It was because of his frequent LSD trips that she kicked him out of the house on Bower Road. His apartment building on Gray was catty-corner from a small clothing store known as the People's Place, the first attempt by a young Tommy Hilfiger to sell clothes—in this case, hip-hugging and bell-bottomed jeans that otherwise would not have been available in Elmira. Hilfiger's store was the site of "happenings." Local radio stations would broadcast live from there. Minor celebrities made appearances. But Hilfiger was not getting rich in Elmira. His store was in the small city's downtown section. Once-thriving business had been sucked away by shopping plazas and malls built on the outskirts. He later complained that there were usually more people hanging around outside his store than were inside buying clothes.

Robert Bruce Spahalski remembered being one of those young people out front and claimed to have been an acquaintance of the man he remembered as "Tommy Hillfinger."

"He was always well-groomed and financially maintained, even in those early years," Robert recalled.

The building that held Hilfiger's store is no longer there. It was torn down in 1999 to make room for the First Arena, the home of Elmira's minor league hockey team, the Jackals.

In the meantime, while Hilfiger was struggling to sell jeans, the residents on West Gray Street were not at all happy with this kid Spahalski who had just moved into their building. The apartment was noisy at all hours— loud music, foul language, doors slamming, stomping Frye boots on the fire escape.

Business was better for Robert, being in the dope trade. He had a whole menu of drugs available, but most sales were exotic weed, coke, or meth.

"I was buying and selling quarter-pounds and half-pounds of weed to all my high-school friends. There was a lot of traffic in and out of the apartment," Robert said.

And it wasn't just traffic that was upsetting to a woman named Mary Huff, who lived across the hall. There was the music. "We were always blasting Black Sabbath," said Robert.

Did he remember Mary Huff?

"Ha! I even tried to get into her panties, being the American I am," he said proudly.

* * *

On June 9, 1973, Mary Huff—who lived in the rear of the building across the hall from the young man she knew as Bruce—left her apartment briefly to get her mail. When she returned, she discovered her pocketbook was missing.

No one had come in or out of the building through the front door while she was getting her mail, so she knew it had to be someone from inside the building—no doubt one of those rowdy boys from across the hall.

Years later, Robert remembered Mary well. He knew she wasn't a Black Sabbath fan. "She always called the police on me," he said.

She certainly called the cops when her pocketbook disappeared. It only had about $10 in it, but there were other items—photographs, Social Security card, medical insurance cards—that she would really like to get back.

Officer Hawley pounded on Bruce's apartment door, but there was no answer.

That didn't mean it wasn't him, Mary Huff told Hawley. Bruce and his "longhair friends" sometimes came and went using the back fire escape.

When the Black Sabbath record was finished, and flipped over and finished, the longhairs in Bruce's apartment listened to ZZ Top, Deep Purple, Ted Nugent, Hendrix, Cream, Mountain, Traffic, Uriah Heep, Moody Blues. Then Black Sabbath again. If the neighbors didn't like it, the hell with 'em.

The following day, Officer S. Miller stopped by and knocked on Bruce's door. This time he was home. Robert explained that he had been away the whole previous day, but he did have friends in the apartment.

He told Miller that he would speak to them and see if they had anything to do with the pocketbook's disappearance. If they did, he would explain that it was really uncool to rip off the lady across the hall, and he would see if he could get her stuff back.

The officer then visited Mary Huff, who said that

she'd done a survey of her apartment and found that some rolls of old coins were also missing. (There was an odd footnote to this story: Mary Huff's pocketbook was recovered seventeen months later behind a building a few blocks away. The contents, including the cash, were still in it.)

Three days after Mary Huff complained of having her pocketbook stolen, Bruce was after larger game. He loved to play guitar, and he desperately wanted to be in a band. He was going to make it so.

Sometime during the overnight, between June 11 and 12, someone broke into Kelly Music Store on West Water Street, on the north side of the Chemung River, between the Main Street Bridge and a dike.

When the store was opened up for business on June 12, an employee discovered a rear window open. An inventory revealed that $286 in cash, three electric guitars—two Fenders and a Gibson—and a 132-pound amplifier were missing. The thieves, it appeared, knew what they were doing, as the equipment taken was the most expensive in the store.

The thief or thieves would have had to climb a small tree to get in that window, which was fifteen feet off the ground. Pretty acrobatic stuff. Scuff marks were visible on the trunk of the tree and on the store's wall beneath the window.

As it turned out, the thief was pretty acrobatic. Years later he recalled the ordeal.

"To steal that stuff, I had to smoke a joint, take forty feet of clothesline rope, and climb up a tall tree. The tree took me to the height of the window, which I opened with a handy crowbar," Robert said.

He cleaned out the cash register, then began tying equipment with the clothesline and lowering it out the window to the ground below.

"I had to climb up and down several times to unhook the equipment from the rope. It took about a half hour to burglarize the place." He lived close by on Gray Street, so he didn't have to carry the stuff far. "I was trying to put a band together, which was a cool thing to do back then, and I gave most of the equipment to the guys I had chosen to be my band members."

The case was broken on June 13 when an anonymous informant, a student at Elmira Free, told police that Bruce Spahalski and his roommate, Terry Potter (pseudonym), robbed the store, and they had been bragging about it. Cops talked the informant into trying to get inside Spahalski and Potter's apartment to see if any of the stolen property was there.

Also trying to be helpful was a janitor at a bank near the music store, who said he saw four males behaving suspiciously "over by the dike" on the night of the burglary. It was suspicious enough for him to write down their license plate number. Police questioned the car's owner, who said he and three friends were fishing in the river that night. The janitor was asked if this scenario fit what he saw, and he said no way. The men were empty-handed, going behind the music store, then carrying long packages when they returned. It turned out that the young men were telling the truth about going fishing, and what the janitor saw had nothing to do with the burglary. He had perhaps melded two separate memories into one.

In the meantime, the store owner was offering a $25 reward for info that might get his merchandise back. An anonymous caller said the theft was connected to a break-in at the Horseheads Junior High music room, and that the stuff was being stored in a house on West Gray Street, a block from Robert's apartment.

Police went to that address and talked to neighbors, who complained of loud guitar music for the past week. The noisy apartment was occupied by David Teeter, who was arrested for burglary and possession of stolen property. Teeter told police he committed the crime alone, although only a portion of the stolen stuff was in his possession.

After another look at the tree and the store window, police came to the conclusion that it would have been impossible for Teeter to rob the store alone. When questioned again, on June 23 in jail, Teeter said Bruce Spahalski had been with him.

Based on this info, a search warrant was granted for Spahalski's apartment. The apartment house's landlord signed a consent-to-search form, which allowed police to search the building's public areas. Lieutenant Dick Wandell, who would later become Elmira's chief of police from 1984 through 1988, was among those who carried out the search.

Before searching Bruce's apartment, police talked to Mary Huff, who was still looking for her pocketbook and its contents. In an effort to retrieve her property, Huff had been going through Spahalski's trash after he carried it outside. She hadn't found any of her own belongings, but she had found a few Kelly Music Store price tags. Since they were for amounts in the hundreds of dollars, she knew they were suspicious, plucked them out of the trash, and kept them.

Huff now handed the price tags over to Lieutenant Wandell. Those tags would eventually help convict Robert Spahalski and send him to prison.

There had been wisdom in Robert's earlier words: it was *indeed* very uncool to rip off the lady across the hall.

The ensuing search of Bruce's apartment and the building's cellar led to the discovery of the remaining stolen merchandise from Kelly's, as well as items that had been reported missing from the junior high school in Horseheads.

On the same day as the search, two anonymous female informants told police that Spahalski, Teeter, and another male had robbed the junior high, the music store, and a Laundromat.

On June 25, 1973, Lieutenant Wandell and his partner located Spahalski at the Red Barn restaurant, where he worked. He was arrested and charged with third-degree burglary and second-degree grand larceny. Wandell read him his rights.

When asked if he understood his rights, Spahalski said firmly, "No!" He refused to answer any questions and was tossed in the county jail to await trial.

On June 26, he managed to get in trouble, even though he was already behind bars. He apparently gave some of his druggie friends permission to use his apartment while he was away. At just before 2:00 A.M., on June 26, a neighbor, perhaps Mary Huff, called the cops to complain.

The apartment was noisier and busier with Robert in jail than it was when he was home. Sergeant Arthur Keith, Sergeant Cortright, and Patrolman Joseph Keough Jr. responded to the call. Inside the apartment, the cops found a twenty-one-year-old, who lived down the hall, and two underage teenage boys. They said they had permission to be there. The cops hauled all three in and contacted Spahalski, who verified that they had permission.

Much to their disappointment, the officers found no drugs in the apartment, but they noted that it seemed to be set up for drug use. The key was a scale that measured in grams, an item that long-haired youths used almost exclusively to weigh out quantities of drugs—most commonly, marijuana and cocaine, both of which were routinely sold by weight.

Talking to neighbors, they learned that there was heavy traffic in and out of the apartment at all hours, apparently for the purpose of taking drugs, and they were getting sick of it.

The problem resolved itself soon enough. Robert was successfully prosecuted for grand larceny and burglary for the Kelly Music crime. The prosecution was handled by

Chemung County DA Bruce Crew. Robert was sentenced to five years in prison.

"That ended my musical career for a while," Robert said.

His landlord on West Gray Street immediately rented apartment number 4 to someone else, who, much to Mary Huff's relief, was much quieter.

"Anyways, as luck would have it, I ended up in Elmira prison, in the same prison block as my twin," Robert remembered. For a few years, Robert and Stephen got to work together in the same shop. "It was a glorious family reunion," Robert explained.

In addition to being with Stephen again, Robert also passed his high-school equivalency exam and received his GED while in the Elmira Correctional Facility.

After serving two and a half years of his five-year sentence, Robert was released in 1975. He tried to get a job in Elmira, but there was doodley-squat.

"I remember when I was released, the Vietnam War was just ending," Robert said. "I tried to join the Marine Corps, but they refused me because of my felony conviction."

He finally found a part-time job as a piano mover, but it wasn't long before he was back to the old "sex, drugs, and rock-and-roll" lifestyle.

The first order of business, with Stephen out of commission, was to acquire someone to replace his twin in his life, someone to compete with.

"I get bored easily, so I got another burglary partner," Robert remembered. He was Peter Manuel (pseudonym), and he served a dual purpose: he was also a guy Robert could play guitar with.

The pair started a fresh crime wave. The wave first formed a blip on police radar on January 19, when Robert was investigated in regard to a fire bomb, although it is unclear from the records if Robert ever actually had anything to do with a bomb.

On April 22, Robert burglarized a house on Fassett Road. On April 27, he struck again, this time on the southside at St. Athanasios Greek Orthodox Church, on Franklin Street.

On May 22, he broke into and stole items from the Seventh-day Adventist Church on Maple Avenue. The very next day, he burglarized a home on Fulton Street.

After taking the month of June off, on July 1, Robert removed items from the auditorium of St. Mary's Catholic Church, on Franklin Street, which was only five buildings away from St. Athanasios.

According to Robert, he and his new partner in crime were very selective when it came to choosing their targets. Instead of taking little things, like jewels and cash, their competition sometimes took the form of giantism. The one who stole the *biggest* item was the winner.

"One day we would steal a refrigerator out of a house," he said. "The next day, we'd take a bed and a La-Z-Boy."

Sometimes, if they were hungry and wanted to make the homeowner feel good and violated, they'd take the food out of a house's cupboard and freezer. "On and on, it went," he said.

Robert remembered a loneliness about that time, a feeling of being left behind by the rest of the world—like hitchhiking on a night when no one's picking up.

"I saw no future on the road ahead," Robert said. "I wasn't climbing socially like everybody else. It was a very helpless and frustrating feeling," he said.

Those feelings were blended with, and enhanced by, his alienation. He'd once felt on top of the world while walking the streets of Elmira. Now that he had to look out for himself, he saw a city that didn't want him, and it hurt.

Robert ruefully said, "I felt totally rejected in Elmira. I remember kicking myself in the ass for not accepting a gymnastics scholarship to West Point. Maybe if I'd done that, the direction of my life would have changed. But drugs deferred my common sense of judgment."

The day after the St. Mary's break-in, July 2, Robert's latest crime spree screeched to a halt. Sometimes Peter Manuel and Robert Spahalski served as each other's look-outs when doing crimes—just as the Spahalski twins had served one another when the stealing game was fraternal.

But on this night, Manuel was elsewhere, and Robert's luck ran out.

According to Patrolman Joseph Keough Jr., at 9:53 P.M., he was informed that the burglar alarm at Southside High had gone off. Keough went to the scene, checked the various entrances to the large school building, and saw no evidence of entry, so he drove to the school janitor's home and picked him up. To search the school properly, he needed the man with the keys.

The patrolman and the janitor entered the building and discovered Robert squatting on the floor of the music room. Keough asked the young man, now twenty-one years old, what he was doing. Robert replied he was "just looking at the musical instruments."

Robert was placed under arrest and charged with burglary. Back at the police station, during interrogation, Robert admitted to the earlier burglaries. He was convicted in court and given a two-and-a-half-to-five-year sentence in Attica for each of the burglaries, all of the sentences to run concurrently. He was in prison from March 28, 1977, until November 13, 1979.

For a couple of years, law enforcement in and around Chemung County had a break from the Spahalskis. As luck would have it, briefly in 1978, Stephen and Robert were again in the same prison, this time the Auburn Correctional Facility.

Robert remembered, "I lived on my twin brother's

company and got into his prison shop, where we built state highway signs together."

Guards had trouble telling them apart. They were still nearly identical and shared the same odd behavior. For example, the Spahalkis apparently had retained their gymnastic skills, and one or the other or both could regularly be seen walking around the prison's exercise area on their hands.

According to prison guards, the Spahalskis' display of gymnastic prowess was not exclusively vanity. They weren't just showing off. And they weren't that off-the-wall, either. Hand walking had a desired effect. The weirdness spooked the other inmates, and rather than being abused, the twins were pretty much left alone.

In July, according to Robert, "I got bored and tried to escape. I built a false bottom on an army truck."

He tried to escape by having his identical twin cover for him. Robert built the bottom on the sly in auto shop. The truck, he knew, was scheduled to leave the prison and travel to a government agency.

"I said good-bye to my twin brother and ventured forward with the escape plan," Robert said.

But someone hip to the plan was a snitch. Prison officials received a tip, then realized only one of the twins was present and accounted for. The truck never left the prison.

Realizing the jig was up, Robert managed to escape long enough to confuse the issue of identity. He left his secret compartment and ran into the prison's auto shop, where both twins worked.

Stephen noted that this escape attempt occurred before he had fully embraced his feminine side and homosexual lifestyle. "I was not wearing makeup back then," Stephen said years later. "At the time, we were in pretty good shape. We looked pretty much the same.

"I got caught and was sent for a year to Attica. I never

saw my twin again, and I never lived in Elmira after that," Robert said.

Thirty years later, he still missed both Stephen and Elmira.

"I was always fond of living in Elmira and had a lot of fun, friends, good memories, and regrets. Most of all, I still consider it home," Robert said.

In 1979, Stephen was released from prison on parole. (Robert was still in.) The local authorities were not informed of Stephen's release.

That's the way it was, back in those days. Police often didn't know when career criminals were out of prison until familiar crimes were committed, and they themselves had to put "two and two" together.

Today both sides are eager to point out that communication between law enforcement and the correctional system in New York State is much better. But back in 1979, it took city and county cops a while to make the connection between a sudden rash of burglaries in Elmira and the fact that there was once again a Spahalski twin in town.

During July 1979, there was a robbery at Glider City Powersports, which sold dirt bikes, ATVs, watercraft, and the like, on Cedar Street, along the very southern edge of the Elmira city limits.

On November 12, 1979, there was another armed robbery, this one at the Beverage Baron, in which a victim had a shotgun held to his head by one assailant while the other cleaned out the cash register.

This brought Stephen Spahalski to the crime for which he would spend most of his life in prison. . . .

14

The Kidnapping

On April 2, 1980, two masked men—one tall, one short—entered a convenience store behind a Hess gas station at the corner of College Avenue and Verona Street in Elmira and announced that this was a stickup.

As per their MO, one put a shotgun to the head of the teenage boy behind the counter, while the other scooped money out of the cash register into a bag. Once the robbers had all the money, there was a quick conversation between the two.

"Let's take this guy with us," the tall one said.

"No. Why?"

"No witnesses!"

"But he can't tell who we are," said the shorter of the two. They were, after all, wearing masks.

"No witnesses. We're bringing him!"

And so they grabbed the guy, threw him into the car, and drove away with the money and their hostage. They drove outside the city and marched the kid into the woods.

"Let's kill him," the tall man said.

"I won't talk. I won't talk! Don't kill me," the victim begged.

The other assailant, the one who didn't want to commit the kidnapping in the first place, talked his partner into giving the victim a puncher's chance.

"Let's just tie him to a tree and leave him," the short man suggested.

"Okay," his partner agreed, and that was what they did.

The victim turned out to be the luckiest guy in Elmira. Gagged and bound and left outside in the cold spring air, he was discovered by a passerby, untied, and taken to the hospital, where he was treated for exposure.

It had been an ordeal, but all in all, it was better than having his head blown off by a shotgun.

Because it was an armed robbery using a shotgun, local enforcement figured there was a good chance that the guys were the same ones who had robbed the Beverage Baron a few weeks earlier.

The case was being investigated by the sheriffs rather than the Elmira police because the kidnapping had taken place partially outside city limits.

As was true with the murder of Ronald Ripley eight and a half years earlier, one of the investigators on the kidnapping case was Pat Patterson, who later recalled the crime.

"It wasn't until the name Stephen Spahalski came up during the investigation, I realized he was out of prison," Patterson said.

At the time of the kidnapping, Patterson remembered, Stephen was living with a wife, maybe a woman he met while in prison. "I got the impression she was one of these prison groupies," Patterson recalled.

Robert met his future sister-in-law once. And it might have been back in high school. She was beautiful. Her name was Joyce Abbott (pseudonym). She and Stephen were married and had a baby girl.

Stephen and Joyce lived on West Water Street, near Lake Street, in a big old Victorian home that had been converted into multiple apartments.

Stephen Spahalski's name was first mentioned to investigators, Patterson said, because he'd been hanging out with another Elmira career criminal, a diminutive and lesser sidekick named Ronny Jones.

According to Patterson, Jones and Spahalski, sometimes with a third accomplice, were drinking, drugging, and "running around doing robberies."

Patterson picked up Jones for questioning regarding the earlier Beverage Baron armed robbery. Stephen, Ronny Jones, and a guy named Lawson had allegedly walked into the store, wearing ponchos and carrying a shotgun.

According to current Chemung County district attorney Weedon Wetmore, Stephen had ordered store employee Mike Hayden (pseudonym) to the floor, and one of the assailants held a shotgun to the back of his head while the others took the money. Wetmore said Hayden still lived in Elmira, where for years he operated a small store across the street from the First Arena in the downtown area. He would never go a full day without thinking about the night the shotgun was held to his head.

Pat Patterson described sidekick Ronny Jones as a classic loser. "He was an inadequate personality," Patterson recalled with distaste.

Jones confessed to the Beverage Baron armed robbery. Patterson wisely followed up the confession by asking Jones what other crimes he'd been involved in.

Once Jones started to squeal, his inadequacy wouldn't let him stop. He said he'd hung with Spahalski and another guy for a series of robberies and burglaries—and they were the ones who left that kid in the woods.

"Taking the guy was Steve's idea," Jones said. "Steve said he was going to kill the kid because he didn't want there to be any witnesses against us. I said the kid couldn't ID us, we were wearing masks. I talked him out of killing the guy, so we just dumped him, instead."

"Talking to Jones, that was how the sheriff's office found out that Spahalski was out on parole," Patterson recalled. "We went to see Stephen at the old converted Victorian house on West Water."

Stephen and his old lady were home. When Patterson asked Stephen about a series of robberies, Spahalski's wife acted completely shocked.

"Robberies? What are these cops talking about, Steve? *Robberies?*" She created a strong impression that she was on a need-to-know basis when it came to her husband's criminal ways.

If it was an act, Patterson bought it. "I gathered from her reaction that he was leading a double life, working during the day, committing robberies at night," Patterson remembered.

Unlike Jones, Stephen wasn't in a talking mood. Patterson asked about the robberies, about the kidnapping, but Stephen would not budge. Lips pressed together, Spahalski admitted to nothing, so Patterson left.

The investigator wanted badly to get Spahalski. Talk about a bad egg. He'd already killed one, left another to die. He was death waiting to happen.

"It was one of those cases where, as investigators, we simply followed the evidence where it led us. But there was a sense of urgency. I think the victim in the woods is the luckiest kid in the history of crime," Patterson said.

He knew Stephen would have slit that kid's throat or hit him over the head with a hammer without an iota of remorse if Jones hadn't talked him out of it.

The guy simply couldn't be out in society. Patterson had to do something. "We set up a trap," Patterson said, noting that Spahalski was completely unaware that Jones had been picked up and questioned by the sheriff's office.

Patterson had Jones leave Spahalski a note. It said

something like, *I've got something important to tell you. Call me at this phone booth from another phone booth so no one can listen in to our conversation.* He gave a specific time.

The sheriff's office would be prepared for the call. Surveillance experts tapped the phone booth from which Jones would receive the call. With Jones waiting, the phone rang right on cue.

Spahalski told Jones that the police had been to see him and that he'd been questioned about some of the robberies and the kidnapping. Jones and Spahalski had a long conversation about that crime.

The pair went over it, step by step. Spahalski said police were just guessing. There was no way the kid could know who they were, because they were wearing masks during the kidnapping.

The law enforcement officers listening in felt chills at the coolness with which Stephen discussed committing crimes and acts of violence. There was no concern for the welfare of others. His focus was completely on *not* getting caught.

"That was how we got Spahalski on the kidnapping. With that evidence in hand, we went back to Spahalski's home, taking a parole officer with us, and picked him up."

The robbery/kidnapping at the Hess station and the robbery of the Beverage Baron were separate charges but were included in the same indictment by prosecutor Bruce Crew.

When the case came up for a pretrial hearing, Jones testified against Stephen. After listening to the surveillance tape, a jury convicted Spahalski of the robbery and kidnapping at the Hess station, but—because that crime was not specifically mentioned on the tape—acquitted him of the armed robbery at the Beverage Baron. Still, it was enough. He went back to prison.

After serving eighteen years for the robbery/kidnapping, Stephen was released from prison in 1999, but he didn't remain free for long. Within weeks a parole violation put him back inside.

It was possible that because he had spent his entire adult life behind bars, freedom was an abstract notion that merely frightened Stephen. This sometimes happened. When given the opportunity to achieve freedom, prisoners repeatedly messed up, clutching to the security of institutionalized living.

For example, Stephen was scheduled for release again during the spring of 2006, but he remained in prison when he failed to complete the required antiviolence course.

New York State Department of Correctional Services spokeswoman Linda Foglia said that Stephen Spahalski refused to participate in the prison aggression-replacement program. Inmates are offered courses focusing on aggression management and finding alternatives to violence. Prison officials enrolled him in the course, but he refused to go.

In 1981, Chemung County law enforcement got to enjoy a Spahalski-free society for only a few months. Stephen was just back in, when Robert got out on parole. Predictably, Robert's stint on the outside was short-lived.

Now twenty-six years old, Robert was arrested with an accomplice, Roger E. Saxbury, when the pair were caught in August 1981 stealing a coin collection worth $15,000. The collection had been the property of an Elmira prison guard's father.

Robert was convicted and sentenced to two and a half to five years. Back to the Attica Correctional Facility, he went. He was in prison from September 1, 1981, to December 26, 1984. Upon his release, he moved to Rochester.

After a couple of years of luck, he was again convicted of attempted burglary in Rochester and was sent back to Attica, from July 29, 1987, to February 8, 1989. When he reemerged into society, he found a new climate of fear on Rochester's mean streets.

Prostitutes were disappearing from the Lyell Avenue strip and being found dumped near the banks of the county's waterways. The Genesee River Killer was in full swing. Small vulnerable voices on the TV news: "We never go with johns we don't know. . . ."

Less than a year after that serial killer was captured, Robert began his own campaign of death, choosing some of his victims from the same weak and vulnerable segment of society as Arthur Shawcross had.

According to Robert, he never went out looking for trouble. His idea of a perfect crime was one in which he got rich and never so much as had to speak to another human being. He didn't care for conspiracies and he didn't like confrontations.

"I liked being a silent thief in the night," he said.

He kept his crimes small. By the late 1980s, he had four felony convictions and four state prison bids under his belt. He knew all about the new three-strikes law and mandatory life sentences.

"I curbed my criminal behavior," he remembered, "mostly to misdemeanors—crimes where the worst they could do to you was eight months in the county lockup." One eight-month stint came after he was caught trying to rob every parking garage in the county at least once of their receipts. This one-man crime wave necessitated a task force, which quickly caught Robert and—boom— eight months.

"I went for nickels and dimes rather than the mother lode," he said.

Getting back to his former lifestyle, Robert developed a coke habit. But, just as had been the case when he was a youngster smoking furry buds of exotic marijuana, and

washing it down with high-octane methadrine, he
needed a steady flow of cash—so he went into business.

It was a lot harder, and more dangerous, to be a drug
dealer than it had been in the old days in Elmira. Here in
Rochester, Jamaicans had that market pretty much sewed
up. Step on their dreadlocks and you were a dead man.

As his addiction grew, selective nickel-and-diming gave
way to recklessness.

He didn't always work alone. He tried to pull a sizable
heist with a Jamaican partner once, and things didn't go
well—for the Jamaican. Although he later told police it
was a "bank robbery," the goal was to steal a bank drop
from a business depositing their daily earnings. The bank
was in Westgate Plaza on Chili Avenue, southwest of the
city. Robert drove a custom Ford F-150 pickup truck to the
bank and let the Jamaican out. As Robert watched, the Jamaican pistol-whipped the employee holding the bag,
and took $3,500 in cash.

The plan was for Robert to circle the parking lot and pull
up in front of the bank timed perfectly so his partner could
jump in without breaking stride. But ticked-off citizens—
indignant suburbanites—ganged up on the Jamaican.

"He never made it back to the truck," Robert said, "so
I drove away from the chaos, looking for a luckier day."
Robert recalled that he was in jail for a week before they
freed him for lack of evidence. "I went to my drug dealer
and got credit on a few bags of crack to straighten my
social perspective out."

Robert maintained that it was never his intention to
be a big-time criminal. The one-upmanship with his twin
was years and years gone.

About a month after the Westgate fiasco, Robert's
truck was still impounded, so his younger brother gave
him a Pontiac station wagon to drive.

"The Jamaican drug crew I associated with," Robert
said, "paid me off in crack cocaine to drive them and do

a drive-by shooting to a neighboring drug gang. Was I out of control? A little bit."

He tried to steal only when it was convenient, and the chance of getting caught slender. Otherwise, it was the streets. Hustling. He was both whore and pimp. "I could always make a buck with my golden cock," Robert boasted.

According to Robert, this was the first time he'd ever really explored his bisexuality. These were loathsome times, and he performed gay *only* because he desperately needed money to buy crack.

"Other than that," Robert said, "I am not interested in men. I'm not gay, nor do I act feminine. I could never be emotionally involved with the male species. I do admit experimenting with oral and anal sex as a curiosity of explore-amentation."

Despite that, Robert still saw himself—sexually, at least—as a regular guy.

"I was still the typical male American, who liked to plow the fields of horny women—without my old lady finding out, of course," Robert said.

As 1990 drew to a close, Robert burglarized an auto safety glass company for $1,200 in their petty-fund account. After that, he binged on crack for three days, which brought him to New Year's Eve.

During the early-morning hours of December 31, 1990, Robert met and partied with a twenty-four-year-old "cute black girl," Moraine Armstrong, in her Lake Avenue apartment

He also said that he brought fifty bags of crack to the party, $500 worth, bought with the glass company money. They were lying, side by side, naked on her bed. Because junkies never share, they each had their own glass pipe.

"I'm so high and sleep deprived that I'm seeing things and hearing voices from my inner demons," he recalled. As Robert hallucinated, Moraine got the heebie-jeebies. "She couldn't sit still," he said.

Robert's focus now was on "saddling her" and giving

her strong sex, but Moraine was spacing out on the crack and grew noncompliant.

"Eventually she got high and stupid enough that she tried to sneak twelve bags of my crack. I busted the move, and the demons inside me exploded."

So he strangled her with an electrical cord. She'd had the audacity to try to steal from him. The death penalty was warranted. She had "blatantly" tried to rip him off, an offense he called "the ultimate betrayal."

"She went to Heaven or Hell wearing only her birthday suit. The party was over," he said. He got dressed, gathered up his drugs, crossed Lake Avenue to his apartment, and continued smoking crack "without skipping a beat. That was how I brought in the New Year of 1991. The murder of Moraine Armstrong was not a planned event. I exploded in a volatile rage that I don't understand myself."

The year 1991 was one in which "I was a paranoid schizophrenic because of hard-core crack abuse—although, at that time, I had yet to be diagnosed."

That year, along with full-blown mental illness, Robert claimed, he also held down a full-time straight job. He was night supervisor at a metal-fabricating company. The place was called Gray Metal Products, and while Robert worked the four-to-twelve shift in the "elbow" department, he stole about $1,000 in petty cash.

"I also sold one of their forklifts for fifteen hundred dollars without them knowing it," he boasted. He said he sold machinery under the table to an HVAC subcontractor. That's short for "heating, ventilating and air-conditioning."

At the same time, he moonlighted for a catering service run by a "pleasant black Indian lady." She hooked him up with a connection at a clothing manufacturer, where he was given the "opportunity" of "picking up" $20,000 worth of duds, which the company used as a tax write-off. The metal fabricator let him borrow a flatbed truck so he could pick up the donation.

It wasn't all stealing, and when it wasn't, he enjoyed

the good feeling of being gainfully employed and contributing something to society for a change.

His girlfriend at the time was thirty-five-year-old Adrian Berger, who lived in a downstairs apartment on Emerson Street, about a block from his place. She was damned cute, in his eyes, and she had other things going for her as well.

"She was employed," he said. "She enjoyed smoking weed and oral sex."

How their relationship ended was something he didn't remember clearly. It was the summer, a hot spell, brutal hot, June or July, and he was on a two-day drug binge.

"I'm hot and horny for some sex, and she isn't in the mood," he said. He said he stripped her naked and attempted to fondle her intimate places. She was moist, but still not in the mood. And his grabbing her there pissed her off even more. They had a loud, wall-shaking argument. Adrian, he said, made her big mistake when she grabbed a frying pan and whacked him hard on the back of his head with it. He saw stars; then he saw red.

"That enraged me into a homicidal mood brought on by my inner demons. A circuit blew in my brain and I ended up strangling her with my bare hands," he said. "This turned me on." He had intercourse with her "in the midst of her ultimate strangulation. She came into the world naked and she left the same way."

Robert was questioned in the case as a "person of interest." But the cops had nothing and he was soon released. That made two unplanned murders, and the police had questioned him after both.

"Luck was on my side," Robert recalled. Financially, everything was okay, but he could feel his mental condition worsening. "There were a lot of psychotic transitions happening inside my head."

He didn't understand them, he couldn't control them, and they scared the hell out of him. "I was losing my social perceptions," he recalled.

He said that he was becoming delusional: "I had already killed two women, and now my mind was toying with the idea of killing a man, to balance things out, so to speak."

The "demons" were voices in his head, telling him lies that he believed. That was what a delusion was—a lie that his demons told him. When the voices said that he had to kill, he couldn't help himself. "It was like being possessed," he said. "And my crack addiction broke down any mental fortitude that I might have had."

Robert remembered meeting Charles Grande. They said it was in a gay bar, but it was really a mixed bar. "He was very attracted to my male personification," he said. "He was obsessed with paying money to perform oral sex on me."

Robert was "tickled" and "amused" by Grande. "I couldn't believe that someone would pay me for a blow job." Even in the context of this unverifiable scenario, he overstated his naïveté.

He jumped at the opportunity to make $60. He learned that Grande was a "successful landscaper" who owned a business under the "DBA of Horizon Landscape."

Robert claimed that Grande was obsessed with him, and wanted him to come to work for him and move into his suburban house. "I politely declined," he said.

Robert came to believe that Grande was Mister Moneybags, with "vast amounts of cash" all the time, on account of his home-business payroll.

Then came the two-day binge in the fall of 1991. Robert, desperate for drug money, arranged a meeting with Grande. "I was on a mission, drug addicts like to call it," Robert said. "I got him naked. My intent was only to rob him. Not to kill him."

Something about the retelling made Robert feel like a porn star. After a vivid description of sex with the victim, he bragged about the size of his own penis.

An instant after the sex act was completed, Robert said, "Things turned ugly." Robert told Grande about his mission. He wanted money. Lots of money to continue his crack binge.

"The mission was to relieve him of his cash," Robert said. "He was just a mark to me, a victim of his sexuality. I didn't expect him to put up a fight. But fight, he did."

Robert found a hammer next to the victim's bed, grabbed it, and gave Grande warning: Back off and "go with the flow of the robbery. He was foolish and he kept coming at me," Robert said. So he swung the hammer.

It felt "automatic." Naturally, he swung directly for Grande's right temple, and hit his mark with deadly accuracy. Grande went down "like a rock, never to know he was mortally wounded. It had been merciful, yet filled with rage," he said.

Grande was probably already dead, Robert figured, but he still had some rage pent up, the pressure cooker ready to blow, so he took it out on Grande's head. He used the hammer to "beat his head in. I wanted to make sure his days on earth were over."

Then came the stillness and the quiet, only the sound of his own breathing, that calm finalness when a victim had died. The fight was over. Robert's heart was about to beat out of his chest. He took the time to try and relax.

"I smoked a cigarette," Robert recalled. "Then I took the keys to his car, and his wallet, which had a thousand dollars in it. I searched his bedroom and found another couple grand. To a drug addict on a mission, I was rich for a day or two." Those dollar figures had gone up since his original confession.

He took off with the money in the victim's car. He remembered that it was a rainy night, windshield wipers flapping, as he drove back to Rochester.

"It was time to celebrate. I picked up some drugs and my favorite black hooker," he said. Next step was to get a motel room at an understanding establishment and party.

Robert and the hooker were cruising, looking for more drugs, when they were stopped by a policeman. "I was sweating bullets," Robert said. The cop asked for license and registration, so Robert pulled them out of Grande's wallet. He was told to wait in the back of the cop car. The cop called in the info. Robert thought it was over.

If they searched the car, they would find a bag with cash and a bloody hammer in it. He tried to think of explanations for the money and hammer, but he wasn't getting far.

"But the policeman didn't do his job right, and he let me drive away with the hammer, the cash, the drugs, and the hooker," Robert said.

The thing that troubled Robert most about the stop was the cop took the hooker's name and address. "She was from my neighborhood and could identify me as Bruce, as the guy who drove Grande's car on the night he was murdered," he said. "I knew I had to kill her to keep her from doing that."

He got the motel room, and Robert brought the hammer into the room with him, but after partying with the hooker, he couldn't bring himself to kill her.

"I guess I couldn't kill someone in cold blood," Robert said, with seeming sincerity.

Whatever happened, the hooker survived. She smoked a few hundred dollars' worth of crack with him and they had sex. Robert bragged about his own oral sex techniques when it came to pleasuring a woman.

He was candid. He'd smoked too much and had had sex only a few hours earlier. In this case, oral technique was all he had to offer. It had been a long day; he couldn't get an erection.

"The angels were on her side that night," Robert said.

According to Robert's recollection, he smoked up the thousands of dollars he'd stolen, smoked it up all in one night, and by the next morning, he took Grande's car and drove back to Grande's house.

"I figured there might still be cash there, or maybe some valuables I could pawn off," Robert said. When he drove past the house, he was surprised to see men there. "There were about eight of Grande's landscaping employees waiting for him to send them out to their destinations." Since Grande only had two employees, Robert must have been exaggerating.

He saw them, and they saw him. They knew it was Grande's car, and he wasn't Grande.

"I got out of there quick," Robert recalled. "They knew something was up. They jumped in their cars and gave chase, but I was long gone, baby."

Robert drove the Volaré back into the city and parked the car in a relatively secluded spot, somewhere near downtown. He wiped it down for prints, checked it carefully for other signs of personal usage, and abandoned it.

Only a week later, Robert was picked up and arrested for criminal impersonation. The hooker had given him up, just like he knew she would. He recounted with glee how he had been acquitted by a jury.

"The homicide officers were really pissed-off," he said. "I'd just beat a murder charge." They wouldn't leave him be. They harassed him on the street. They contacted his employers and asked questions.

"Once, they told my boss that I was a murderer and he should lay me off for his own safety," Robert said. He lost jobs, until he couldn't get a new job. The cops' harassment drove him underground.

"I disappeared off the social radar," Robert said. He had to be innovative in order to make money. He should have left town, but no way. His drug dealers were local. He couldn't leave his comfort zone.

"I wasn't completely stupid. I knew that I was a person of interest in three homicide investigations. My name kept popping up," he said.

When society wouldn't allow a person to be a climber, he had to be innovative to make ends meet. Robert made money as the neighborhood drug runner. To avoid possible troubles with Jamaicans, he limited his clientele to middle-class folks from the burbs who happened to be drug addicts.

Robert called them "weekend warriors." They wanted to party without hassle, and he provided that service. He gave his clients a "safe haven."

They all seemed to come from towns that ended in "port." Brockport. Spencerport. They would introduce him to their friends. Business grew. Robert called it a "snowball effect." He made tons of money and partied for free.

Robert became a very well-known individual around town. He knew all the drug dealers, all the gang members, all the hookers—all the undercover cops. It was around this time that he became known as "Bikeman." Christine Gonzalez would see him going here and there on his bike, and for a time, she couldn't figure out what in hell he was up to. Later it all became clear.

Being with Christine really helped Robert function. "She helped to keep me grounded," he said. "She kept me healthy and helped me maintain my social responsibilities. She made sure I ate correctly. Discipline was the name of the game."

Not long after he moved in with Christine, he confessed to her that he was bisexual on occasion, and she said she was cool with that. Her attitude was, whatever, as long as his promiscuity didn't involve other women.

According to Robert, his gay side wasn't big, but it was entrepreneurial as hell. His gay side was *enterprising*. He had a friend who was a gay business owner. The man helped Robert recruit gay clients.

The gay clients would pay big bucks for sex, so Robert started a business called Behind Closed Doors, set up for businessmen who were looking for a little sump'n sump'n that they couldn't get at home.

"I specialized in domination, submission, and the teaching of humiliation," Robert said. "My target clientele was married professional bisexuals who desired secret, discreet sessions with their master, their daddy."

He used the name "Adam Tai-chi." If cops asked a client his name, that was the only one they could provide. No link with Bruce and the three killings.

"My clients included doctors, lawyers, accountants, a police officer, and even a priest. It wasn't just the money. It amused me," he added.

The business allowed him to "study and psychoanalyze people's perversions. I provided therapy to those people, and I know they secretly still miss their master."

For about five years, his life became a little easier. In addition to his business, he was collecting Social Security. He did a stint in drug rehab. Then came 1996, and Christine was understandably running out of patience.

"She was getting really pissed-off and irritable over all the people trafficking in and out of her home day and night," he said. "Sometimes money is not worth privacy and peace of mind."

So Robert sought to appease his girlfriend. He cut back on the number of clients he serviced, down to a "rich few." He was proud to say that as of 1991, Robert stopped forever being a taxpayer.

He had his own version of Economics 101. He didn't owe Uncle Sam anything. "I was socially ostracized and therefore null and void," Robert theorized.

Looking back on the highlights of his life, Robert feared his legacy would be that he was a "homicidal, whacko, out-of-control crack addict." That was only *on occasion.* Readers, he said, would be stunned to know how normal things were.

He said, "After my killing binge of 1991, I lived my life discreetly, away from the prying eyes of the homicide detectives. But never too far away. Those eyes always seemed nearby—lurking." (Perhaps he was thinking of the pseudofriendly drive-bys of Tony Campione.)

For the most part, he was a peaceful student of life. He said, "I enjoy the magic of learning new things, utilizing and applying what I learn—no excess mental baggage, please. When I wasn't smoking crack, stealing, or killing people, I lived a normal life in Rochester."

He worked straight jobs, but they were always off the books. He installed floors, papered walls, painted houses. Drywall, roofing. He steam-cleaned carpets.

"I sold, stole, and installed a lot of ceiling fans," he recalled. "I like the way they go round and round."

It wasn't that his urge to kill went away during the fifteen years he took off. He felt the urge every day. It was like anything else. He had to take it one day at a time. Not killing was like staying off a drug. One day at a time.

"I kept rein on my inner compulsiveness," Robert said. He never stopped being a small thief. Truth was, he enjoyed stealing stuff. It wasn't just a matter of survival. It was fun, too.

He liked stealing items from the straight world because they had all of the advantages, anyway. Why shouldn't he have some of their stuff?

It was just like back in Elmira. He still loved the notion that he was a thorn in society's side. "I was the guy you cursed on your way to work that morning, only to later find the tires missing from your car. I was the guy just going to bed while you were getting up to go to work," Robert said with a laugh. He had fun in his "backyard called life."

Christine might have been a stabilizing factor in Robert's life, but she drank a bit. His fondest memory of trying to do her a favor came when he robbed a newly renovated bar/club soon to open under new management. There wasn't any cash yet, but it was fully stocked with booze.

"I stole every bottle behind the bar. I left only a half-drunk bottle of vodka. They must have cried. I did the exact same thing with two downtown bars three blocks from the police station," he said.

He didn't just take the booze—and the cash and food, if there was any—but he also copped eleven antique mirrors and some ceiling fans.

"My old lady was ecstatic," Robert remembered. "She never asked any questions. She knew I was the alley cat of the night."

Luckily, Robert was a bit of a voyeur, and sometimes observing people without their knowledge opened up opportunities for profit.

"I enjoyed studying people's habits at night with a pair of binoculars," he said. "I observed women stashing their purses and valuables underneath the front seat of their cars."

By the time they returned, of course, a car window was broken and the valuables were long gone.

"I love a woman's purse," he said. "It holds so much stuff like gold jewelry, cosmetics, credit cards, bank cards. You wouldn't believe how many of them left their PIN numbers on slips of paper tucked inside their purses somewhere. When that happened, off to the bank I would go."

In the summer, he liked to smoke a joint and take the bus to the picturesque University of Rochester campus on the east bank of the Genesee, south of downtown. He brought a pair of bolt cutters with him in an army bag. He'd lift a high-end bike from somewhere on campus, then unload it on one of his clients for $40. That was *another* reason they called him Bikeman.

Being a thief was in his blood, his God-given calling. He could feel it in the adrenaline rush he experienced when he was swiping stuff.

And even when he wasn't stealing, his lifestyle was intrinsically adventurous. "There was a lot of danger in being a drug addict/dope runner in the 'hood," he said.

Point was, for the fourteen years after he murdered Charles Grande, the "Christine Years," he didn't kill anybody, he was never homeless, he was never hungry, and his bills were always paid on time. "All the bills, except the cable bill, of course. I screwed them on principle," he said.

Those were the best years, because he was not only getting by, he was doing it without having to deal with the straight world. He did it outside the constructs of society. No nine to five. Just freedom. Joy.

"It was a blessing. I could do what I wanted," he said.

Christine had faith in him, she trusted him with her life, and for years he didn't let her down. He promised her he would come home at the end of each night, and he did.

Somewhere near the end of 1999, Robert met Vivian Irizarry for the first time. He and Christine were living at the time in a house on Fulton Avenue, near the crux of Lake and Lyell Avenues.

"Vivian was introduced as Christine's best friend. I thought she was beautiful," Robert said.

Christine was in the room the first time Robert ever copped a feel off Vivian. According to Robert, he gave Vivian a hug, and then reached down and squeezed her buttocks. Vivian called for Christine and ran out of the room.

She may have run off like she didn't like it, but an important message had been sent. "She now knew the cat wanted the mouse," Robert recalled.

Robert and Vivian became good friends, but only sometimes lovers. In the six years he knew her, he'd only bedded her three times. "But they are sweet, intimate memories," he said.

For the most part, he loved Vivian like a sister. His best memories were of scheming and eating and riding bikes with Vivian.

"I even let [a relative of hers] live with us for several weeks when he was homeless and unable to stay elsewhere because of relationship problems," Robert said.

As the new century began, Robert could feel his luck

running out. The years of crack abuse were starting to take their toll on his health, particularly his mental health.

His daily routine consisted of running to the ATM for clients, cashing in their gold and diamonds at the diamond exchange, selling their guns, TVs, computers, stereos, and antiques. He converted items into cash so his clients could buy more crack.

The demons, the voices in his head, were back. At first, they were still distant—garbled subliminals—but they were back, and they grew.

His crack habit was out of control: $3,000 to $5,000 a month. He and Christine were getting nowhere. They were barely maintaining their dysfunctional lifestyle.

Robert was reduced to seemingly reckless con jobs, like trying to pay for drugs with play money, counting on the fact that the guy he was buying the drugs from was just as bleary and out of it as he was.

The trick with the fake-money scam was that he couldn't use the same dealer twice, and he was making enemies for life out there on the street, where it was dangerous enough without burning dealers.

Bikeman didn't blend well, and so, if drug dealers were looking for him, they usually found him. One time he used a fake $50 bill to buy six bags. "I folded it so it looked real," Robert said.

When the dealer discovered the trick, a posse was sent out to teach Bikeman a lesson. "They dragged me inside their house and pistol-whipped me," Robert said.

To make it up to the dealers, Robert paid them what he owed them the next morning, and he spent another $100 on crack to help smooth things over. A man had to be alert, conscious of street politics at all times—and he had to cover his tracks.

He would pass the fake cash in dope houses at three in the morning, when he knew the dealers were least alert. It was during that string of sad scams that Robert learned the "don't go to the same dealer twice" rule. He did try to scam the same guy twice, and it was a mistake.

"This big bastard pulled a machete on me and told me to take off all of my clothes," Robert said. "He took my money and my bike, and I had to walk home naked. But I was a good customer, so he didn't tell me I couldn't come back."

Some of Robert's stories sounded straight out of "*Penthouse* Forum." For example, there was the time he went to the Jamaican dope house and the guy answered the door naked, "his flag waving."

Jamaican said, "Come in, Bikeman." So Robert entered. Inside was a gang bang—six naked Jamaican men and an "exquisite naked girl" on a bed.

The girl had gotten paid ten bags of crack. Robert was asked to participate and he accepted the invitation.

According to Robert, he participated, but only later did he realize how humiliating the experience was . . . for himself. He had just wanted respect from those gang-bangers. "What a price to pay, huh?" he said.

Then there was the time he was sauntering past Kodak regional headquarters, walking down the street minding his own business, when a stretch limo pulled up beside him, a tinted window rolled down, and a naked blonde popped her head out. A cloud of weed smoke puffed out with her.

"Excuse me," she said. "Would you be interested in having a threesome?"

Robert said sure. "Being American, I had a duty to perform for mankind," he recalled. That was the only time that ever happened to him, but he never stopped thinking about it. He wanted more of that three-way action.

Another "funny" one: One night he was out scoring drugs for himself, Vivian, and Christine. He was trying to get the security door to his apartment open when two thugs jumped him, held a sharp knife to his throat, and demanded his drugs and money. Robert got so scared that he shit his pants. The thugs got the cash but did not find the stash in his secret pocket.

When he got home and told Vivian and Christine that he'd literally had the shit scared out of him, they fell to the floor, laughing. Robert thought it was funny, too, and paused for a hit of crack before hitting the shower.

One night an angry dealer tried to run over Robert on his bike in the street. Robert jumped off in time, but the last he saw of that bike, it was crumpled and being dragged down the street by the hit-and-run vehicle.

On another night, Bikeman was riding south on Lake Avenue toward Lyell. As he passed a large black man walking north, the guy punched Robert dead in the face, stunning him. He didn't fall off the bike, but his bones were seriously jarred.

"I circled around him and made a beeline for my apartment," Robert said. "I picked up my stolen .380 automatic, then caught up with this asshole." The first shot "just missed," and the guy ran for his life. Robert fired a few more shots at the fleeing man's ass but didn't know if he hit him. It was pretty satisfying just seeing the guy run in terror like that. Taught him a lesson. He never saw that guy again.

Point was, Robert pushed the envelope, lived on the edge—just like the days when he and Stephen were doing handstands, walking upside down on the edge of some mind-blowing abyss.

Now, in adulthood, though, there wasn't a real abyss. It was more theoretical, more hypothetical. Foul up now and he would be a fatality on the sidewalk or forever incarcerated. That was enough risk to keep the juices flowing.

Plus, truth be known, he was always a two-woman man. Fidelity didn't compute. One woman was Christine. The other was whatever crack whore he happened to be with.

During much of the 1990s, Robert saw his share of sideline action, using the uncomplicated world of crack

whoredom to satisfy his "dark side," while still enjoying
the domestic comfort of being Christine's boyfriend.

Eventually it got to be 2003. "Christine was working
full-time and I was collecting Social Security disability for
a mental defect," he said.

The heat returned.

"There was a black girl downstairs who got herself murdered in a way that fit my MO. She was found dead and
naked, and the detectives were at my door again," Robert
said, referring to the murder of Hortense Greatheart.
"The detectives weren't satisfied, but what could they do?"

Then, two years later, there was a bit of an upheaval.
The landlord on Lake Avenue gave Robert and Christine
their walking papers. According to Robert, the charges
were that the couple engaged in too much "people trafficking." Things hadn't changed that much since he had
his first place of his own on Gray Street in Elmira. His
neighbors were still complaining because of all those
footsteps, in the hall, on the steps, and the vulgar voices
of strangers at all hours. Robert and Christine had thirty
days to find a new home.

About ten days after they received their eviction notice,
Robert put down a deposit for a two-bedroom apartment
on Spencer Street. Among those who helped Robert and
Christine move was Vivian Irizarry.

Along with changing residences, Robert took a crack at
altering his lifestyle as well. As he had done once before,
he drastically reduced his number of clients. "We cut
down on ninety percent of the traffic," he said. "We were
tired of all the games and crack abuse. We were trying
hard to be a normal couple."

Only four people were allowed to visit the apartment
on Spencer Street, and one of them was Vivian. The voices
in his head were growing loud again, and Robert was on
the second day of a crack binge, on November 4, 2005,

when Vivian came to visit while Christine was at work.
Vivian was dropped off in front of the Spencer Street
house that Friday morning. She arrived at 11:00 A.M.,
happy and smiling.

She gave Robert $40 and asked him to buy them a
"morning wake-up," which meant one $20 bag of crack
each. In retrospect, Robert realized that this must have
been some serious kick-ass crack he bought that morning for him to jump off the cliff the way he did.

They had a routine and assumed their usual positions.
Vivian liked to smoke in the pantry, where there was a
table to set down her things. Robert smoked in the
kitchen, giving Vivian some space to zone out in private.

Robert took one major blast off his pipe and the
voices in his head got louder and louder, screaming
helter-skelter, until they overwhelmed everything else.
He didn't remember walking into the living room and
picking up the hammer.

"The next thing I know, I'm standing in the kitchen
again, looking stupid at the hammer, not comprehending
what was actually happening," he said. "Then the voices
shouted, 'She's a demon! A devil! Kill her! Kill her now!'"

He heard a distinct click in his head and snuck up
behind her as she smoked.

"I sunk the hammer deep into her skull," he said.
"Time stopped for a while. It seemed like sixty seconds
before I heard her hit the floor. That snapped me out of
it and I heard myself call out her name."

He cursed himself for being such a dumb ass. He
knelt down beside Vivian and instinctively knew that she
was brain dead, in a coma from which she could never
come back. She'd soiled herself.

"I took off her clothes and cleaned her up, best I
could, and lifted her up like a parent would pick up a
sick child. Oh so tenderly, I put her in my bed," Robert
recalled.

He was crying and scared. There were about two

quarts of blood on the pantry floor. His pillow and blanket were getting all bloody, too. He tried reviving Vivian by talking to her and using cold water, but it was hopeless.

She was practically dead, which is technically still alive, so he decided to take her out of her misery and slowly tightened a ski rope around her neck.

He felt a sense of responsibility as he choked her: "I had to make the judgment call and send her to Heaven. She stopped breathing and died naked in my bed," Robert said. He carried her into the basement.

Robert spent an hour cleaning up the pantry, as best he could, and then bundled up all of the bloody and soiled stuff, the pillow, blanket, Vivian's clothes, the towels he used to clean up. He then carried the bundle over to the Genesee River and tossed it in so it could be "washed away into all eternity."

When Christine got home from work, Robert told her that Vivian had been there for a while but had left. Christine had the next three days off. Those were very long days. He had no opportunity to move the body, and Vivian's boyfriend and son came looking for her, concerned that she was missing.

Robert and Christine smoked crack for three days, and the whole time, Christine kept wondering out loud where Vivian could be. It wasn't like her not to tell anyone where she was. Robert felt the pressure and stress building up inside him.

At night, as Christine slept, Robert went to the basement. "I visited with Vivian," he said. "I would cry and talk to her and tell how sorry I was."

Vivian was killed on a Friday afternoon. By Sunday night, Robert was so distraught that he swallowed an entire bottle of antidepressants. They almost took him over the edge, but not quite. Monday came and went. The search for Vivian continued.

On Tuesday morning, Christine had to go to work, and

Robert insisted on walking to work with her. That gave him an opportunity to tell her how much he loved her.

"Deep down inside, I knew I was never going to see her again," Robert said. "I thought, 'The shit is going to hit the fan now.'"

From 1991 through 2005, Christine was his anchor. He battled the demons daily but got by because of her influence over him.

"She gave me focus, and a sense of direction and belonging. Without her I would have succumbed to more murders," Robert admitted. "This, in my heart, I know to be true."

Walking home for the last time, his feet were heavy with melancholy and he walked slowly, trying to feel alive, even though he knew he was a dead man.

"I borrowed a twenty-dollar bag from my upstairs dealer and smoked my last crack," he said.

The voices returned immediately, a cacophony of irrational anger and bad advice. He was shaking, having an emotional breakdown.

"I went into the basement and kissed Vivian goodbye," Robert remembered.

He didn't remember the walk to the police station. But he recalled the waves of sensation on his shoulders and in his lungs that came with the realization of "last-time freedom."

He remembered that there was blood on his hands. His bloody hands raised in surrender! There was blood on his sneakers when he turned himself in to the homicide cops. Party over. Seemed like the next thing he remembered was wearing nothing but a skimpy gown and being held for forty days in a "suicide cell."

Looking back, Robert felt that going to the police station might have been an error. He should have surrendered to a mental institution. Given the disorder of his mind, he wouldn't have had to fake anything. He would have gotten "more mercy" from the law if he'd played it that way.

"I don't remember being interrogated, and I don't remember signing any confessions," Robert said. The police were exploiting his confusion. He was having a mental breakdown, and they made the most of it.

In the days and weeks following Robert's confession, police and reporters alike tried to stitch together a full biography of Robert Bruce Spahalski—but they didn't have much luck. His family had circled the wagons, and, *until this book*, Robert had not cooperated with writers.

Those reporters knew only one angle on Robert. They knew his criminal history, but that was about it. His activities between arrests were a blur.

Robert's longtime girlfriend, Christine Gonzalez, refused to talk to anybody about anything. She told her friends that she was planning to get the hell out of Rochester.

PART THREE

15

Witnesses Emerge

Police could find no evidence to refute Robert's claim that he'd earned most of his money illegally during his quarter of a century in Rochester. According to available paperwork, Spahalski's only "real" job—for a legitimate business, and on the books—was for the City of Rochester.

When the *Democrat and Chronicle* published Spahalski's skeletal work history, there were squawks from many portions of society. A future serial killer's wages being paid for by local taxpayers! The very idea!

Handy enough to build a false bottom on a government truck in his prison's auto shop, Robert got a job as a mechanic's helper, and later a maintenance trainee, at an operations building on Andrews Street, just west of downtown. He was hired to the entry-level position on August 4, 1980.

Robert's employers may or may not have been aware of the full extent of his prison record, dating back to the age of sixteen. The truth was, he'd only *just* been released from Auburn Correctional Facility.

These were the old days. Officials at Rochester's City Hall agree that today an extensive computerized background check of Spahalski would have been done, even though he was applying only for an entry-level position, and the chances were good that he would not be hired by the city.

The city job lasted for a year. But then Robert was arrested again and was soon thereafter fired for failure to show up for work. After that, he apparently earned his money either on the streets or off the books.

Carlos Rodriguez, the eighteen-year-old youngest son of murder victim Vivian Irizarry, said his mother had been friends with both Robert and his girfriend Christine—although he noted that the man had usually used his middle name, Bruce. He'd known him as Bruce.

Rodriguez said, "I used to see him when I dropped my mother off at his apartment building. He was a nothing. All he did was do drugs. He told me he was HIV positive."

The Edgerton Park neighborhood was thoroughly canvassed, and police located several people who were willing to admit they'd seen Spahalski around.

One was Kassem Saleh, who owned a grocery store called Lyell 1 Deli and Grocery, on Lyell Avenue, across the street from a Sunoco gas station and not far from Spencer Street. Saleh said he'd seen Spahalski buying crack from the young dealers who loitered near his store.

"He was in my store all the time. He liked the same thing for lunch every day. Ham and cheese sandwiches. That was his favorite. Sometimes he also bought Lotto tickets," Saleh said.

During the spring of 2005, for some reason, Saleh was operating his store without his beer license. It was taking him some time to get it renewed. This frustrated Bruce Spahalski to no end.

"He told me I had to hurry up and start selling beer.

I asked him if he liked beer and he said no, he never touched the stuff. He said he only bought beer 'for the ladies.' He told me if I started selling beer, he'd see that I got a lot more business," Saleh said.

Saleh always went out of his way to be cooperative with the police. He'd had trouble relaxing around "the Man" since the days after 9/11, when it didn't pay to be a Yemenite. In fact, it was terrifying.

In September 2001, Saleh traveled to Dearborn, Michigan. While driving in a car with two other men from Yemen, he was stopped by police, and—for no other reason, he learned, than their ethnicity—the car was searched. Police found three pocketknives—legal in New York State, but not in Michigan—and that was all they needed. The three Arab men were arrested, and subsequently interrogated for days by the FBI. The men—who repeated again and again that they were very sad about those who died in New York, Pennsylvania, and Washington, DC—were told that they couldn't be released until immigration officials had a chance to ask them questions, and that was going to take a few days.

By the end of the month, Saleh was released and allowed to return to his Rochester deli. He came home to find his store broken into and robbed. Thieves had ransacked both the store and the apartment upstairs. Cash, cigarettes, and beer were stolen from the store. From the apartment, electronic equipment was taken, along with the immigration green card of one of Saleh's friends. It was a few days before Saleh could reopen his store. He had to replace the safe.

Saleh wasn't the only store owner who remembered Spahalski. Another was Jamil Shaibi, who owned the S&S Mini Mart. He remembered Spahalski as an edgy, pushy customer who often purchased Midnight Special rolling tobacco and rolling papers.

"I guess he rolled his own cigarettes. His hands looked like he did. All yellow," Shaibi said. Spahalski didn't ask for the things he wanted. He demanded them.

"He got upset if I didn't have something he wanted," Shaibi said. "He was easily frustrated when things he wanted were unavailable. I remember one time he got angry when I had run out of matches."

There was nothing relaxed about him, Shaibi recalled. His jaw was always clenched and working side to side, like he was grinding his teeth—and he walked with his head thrust forward, so he looked like a hawk.

Some neighbors remembered Spahalski because it was unusual to see a man that large riding a bicycle, which he often did. No one called him Robert. He was always Bruce or Bikeman.

Police reinterviewed Kevin Turner, the Spencer Street landlord who was first questioned only minutes after the discovery of Vivian Irizarry's body. Turner now offered more detail: Spahalski and his girlfriend moved in some-time during the summer of 2005. They'd only been there for about four months. They were a quiet couple with a cat. Maybe the victim was related to Bruce's girlfriend, not sure how. He'd seen her a few times visiting the house on Spencer. He last saw her Thursday or Friday, when her brother [actually her son] dropped her off in front of the building.

"She was a nice-looking girl—very attractive," Turner said. As for Spahalski, he noted, "There was no indication he was a murderer. He never raised his voice. He was soft-spoken. I never even heard him say a curse word."

Did Spahalski have access to the basement? He did, but he had no reason to be down there.

This train of thought caused Turner to remember an-other encounter he'd had with the accused killer: "I talked to him once about some wires that were torn out of the furnace down there in the basement, and he said that his cat must have done it."

A check of the Department of Motor Vehicles revealed that Spahalski had his own driver's license and a series of automobiles during the 1980s, but lost his license in 1991. Before living on Spencer Street, Robert and Christine lived in the same Lake Avenue building in which Hortense Greatheart was murdered.

A reporter canvassed that building and talked to Susan Servanti, a former neighbor. "I'm just in a state of shock. I'm totally blown away," Servanti said. "I've been in his apartment. He was quiet and polite. I can't imagine him being violent."

She recalled that he enjoyed feeding nuts to the squirrels in the backyard. She and he would chat, nice and relaxed, talking about things that were happening in the apartment building, or whatever. She didn't know for sure if he was a drug addict, but she'd had her suspicions that he might be "on the pipe." She'd never had the slightest inkling that he could *ever* be violent, but there *was* that one time.

"I once warned him that he should lock up his bicycle when he went inside the grocery store down the street, because the neighborhood was bad and somebody might steal it. He flared up and said, 'If anybody steals my bike, I'll kill them. They don't know me. I'll kill them.' But I didn't believe him. You can't expect a person to believe it when they say something like that."

She didn't want to hear the phrase "serial killer." She couldn't imagine him being one of *those,* even if he had killed someone, or even more than one person. She couldn't see him as a predator, stalking his victims to get his kicks. That wasn't Bruce.

"If he did commit these murders, he must have been provoked," the former neighbor concluded.

* * *

Robert and Christine did not move from the Lake Avenue apartment to their new home on Spencer Street voluntarily. They had been evicted. In Robert's version of the story, he and Christine were given the boot because of the twenty-four-hour comings and goings. His neighbors recalled it being more a matter of hygiene. It appeared, those neighbors said, as if the Lake Avenue apartment had never been cleaned the entire time they had lived there. Dirt was layered thick upon surfaces hideously crawling with cockroaches.

One neighbor, who was intimately familiar with the mess because she had helped clean it up after the pair left, said food and cigarette butts covered the floor, and there was a stain, like splashed spaghetti sauce, all over one wall. They had to go.

Although Spahalski's Lake Avenue landlord may have wanted him and his girlfriend out, he wasn't going to do anything to hurt the couple's chances of finding a new place. When Robert and Christine applied for the apartment on Spencer Street, Turner called the old landlord to ask if there had been a problem. The landlord said nope, no problem at all. When asked why Robert and Christine were leaving the Lake Avenue apartment, the landlord said, vaguely, that he'd had a few problems with some of the residents there.

Turner later said that the Spencer Street apartment was "impeccable" after the couple moved in. Never a mess. Always spic-and-span.

The thirty-eight-year-old landlord recalled "that day" vividly. It was a Tuesday afternoon, and he looked out the window and saw firemen on the lawn. Running outside, and then around the corner to the side of the building, he saw they were about to break a basement window. He remembered he still had his lunch in his hand, and asked what they were doing.

A fireman replied, "We got a call, and there's a body in there."

"You've got to be joking," Turner said. "Don't break that window. I've got the key. There's not a lot of light down there, and I'm the only one with a key, so I know there's no body down there."

He followed the men down the stairs and into the basement, but before he got far inside, he smelled death. A fireman ordered him to return outside. They'd found something. After that, the circus really began.

During the early-morning hours of November 9, 2005, Robert Spahalski was arraigned twice. First in the Webster Town Court for the murder of Charles Grande; then in the city for the murder of Vivian Irizarry.

The second arraignment was presided over by Judge David T. Corretore. At that court hearing, Spahalski's confession was read into the record.

Rose Grande was there and told a reporter that her family had known Spahalski was a suspect in her brother's murder, right from the beginning. They could only watch, frustrated.

"They didn't dare charge him unless the case was iron-clad, which it was not. We knew—and he knew we knew—but there wasn't anything we could do about it really. We could just wait for time to pass," Rose said.

She pointed out that she had known about Robert Bruce Spahalski for fourteen years, but had to be patient and wait for police to build a strong enough case to make an arrest—and that was a long, long wait.

"But it's finally over," she said. But there was no sigh with her words. No *amen.* "I'm not happy or anything. But justice is justice, if it comes in fourteen days or fourteen years. I'm glad that part of it is over."

Rose said she wouldn't have had the strength without her husband, Scott Van Dusen. "He was my rock for fifteen years, until this was over. It isn't easy on a spouse, but he hung in there. Scott has been through a lot. 'Unkle' Roger McCall, the all-night guy from WCMF, was murdered a few years back, one of my husband's best friends. There are no leads, as far as I know. It was horrible."

Rose wanted to make it clear that she and her family had nothing to hide. If a reporter had a question, she would answer it. Now that she'd heard what Robert Spahalski had to say about her big brother, she was more determined than ever to set the record straight.

"I wouldn't want a sociopath's distorted view of Chuck to be the last word," she said. "Heaven knows my family had more than enough of that with the media around here. He was a special, beautiful, well-loved human being." She said that a hatred of violence was something that she and her brother had in common. "The violent and senseless murders in Rochester disturbed my brother and I very deeply. We were two years apart, grew up together, and both of us abhorred violence. There's too much of it in Rochester," she said in 2009. "I'll never believe what Spahalski said about my brother in his confession. It was selfserving and I'll never believe a word of it, that he refused to pay full price for a sex act. The story is just ridiculous. I don't know how it happened," Rose said, "but it didn't happen that way."

Rose theorized that perhaps Robert Spahalski had been looking for work. He was a well-muscled guy. Chuck did landscaping and might have been looking for someone to do some heavy work, looking perhaps to save a drug addict, to save a lost soul. Not everyone who worked for Chuck was an upstanding citizen. That was certain.

"We'll never know," Rose concluded. "Sociopaths are geniuses at taking reality and mixing in their own fantasies to come up with a mixture that serves their own interests best, even when those interests are nothing more complex than pure sadism. They want to hurt people, and they know how to do it well. They know how to create a compelling story that—though bullshit—everyone is going to believe," Rose concluded. "Chuck was completely nonviolent. He was completely antiviolence—and he believed there was good in everyone. I believe that his trust might have been his fatal flaw. He knew all sorts of people, and he didn't care if they were drug addicts or alcoholics. He was very outspoken about the evils of drugs. He would lecture people about prostituting themselves and doing drugs." Maybe that was why Spahalski was in Chuck's Phillips Road house. Maybe Chuck was trying to save him.

Rose stood up to Spahalski when he got in her face at the criminal impersonation trial and she wasn't going to stop now. She was angry with the local newspaper when they left Chuck's name off their list of 1991 murder victims, and now she was angry again. The paper printed the information in Spahalski's confession like it was chiseled in stone and came from "on high." Chuck was killed because he shortchanged a male streetwalker. The possibility that it was a fabrication was never considered, certainly not emphasized.

"They couldn't stop themselves from going with the story the way Spahalski told it, for the simple reason that it was juicier than juicy," Rose said. "And it wasn't just Chuck. They were vicious toward Vivian Irizarry, too, saying that she was nothing but a cocaine addict. That's ridiculous. She was a fabulous woman. The only way I could get through this was to turn off the media completely. I stopped talking to reporters. I wouldn't even look at them. They got so miffed. They got nothing from us. It had to be that way. You can't do what they did. You just can't do it. This person and that person, they're not here to defend themselves. They were impugning Chuck's integrity and his entire life, reducing it down to a twenty-dollar transaction for a sex act. His entire life!"

Why does Rose think Robert Bruce Spahalski killed her brother?

"I think there was something about Chuck that drove

Spahalski nuts, something that he couldn't stand. I believe it was some kind of a jealousy. Everything that he said about Chuck seemed slightly exaggerated. He said Chuck's house was beautiful. His car was beautiful. I mean, Chuck had a great house, but his house was a *mess*. He was a *bachelor*! His car was old and it was a little bit beat-up. Spahalski talked about Chuck like he was the one in love. 'Chuck was so strong.' Well, it's true that Chuck was strong, because he was a landscaper, but he wasn't muscular. He never worked out or anything. He wasn't *that* strong."

16

Burned Fingertips

Back when multiple serial killers were active in Rochester's west side, the Monroe County DA was Howard Relin. In the DA's office since 1968, he was elected DA for five terms, from 1983 through 2003. That made him the longest-serving DA in county history. His decision to retire came after several "very heavy" discussions with his wife.

"My love of family won out," Relin later recalled. Following his retirement, he took a teaching job at the Rochester Institute of Technology.

Relin came from a family of lawyers. His father, two uncles, and two cousins—all lawyers. His intentions as a youngster were to become a historian, and he was halfway toward a master's degree in history at Columbia University when he decided on law school.

During his more than two decades as the county DA, Relin's office recorded six hundred murder and thirty-six thousand felony convictions. Among his greatest accomplishments was the arrest, trial, and conviction of Arthur Shawcross. The Genesee River Killer, Relin recalled, had a tremendous impact on people living in the Lyell Avenue area.

"Those people were scared to death," he said. "There was a serial killer on the loose for eighteen months and it really frightened the community in the most horrible way. So having him put away, and having the trial on television, too, became one of the great educational things that we ever had in our community."

Following Relin's retirement, the "new" DA was Michael Green, who had in 2003 switched political parties—from Republican to Democrat. Relin had done the same thing twenty-one years earlier. Green was elected and took office on January 1, 2004. Although relatively new to the top job when Robert Spahalski confessed, Green was hardly new to the DA's office. He'd tried more than one hundred jury trials, and prosecuted more than thirty homicide cases. He was lead prosecutor on four first-degree murder cases, including one of the few capital cases to end with a death sentence in New York. As district attorney, Green personally continued to prosecute homicide and other high-profile cases.

But not this one.

On the evening of Robert Bruce Spahalski's confession, Green assigned Assistant District Attorney Kenneth "Ken" C. Hyland to handle the Spahalski case. Hyland had worked in the Monroe County DA's office since October 7, 1978. He'd been promoted to head of the Violent Felony Bureau in 1987, was named second assistant DA in 1993, and since 2004, he had been the first assistant, or second in command, in the DA's office.

Unlike some of the police investigators handling the case, Hyland had never heard of Robert Bruce Spahalski before he confessed.

"It was Election Day," Hyland recalled, "so it was a day off for us. My wife and I were at our cottage in the Southern Tier, closing it up for the winter, when my pager went off. It was RPD. I called them and they told me this guy had just walked in off the street and said he killed somebody, and when they checked it out, it turned out he had."

That was the end of Hyland's day off. At the time of the phone call, Spahalski had only confessed to killing Vivian Irizarry. Hyland and his wife drove the ninety minutes back to Rochester, and he called in again. By that time, the guy had admitted to killing Charles Grande as well.

"They informed me, at that time, that he was a suspect in a couple of other cases as well," Hyland said.

When details of Spahalski's confession were leaked to the press, one of Hyland's first duties was to answer questions from reporters. Hyland was asked if Spahalski's claim that he "choked out" Vivian Irizarry to end her discomfort—that it was a mercy killing, in a sense— could be considered a mitigating circumstance when charging him.

The assistant district attorney said it would *not*. The question struck him as a tad absurd. Hyland calmly explained that the "mercy" aspect of Spahalski's violence was moot, because Spahalski was the one that caused the victim's agony in the first place. Besides, euthanasia was every bit as illegal as any other homicide.

"He said the strangling was to put her out of her misery. Even if that were true, and his statement was taken at face value, that's still intentional murder," Hyland said. "And there's still the question of whether mercy was an *actual* component of the killer's mind."

That night Hyland met Spahalski for the first time. There was a problem getting Robert's fingerprints. When he was booked earlier in the day at the Monroe County Public Safety Building, his prints were taken in the conventional way, but they were unreadable.

"It was bizarre," Hyland said. Along with having sores all over his hands because of trying to light a crack pipe off the stove, Spahalski's fingertips were covered with scar tissue. "The fingertips were burned from the crack pipe, and the prints we were getting were no good. I had to get a court order to try and get his fingerprints in a high-tech way."

So, several days after the first attempt to take Robert's prints, Hyland and his co-counsel on the case, Tim Prosperi, along with Spahalski and his attorney, Jeffrey A. Jacobs, went to the Monroe County Sheriff's Office, where another attempt was made to get the defendant's fingerprints. An electronic scan was tried, again with less than stellar results. The little ridges and whorls that make people unique as snowflakes were, on Spahalski, largely gone.

But it was the twenty-first century, and technology almost always won. Partial prints were obtained from a couple of fingers by using the electronic scan. As luck would have it, this was enough to match prints found in Charles Grande's Webster home.

Throughout the process, Spahalski behaved himself. This wasn't the same man who had once used his brute strength to break a pair of handcuffs and climb into the drop ceiling of the Public Safety Building. He had surrendered completely, conceded to his fate.

17

The Double Initial Killer

When Arthur Shawcross began his campaign of terror, and the *Democrat and Chronicle* ran its daily headline about a "serial killer at-large," the locals felt a strange sense of déjà vu. This wasn't the first serial killer to plague the city. Rochester, it seemed, was a fertile environment for killers at play. Weary police joked: "Maybe it's something in the Cobbs Hill Reservoir."

The most famous serial killer to strike the region was a monster whose deadly exploits were the subject of a 2001 Discovery Channel documentary, and were heavily fictionalized in the 2008 movie, filmed in Rochester, *The Alphabet Killer*, starring Eliza Dushku and Timothy Hutton.

Using a signature reminiscent of the 1936 Agatha Christie novel *The ABC Murders*, this killer raped and murdered little city girls who had the same first and last initial, and then dumped them in a Rochester suburb that also began with that letter.

Long before anyone caught on to the initials angle, the killer worked his way into Rochester's nightmares. The bad dream started with his very first kill on November 16, 1971, a week before Stephen Spahalski killed the Reverend Ron Ripley in Elmira Heights.

The victim was eleven-year-old Carmen Colon, who disappeared from the Bull's Head section of Rochester, just southwest of downtown.

She'd been running an errand for her grandmother, going to Jax Drug Store on West Main Street. She made it to the drugstore all right, but somewhere between the store and her home on Brown Street she vanished.

Carmen wriggled free from her killer at one point and jumped out of his car. Naked from the waist down, she ran hysterically down the shoulder of Interstate 490, screaming for help. She fled from the car—perhaps a dark Pinto hatchback—backing up along the shoulder of the road. It was rush hour and scores of cars drove by, observing the youngster in distress. Not one stopped.

Carmen's killer caught her and dragged her back to the car. Her body—severely scratched by fingernails, strangled, and sexually assaulted—was found two days later in a gully against a rock in a wooded area off Stearns Road, outside the village of Churchville.

The murder dominated the news for weeks, but the commotion had died down by April 2, 1973, a rainy Monday, when eleven-year-old Wanda Walkowicz disappeared while running an errand for her mother.

Wanda went by herself to the Hillside Deli on Conkey Avenue. As was true in the Colon case, it was late afternoon, about five o'clock, Wanda made it to the store, purchased groceries for that evening's dinner, and vanished on her return trip to her Avenue D home.

Her body—sexually assaulted and strangled, perhaps with a belt—was found on the morning of April 4, just west of Irondequoit Bay, on a hillside next to a Route 104 access road in the town of Webster.

Wanda was last seen talking to someone in a car outside the deli, where she had shopped, but nobody saw the driver.

The similarities in Carmen's and Wanda's murders were obvious. Plus, there was more. The initials motif was noticed at this point. Instant infamy. It was like Rochester had its own "Zodiac."

Young girls in the area with the same first and last initials were afraid. They looked at maps, trying to figure out where their bodies would be dumped.

Fear turned to terror, and terror to panic, on November 26, 1973, when ten-year-old Michelle Maenza disappeared the Monday following Thanksgiving.

Michelle lived on Webster Crescent, on Rochester's east side. She disappeared while on an errand for her mother. Mom had left her purse at a store in the Goodman Plaza, near their home, and sent Michelle by herself to retrieve it. Michelle made it to the store, retrieved the purse, and was returning. At that time, she was seen by her uncle, who offered her a ride. She declined.

She was next seen in the suburban town of Penfield, outside a fast-food restaurant. Michelle was portly and her abductor had fed her.

Michelle was last seen in a car that was parked on the shoulder of Route 350 in the town of Walworth. The car had a flat tire but had not yet been jacked up.

Several passersby, one of whom stopped and offered help, noticed the car and the girl sitting inside. The driver of the disabled car made it clear he wanted no help, so the Good Samaritan went on his way.

Michelle's body, raped and strangled, was found two days later in a ditch about eight feet from the shoulder of Eddy Road in the town of Macedon in Wayne County.

The autopsy tended to verify the sighting at the restaurant, for it was discovered a hamburger had comprised her final meal. The Route 350 witnesses came forward, and working with a composite artist, they produced a drawing of the suspect.

Despite a huge task force assigned to these cases, the Double Initials Killer was never caught.

Kenneth Bianchi, who would later be arrested as one of L.A.'s Hillside Stranglers, had lived in the Rochester suburb of Gates at the time of the initials killings. Kenneth had lived his whole life in and around the city, growing up on Hague Street in the Dutchtown section of Rochester—where, for one year, he attended the same school as the author.

Bianchi's car resembled the one seen on I-490 at the time of Carmen Colon's attempted escape, and he left the area, moving to California, soon after Michelle Maenza's murder. (Bianchi's cousin Angelo Buono, the other Hillside Strangler, was also from Rochester.)

Another suspect was a fireman, an alleged serial rapist who committed suicide in 1974, while fleeing from the police. He hid in a parked car outside a home on Fieldwood Drive on the city's far east side and shot himself.

In 2007, with a warrant from the Monroe County Sheriff's Office, the fireman's body was exhumed from Holy Sepulchre Cemetery. His DNA did not match that found at one of the crime scenes. (All three victims were also buried at Holy Sepulchre on Lake Avenue.)

Long before Wanda and Michelle died, Carmen Colon's uncle was a suspect in her murder. He committed suicide in 1991, not long after shooting and wounding his wife and brother-in-law. After begging police to kill him, he turned his gun on himself.

Another suspect in the Colon murder was a known child molester who worked in the Bull's Head area. The man, now dead, couldn't account for his whereabouts at the time of Carmen's disappearance.

Some theorize that there was no serial killer, that two or three different homicidal pedophiles were at work here, perhaps choosing their methods to throw police off and force police to assume that they were looking for only one murderer.

There were differences in the murders. Colon was strangled manually from in front. The other two were strangled with a belt from behind.

People have tried for years to find a connection between the three victims that would point toward the killer. It was the kind of case that used up detectives. What was a pattern? What was a coincidence? Who knew?

Some believed the initials motif to be a media construct, one that betrayed itself by bending geographic boundaries. Carmen Colon had not been dumped in Churchville at all, but rather in the town of Riga. This was countered with, yes, but it was very close to the Chili border. Maybe the killer thought he was in Chili.

All three victims were poor, Catholic, lived with single moms, and had learning disabilities. The Walkowiczes and the Colons once lived two doors apart. All three were abducted in the late afternoon, picked up urban and dumped rural.

By the late 1980s, when the Genesee River Killer spread terror, Rochesterians were all too familiar with the concept of serial killer. By the end of 1990, when Robert Bruce Spahalski committed his first known murder near Edgerton Park, the presence of serial killers in Monroe County was practically assumed.

18

Probable Cause Hearing

On Monday, November 14, 2005, only ten days after the murder of Vivian Irizarry, a hearing was held in Rochester city court, before Judge Stephen K. Lindley, to determine if there was reasonable cause to try Robert Bruce Spahalski for the murders of Vivian Irizarry and Charles Grande. Coincidentally, Judge Lindley also signed the search warrant for the downstairs apartment on Spencer Street.

Years later, Judge Lindley recalled little about the man who had just confessed to killing four. "I just remember he was calm and demonstrated demur," the judge said.

As Ken Hyland presented the highlights of his case for the prosecution, portions of Spahalski's written statement were read aloud. The court learned the sad state of Spahalski's self-described mind at the time of the Irizarry murder: how Irizarry had been a friend of Spahalski's but had morphed into a demon in his crack-drenched mind, a demon that needed to be vanquished; how he had failed to kill her in his first explosion of violence, but later, after his cocaine high had settled down a little bit, he finished the job to end her agony; how he stripped and bathed her after she soiled herself during her murder; how he left her in the coolest spot in the house so that decomposition would be slow, and there also would be a better chance of Vivian leaving a pretty corpse.

Investigator Glenn Weather testified regarding Spahalski's confession, noting that Robert Spahalski admitted to hitting Irizarry three times in the head with a blunt object, driving her downward with his blows until she was on the floor of his apartment's pantry.

On cross-examination Jeffrey A. Jacobs laid the groundwork for a potential insanity defense by making Weather reiterate that during his confession, Spahalski had admitted to hallucinating before the murder of Vivian Irizarry.

Acting Rochester police chief Cedric Alexander said that in addition to Irizarry and Grande, Spahalski implicated himself in two other killings, but he did not specify which two cases they were.

Police Sergeant Mark D. Mariano was called to the stand and testified that he was the one who went to Spencer Street during Spahalski's confession to see if there really was a body there.

"You went to that address?" Hyland asked.

"Yes, sir."

"How did you get in?"

"The landlord had a key."

"And what did you discover?"

"I discovered a body of a female in the basement."

"No further questions, Your Honor."

"Mr. Jacobs?" Judge Lindley said, looking toward the defense table.

Jacobs turned to the witness and asked, "What led you to believe she was dead?"

"Twenty years of police experience in looking at thousands of dead bodies," Mariano replied.

Later, regarding Irizarry, Hyland said, "There's no question. It was a horrible murder. The scenario for how it happened is based exclusively on Mr. Spahalski's version of events. It remains to be seen just how true that version is. He claims to have been hallucinating and out of touch with reality when he killed Vivian Irizarry. The simple fact is that we may never know what his actual state of mind was at the time of that murder."

Judge Lindley ruled quickly. Indeed, there was probable cause to believe that Robert Bruce Spahalski had committed the two murders. The judge ordered Spahalski placed in the Monroe County Jail with no bail, and instructed the grand jury to consider charges.

The public release of the confession was hard on the families. He had treated the women like pieces of meat, and had tried to elevate his role in Charles Grande's life practically to that of boyfriend. Homosexuality remained a social stigma, and Chuck's relatives had that additional burden to deal with.

The confession implied that Grande and Spahalski had contemplated cohabitation. This, of course, was astounding to his family, even to Rose, who knew more than the others about Chuck's bisexuality.

Despite the picture of Chuck that the killer painted, Rose Grande felt a huge upside to attending this hearing. "We had been trying to get this guy behind bars for fourteen years, and just got screwed every step of the way," she said. Seeing Spahalski as a captive pleased her. Luck had turned: hers was improving, and his was done.

There was a poignant moment at the probable cause hearing when Rose and her husband, Scott, first found themselves in the same room with Vivian Irizarry's family. Rose recalled: "I said to them, 'I'm so sorry. We tried so hard for so long to put him behind bars, because we just knew he was going to kill somebody again. And we failed. We just couldn't do it. The justice system couldn't do it.'"

Despite Robert's insistence that he was not a serial killer, police categorized him that way, anyway. Sure, his victims varied by age and gender. Sure, his murders were irregularly spaced across time. But there were strong common denominators. They were all drug-fueled sex crimes. He was a serial killer.

The New York State legal definition of serial killer is anyone who has murdered three or more victims using a similar method of killing. There has to be time between each kill, but not too much time.

If the killings had occurred all at once, the killer would be defined as a spree killer. If too much time separated the killings, then it was considered a stretch to think of the murders as part of a pattern. Spahalski thought he was exempt for the latter reason.

This legal definition is not shared universally by experts in serial killing. Katherine Ramsland, an assistant professor of forensic psychology at DeSales University in Pennsylvania, who has written books about serial killers, says that a serial killer may only have two victims, if caught before he or she had an opportunity to kill more.

For two months after Spahalski's surrender, the discussion about what did and didn't constitute a serial killer continued. Every year a wider range of serial killers was caught, and old rules no longer applied.

Some experts said that the portion of the New York State law that necessitated a certain time frame between the kills was obsolete. The belief once was that serial killers couldn't stop, their compulsion to kill too strong for them to ignore for long. They were murder addicts. But in the first years of the twenty-first century, this was proven to not be true in all cases.

The cop-taunting "BTK (Bind, Torture, Kill) Strangler," of Wichita, Kansas, demonstrated that serial killers could kill for a while, retire for many years, and then come out of retirement to kill again.

Unless there were homicides involved that law enforcement didn't know about, Robert Bruce Spahalski—like BTK—lasted for more than a decade before returning to his killing ways. His years with beer-loving cutie-pie Christine Gonzalez had been largely peaceful ones.

The stereotype is that all serial killers are sociopaths, but some serial killers do feel acute guilt following each murder, but the thrill overrides that guilt.

Then there are odd ducks, like Robert Spahalski, who didn't appear to feel remorse about committing murder, although he was, he claimed, pestered by unpleasant thoughts involving the decomposition of his victims' bodies.

According to Ramsland, guilty consciences of any sort in serial killers was rare. More often than not, those who expressed remorse were trying to fool authorities.

Serial killers came in all types. They killed with a gun, with poison, with a knife, or with their bare hands. Some smart serial killers used different methods to throw off the police.

Some were predators. Some had compulsions they couldn't control. Some were indifferent to all human life, other than their own. Robert claimed to have compulsions, but some experts thought he was merely indifferent. Someone got in his way, someone died. Simple as that. It was as easy as shooting his dad's pig in the head.

* * *

On December 16, 2005, a Rochester television station reported that Robert had a twin, who was also a confessed killer. To follow up, *Democrat and Chronicle* reporter Gary Craig went to Attica to talk to Stephen.

Stephen—after years in the corrections system—was now embracing his feminine side. He appeared for the interview wearing homemade eye makeup, nail polish, and glasses.

For a time, there were rumors circulating in Chemung County government about Stephen's gender issues. Word was that one of the reasons Stephen had purposefully delayed his release from prison was that he was hoping to receive "gender reassignment" surgery on the taxpayers' tab. In fact, it had been said (by what would normally be considered a good source) that the surgery had already taken place, that Stephen and Robert were no longer identical, that Stephen could now appropriately call himself "Stephanie."

When David Ripley, eldest son of Stephen's homicide victim, was informed that Stephen might have received gender reassignment surgery in prison, there was a long pause before David asked, "Was it voluntary?"

The rumor caused a ripple of outrage as many couldn't believe that a long-term prisoner in the state correctional system could become a post-op transsexual, while New York State's taxpayers footed the bill. Everyone who'd seen it remembered that horrible, nightmare-inducing videotape of Chicago's mass murderer Richard Speck frolicking in prison, sporting a new pair of breasts growing out of his chest.

A closer look at Stephen's medical history dispelled the rumor, however. New York State might allow Stephen to embrace his feminine side, but they weren't about to pay for surgery to remove his masculine side.

The reporter asked the six-foot-two transvestite what his reaction was when he heard that his twin brother had turned himself in and confessed to killing four people.

Stephen said that his brother's arrest was a shock to him. He'd had no clue.

"I never knew he killed someone," Stephen said. "He never told me. He never mentioned it to me. I thought I was the only murderer in the family. I don't know what made him do that."

The reporter asked Stephen about showing up for the interview in makeup. Stephen said he'd come out as gay while in prison and had been incorporating elements of drag into his personal style for about ten years.

"Do you have a prison nickname?"

"Yes. Christmas."

"Why do they call you that?"

"It's my favorite time of the year," Stephen replied.

Robert's twin said that he'd received a letter from Robert just a day or two before he heard about Robert's arrest.

"In the letters, he sounded normal," Stephen opined. "So when I heard that he was seeing demons, in the letters, he didn't appear like that."

Stephen made it clear that although he and Robert might have identical bodies and facial features, they did not have identical brains. Robert, apparently—although Stephen still found it hard to believe—was the type of guy who would turn himself in because his conscience was bothering him. That didn't compute as far as Stephen was concerned.

"Why would he turn himself in?" Stephen wondered aloud. "I would never turn myself in!" Then, after some thought, Stephen added, "It might have weighed on him. I don't know. I'm not a psychiatrist. Maybe he's sorry for killing them. He wanted it off his chest—it's off his chest."

Stephen was realistic about his twin's prospects: "He'll never see the streets again. I assume he's gone forever. He'll never see home again. He's gone."

Stephen told the reporter he hadn't had contact with Robert since Robert's arrest, and his only access to information about his brother came from news reports. He was in Attica.

But it wasn't all gloom for the killer in drag. There were small pleasures for him to enjoy in prison. Recently, for example, he'd had an opportunity to see one of his favorite movies, *The Wizard of Oz*, on TV.

"It's part of home, *The Wizard of Oz*," he said. "It's just part of everybody's home. That's why they put it on every year."

Stephen recalled that when he and his brother were young, they shared a sort of sixth sense about one another. He often knew where his brother was, and what he was doing. And vice versa. When Stephen went to prison as a teenager for killing Ronald Ripley, Robert visited him regularly.

But they didn't communicate that frequently anymore.

"We're still close," Stephen said, although it was hard for a non-twin to fathom what he meant by that. "We don't write too much anymore. There's only so much to discuss out there."

An attempt by the same reporter to interview Robert in prison proved problematic. At first, Robert said that he would need to be paid to talk. The *Democrat and Chronicle* didn't pay for interviews. Then the state prison system put Robert on a "temporarily in transition" list, a category that forbid interviews other than those by law enforcement. Robert was being moved from the Clinton Correctional Facility in Dannemora, New York, to the Great Meadow Correctional Facility in Comstock.

Nurture or nature? Still a mystery, Craig wrote. But, he noted, there was a strong difference in the way the twins regarded their victims. Robert claimed to have felt remorse. If Robert's regret was real, he must have reached a tardy epiphany as he stood over the lifeless body of Vivian Irizarry. But even if he didn't feel any actual remorse, he was smart enough to claim he did, aware that it might make a difference in how others regarded him.

Robert could see himself in a social context. Stephen, not so much.

Thirty-eight years after committing his only known murder, Stephen still felt that the Reverend Ron Ripley deserved to die. What's more, he was convinced that Robert's victims must have deserved it as well.

19

New Indictment, New Judge

By the end of 2005, Robert Bruce Spahalski had been indicted for all four of the murders that he'd confessed to, and a new judge was assigned to the case. She was the Honorable Patricia Marks, a Monroe County court judge, as well as a wife and mother.

Judge Marks once presided over the successful prosecution of Kevin Bryant, a lawyer who lived in the same town as she, Penfield, New York. Bryant had hired his brother-in-law to murder his wife. So brother (actually half-brother) killed sister, using both a gun and a knife, for drug money. The case was the subject of *Betrayal in Blood*, by this author.

At Robert Bruce Spahalski's January 3 court hearing, the charges were read aloud. Judge Marks asked Spahalski how did he plead.

The gaunt defendant replied, "Not guilty."

Rochester district attorney Michael Green unsealed a new

indictment brought by the grand jury against Spahalski. There were now five charges: for killing Irizarry, Grande, Berger, and Armstrong—and for stealing Grande's car.

On January 11, Judge Mark's courtroom again convened on the matter of the *State* v. *Spahalski*. This hearing set out to determine if the county's public defender's office would continue to represent the defendant. That office, it was revealed, had contact with several people who were scheduled to be witnesses at Spahalski's trial, and the hearing would determine if that constituted a conflict of interest.

Ken Hyland explained that one of the witnesses he planned to call at Spahalski's murder trial had been represented by the public defender's office on a minor criminal charge, and another had been represented when he was considered a suspect in one of the murders Spahalski was now charged with.

When Judge Marks explained the situation to Spahalski in court, and offered to appoint new counsel for him, Spahalski surprised her by saying that he did not see a conflict of interest and wanted to keep Jeffrey Jacobs as his lawyer.

Jacobs agreed with his client that there was no conflict. "Your Honor, I have discussed the issue with public defender Edward J. Novak, and we agreed that there is no conflict," Jacobs said.

"Mr. Spahalski," Judge Marks said, "do you realize that you are discarding a defense your lawyer could use to challenge the witness? I'm prepared to assign another attorney to represent you."

"I understand," Spahalski responded.

"Look, I am going to allow you time to reconsider," Judge Marks said. "I want your lawyers to have more time to review the information from the prosecution. I want everyone back here on February first."

After the hearing, Ken Hyland expressed concern over Spahalski's decision not to change counsel.

"He has the right to waive a conflict of interest with

the permission of the court," Hyland said, concerned that the move could create an appellate issue that could reverse a conviction, worried that the defendant could argue that he had ineffective assistance of counsel, and the case could come back years later.

As it turned out, this was the last time Jeffrey Jacobs appeared on Robert Bruce Spahalski's behalf. He was battling serious health problems and was replaced by Joseph Salvatore Damelio, who had been practicing law in New York State for close to twenty years.

In attendance at that January 11 court hearing was Dorothy Hickman, the mother of victim Moraine Armstrong. She expected to be overwhelmed with anger in the courtroom, but she felt something else, something akin to relief, instead. They had the guy. After all that time, they had the guy, just when she had begun to think her daughter's murder was *never* going to be solved. She sat there and hoped that the guy would confess to even more murders, so more families would be able to feel the way she felt. It was so much better knowing than not knowing—knowing that the killer of a loved one was off the streets. She didn't know how many people this guy had killed, but she wanted all of the families to have closure. It was funny, in a way. She had read about this guy Spahalski for a long time—months, right from the time he turned himself in—but nobody told her he was a suspect in Moraine's murder. She hadn't associated him with her daughter. Some major official had said after Spahalski had surrendered that they'd look back ten years, and Moraine's murder was before that. She thought that Moraine's murder was too old, too cold. She'd thought this guy had been after Moraine's time. Instead, her dream came true. Closure.

Melanie Armstrong, sister of Moraine, accompanied Dorothy. Melanie was of two minds regarding Robert Spahalski's arrest. On the one hand, Melanie was pleased that there was a suspect in custody and the odds were good that he wasn't going to hurt anyone else. On the other hand, she was angry that it took so long. Fifteen years! All of that time, the guy had been free to come and go as he liked, free to enjoy the fresh air and sunshine—while all that time, her dear older sister, Moraine, was cold in the ground. Maybe her mother was feeling peaceful, but Melanie wasn't. She hated the guy. She hoped that they would change the law and make the electric chair legal again so they could strap him into it. She wanted to be there and watch the sparks fly. Some people thought it immoral for the state to execute murderers. Melanie Armstrong didn't have any problem with it at all. That man, that *monster,* had taken something from Melanie—something she would never get back. She only had one big sister, and that was Moraine, and he'd taken that away from her. Sure, Moraine had made some bad choices in her life. She'd gotten into drugs and developed a bad habit, and then she turned tricks to support that habit—but she was never bad, never mean. Her character didn't change. Even when her life was spiraling madly downward into the abyss, she was still nice, even considerate. She was still the sweetest person Melanie had ever known, still the girl who loved to throw back her head and laugh at the ridiculousness of the world.

Was Melanie shocked when she learned Moraine had been murdered? Truthful answer: no. Melanie knew about the world Moraine was living in. She wouldn't have been shocked if Moraine had been found dead of a drug overdose, or had caught AIDS and then died. So she couldn't say she was shocked about the murder. The life expectancy of a drug-addicted prostitute wasn't great, *especially in Rochester back in those days.* Melanie doubted that Moraine was shocked, either. During those agonizing moments when she knew that she was being murdered, and her life was coming to an end, she must have felt sad, but hardly surprised. Moraine knew one day her number would be up—sooner rather than later. She and Melanie had talked about it. She had grown more tired than frightened of life's dark side. That was the only side she ever got to see anymore. Moraine still wanted to get off drugs and turn her life around, but she knew she lacked the strength, just as she lacked the strength to fight back when Spahalski throttled her and snuffed out the beautiful spark that was Moraine's life energy.

Melanie had only recently become certain that Robert Spahalski had killed Moraine. Initially police misdirection cast doubt on Melanie's gut feeling. The commissioner said they were looking back ten years. That eliminated Moraine, her family thought. The commissioner—sorry if anyone was misled—later admitted to speaking in overly general terms. Still, in her gut, Melanie knew, from the instant she first saw that face. Melanie recalled the day she read about Spahalski in the papers, probably when he confessed, and she felt the hairs at the back of her neck move. Now, Melanie silently pledged, she was in it for the long haul. She was going to come to court every day. Every time Spahalski was in the courtroom, she was going to be there, too. A reporter outside had asked her if this gave her closure. Her mother said yes, definitely, and she'd agreed out loud, but in her mind, she wasn't sure. They could fry the guy in the electric chair, and *still* she wouldn't have her big sister. Moraine was never coming back. That was the real bottom line.

At the hearing, Judge Marks noted that this was an ex-tremely complicated case. Any murder trial was compli-cated, but multiple murder cases were particularly difficult to prepare for on both sides. She ordered the defendant to be held without bail, and set a date during the late spring for the parties to reconvene. The trial, she said, would begin in July.

* * *

After the hearing, DA Michael Green deftly fielded questions before an assembly of the press. He was asked if the Spahalski case was now closed. Green shook his head. On the contrary, he said, "you never close the book on anything."

"What would be Spahalski's sentence if he were found guilty on all charges?" a reporter asked.

"One hundred years," Green replied.

Just like his boss, Hyland refused to say that four was the final number. Four was just the number that the DA's office thought they could prove beyond a reasonable doubt. Could the number change? *You bet.*

When asked, Hyland said he couldn't comment on motive.

RPD lieutenant Todd Baxter also indicated that they weren't about to give up when it came to Robert Spahalski. Baxter said that investigators were still "looking at everything." Spahalski had confessed to killing over a fifteen-year time span. There were plenty of bodies during those years, so there was plenty of everything to look at.

Armstrong, Grande, and Irizarry had relatives on their behalf in the courtroom, but there was no one there from Adrian Berger's family. So, to get a quote, reporters had to do a little hunting.

Speaking via telephone from his home outside Philadelphia, Adrian Berger's father, Martin, told a reporter, "We have been waiting fifteen years for a satisfactory answer, and we hope this will end our unhappiness and sadness over the loss of our daughter."

20

Admissibility Hearing

On Monday and Tuesday, June 5 and 6, 2006, a pretrial court hearing was held before Judge Marks. Defense attorney Damelio moved to have the charges against Spahalski tried separately. He argued that crimes fifteen years apart shouldn't be lumped together and tried before a single jury.

Judge Marks did the court schedule a big favor and ruled that there would be one trial, and one trial only. Her excellent reasoning: one confession, one prosecution. Either the confession was true and admissible, or it wasn't. Damelio argued nay by bringing up a letter he had subpoenaed, a letter written almost fifteen years before by Robert's then-lawyer, Richard Marchese, warning the various area police departments not to discuss murders with Robert, unless Marchese was there. The letter's message was clear: "Don't question my client about any homicides."

The defense claimed that the letter had been copied and was sent to both the Webster and Rochester Police

Departments. Damelio was forced to admit, however, that he had discovered the letter initially in the files of the public defender's office, not in a file room of either of the pertinent police departments. The RPD said it had been unable to find its copy.

The bottom line was that Spahalski's defense wanted his client's confession to be suppressed—none of it allowed in as evidence at the trial—because police had been instructed by Spahalski's previous counsel not to ask him about killing people. Here, Damelio argued, was proof that the police knew they shouldn't ask Robert questions about any murders without counsel present, and yet they did it, anyway.

During the two-day court hearing, twelve witnesses testified. Among them was Marchese, who said that he had represented Spahalski on criminal impersonation and mischief charges in the early 1990s, but he was not assigned to defend him in any homicide cases.

In response to the defense's motion, the prosecution called a witness, Investigator Glenn Weather, the man whose fourth-floor office had been used for a portion of the long interrogation of Spahalski after he turned himself in. Weather testified that he never saw the 1991 Marchese letter, and that it wouldn't have mattered if he had, because Spahalski willingly spilled the beans.

Officers Maria Graves and Lourdes Baez both testified that Spahalski had voluntarily entered the Public Safety Building and confessed, saying, "I killed someone . . . someone I was doing drugs with."

The prosecution argued that the interrogating detectives didn't know of the letter's existence, the fourteen-year-old letter was no longer valid, and Marchese was no longer representing Robert Spahalski.

Legal eagles on the scene scurried to find law precedent that might predict Judge Marks's decision, and found just what they were looking for in *People* v. *Bongarzone-Suarccy*, 2006 New York Slip Op. 01044.

That case engraved guidelines for determining what the relationship was between previous defense attorney instructions and current urges to confess. The decision read: *The length of the passage of time; whether a record of the earlier communication exists in the files of the police agency conducting the questioning; whether the failure of such record to exist was the result of any bad faith on the part of police; whether any of the same officers were involved in the earlier and later investigations; whether any action was taken against the suspect in the aftermath of the original investigation; and whether the entering lawyer continued to have any contact with prosecuting authorities on the matter after the initial communication.*

At the conclusion of the hearing, Judge Marks asked both the defense and the prosecution to submit their arguments regarding the admissibility of the confession in writing, and said that she would have a decision in a couple of weeks.

The decision, as it turned out, was not made until close to Labor Day, when Judge Marks declared the confession admissible.

During these same June court hearings, the Rochester Police Department formally requested that fourteen-year-old court records regarding Spahalski's acquittal on impersonation charges be unsealed. Investigators believed the sealed records contained information pertinent to the current charges against Spahalski.

The prosecution also wanted permission to use transcripts from Robert Spahalski's 1992 criminal impersonation trial as part of its case.

Ken Hyland said the defense shouldn't argue against usage of those transcripts and other pertinent documents regarding the impersonation case. "Frankly, those transcripts are more important to the defense than they are to us," Hyland said. He explained that once admitted into evidence at a murder trial, the defense would be able to use each and every quote within them to cross-examine prosecution witnesses.

Judge Marks said she would reserve her judgment regarding the sealed files. As it turned out, by the time the files were unsealed, another judge would be in charge of the case.

In June, Damelio asked Judge Marks for more time. The delay, Damelio explained, would allow mental-health experts to examine his client and determine if Spahalski suffered from any mental illnesses that might absolve him from all, or a portion of, criminal responsibility for the four killings. He fully intended to be fair. Damelio said, "The prosecution has an absolute right to conduct their own testing, to interview my client, to do whatever testing they deem necessary in response to what we produce."

Judge Marks agreed that the defense needed more time to decide if they wanted to offer an insanity defense. And if the defense wanted Robert tested, then the prosecutor would want to test him, too. All of that would take time.

21

Insanity Defense

At the end of August, Joseph Damelio announced his strategy. He planned a psychiatric defense for three out of the four murders. For those three at least, he hoped a jury would find his client not guilty because of mental disease or defect. He expected to file the necessary paperwork at the next scheduled court hearing, which was a week away. Robert Spahalski was analyzed by defense psychiatrists.

Outside court, Kenneth Hyland noted that prosecuting against an insanity plea was actually easier because the burden of proof shifted. Against a typical "not guilty" plea, a prosecution had to convince a jury beyond a reasonable doubt that the defendant committed the crimes. But when prosecuting a "not guilty by reason of insanity" plea, the burden for the insanity claim was on the defense. They had to prove he was insane.

Damelio said that the psychiatric plea was only being planned for the murders of Irizarry, Armstrong, and Berger. He decided not to use that defense with the

Grande murder after discussing the matter with a forensic psychiatrist and a neuropsychiatrist, both of whom had interviewed Spahalski.

Damelio noted that Spahalski had admitted to being whacked-out on drugs when committing the murders and that a "drug-induced psychosis/diminished capacity" defense had not been ruled out.

In September 2006, Judge Marks ruled on the admissibility question that had been the subject of the two-day hearing back in June. The police officers who interrogated Spahalski during his confession were not bound by the Marchese letter because there was no evidence that they knew the letter existed.

Near the end of September, Damelio announced that he was dropping his plans to present an insanity defense on Spahalski's behalf.

"They served a psychiatric notice and then very quickly withdrew it," Hyland later recalled. "The notice was withdrawn before we had a chance to have our mental experts examine Spahalski. I would like to know why they did that."

Wasn't insanity Robert Spahalski's only shot at a sentence less than life in prison?

"They had what are called ex parte conferences, conferences that Damelio had with Judge Marks that I was not a party to," Hyland said. "They are allowed to do this in some circumstances when they don't want to reveal their strategy. So it is possible that Judge Marks told Damelio something at one of those meetings that discouraged him from attempting an insanity defense."

During the short period of time that Damelio was pursuing an insanity defense, the prosecution was busy in response, subpoenaing Robert Spahalski's mental records.

"We did get some mental-health records on him, but I don't remember anything of any great value. There was a

lot of rambling and some threats and things like that."
Nothing that the defense could latch onto. He wasn't
taking orders from his neighbor's dog or anything like that.

Perhaps the problem was that Damelio had to defend
his client against charges on four murders, and would have
to prove that Spahalski was legally insane at the time of
each murder. It is difficult to get clients acquitted with an
insanity defense even in single-murder cases—almost impossible, in fact. Damelio felt that he had a good chance of
convincing a jury that Spahalski was insane at the time of
the Irizarry murder—the "transformed into a demon"
story might carry weight with a jury—but for the other
three murders, his prospects were not nearly as bright.

With Grande, he beat the man's head in because he
felt shortchanged, if one believed his story. It was a
demonstration of an acute anger-management problem,
for sure, but not insanity. That was why there would be
no psychiatric defense for the Grande murder.

Hyland noted, "After killing Grande, he steals his car
and drives around, picking up a hooker and buying
drugs." Loathsome, but not insane.

Even if a juror took Spahalski's explanation of Adrian
Berger's murder at face value—that he gave in to an overwhelming urge to choke out Adrian during a sexual frenzy,
a person could not conclude he was insane. He saw a
blend of sex and death as fun. Evil, yes. Poor impulse control, yes. But not insanity. And the prosecutor *did not* take
Spahalski's explanation of Adrian Berger's murder at face
value. Not at all.

"I always felt there was some part of that murder that
Robert was leaving out," Hyland said. "I think there was
a monetary angle. We talked to some of Adrian's friends
and it was pretty clear that she was fed up with him. She
was sick of him mooching off of her. Unlike Moraine
Armstrong, as far as we could tell, Adrian Berger did not
have the same kind of lifestyle as Spahalski. She had a
job. She wasn't doing drugs—and he was. She was giving

him money for drugs and she shut him off, and I think that is why he killed her."

Afterward, he moved Adrian's car to help cover his tracks. There was particularly nothing insane about that. It was, in fact, a sign that Robert understood very well the nature and quality of his actions.

And with Armstrong, it was another business transaction that went horribly wrong, brutal murder replacing discussion and negotiation. Again, evil, maybe—but not insane.

Hyland said, "He smokes crack with her, has sex with her, she demands money from him. He says, 'What are you talking about? We just did one hundred dollars' worth of crack.' She gets up in his face and he kills her."

Not insane.

Hyland noted that even when a defendant does exhibit peculiar behavior and is obviously suffering from some sort of mental illness, juries still do not like an insanity defense. "The problem with the insanity defense is that the defendant has to admit he did it. He has to say, 'I killed this person, *but* . . .' And juries do not like that," he said.

When claiming insanity, the defense inevitably relies on the testimony of experts, and the prosecution has a lot of leeway in terms of cross-examination—getting hearsay in the record, for example—that they normally wouldn't have.

"We could ask, 'Doctor, did you consider this when you came up with your opinion, did you consider that?' And the jury gets to hear a lot of things that they wouldn't get to hear otherwise," Hyland noted.

Also, an insanity defense opened up all kinds of medical records to the prosecution, records that could hurt the defense's case more than help.

Spahalski didn't have high hopes for an acquittal. He had admitted he'd killed four people and—with the possible exception of Vivian Irizarry and his "she turned into a demon" story—he didn't even have a *but*.

Still, it was Damelio's difficult job to try. He hoped

he could convince some of the jury that some of the murders had occurred when Spahalski was suffering from some mental problems, that Spahalski suffered from a diminished capacity to tell right from wrong. If Damelio could pull that off, the law said the jury might convict Robert Spahalski of a lesser charge, first-degree manslaughter.

Judge Marks had delayed Spahalski's trial for the last time. It was now scheduled to begin in November. Jury selection on the first and second of the month, and opening statements the instant that voir dire was completed and a dozen of Spahalski's peers were impaneled.

Judge Marks did not anticipate difficulty finding twelve impartial jurors. The veniremen—all residents of Monroe County—had not been inundated by press about the case. The story made the paper, of course, on the front page a couple of times—but it was nothing like Shawcross's coverage.

22

The Trial

On the morning of November 2, 2006, the murder trial of Robert Bruce Spahalski began in the Monroe County Hall of Justice, adjacent to the Public Safety Building. The courtroom, the largest in the building, was on the second floor.

Unlike most courtrooms, which had one aisle down the middle, the seating here was divided into three sections: right, left, and middle. The jury sat along the left wall. The prosecution team was set up in front of the left seating area, with friends and relatives of the victims immediately behind them.

The defendant and the defense team were on the right, farthest from the jury. Friends and relatives of the defendant were to sit in the front of the right section, if they existed. As far as anyone could tell, Spahalski never once had a supporter in the courtroom.

Everyone had to pass through a tight airport-style security check to get into the building, walking through the metal detector. Those who made it beep were searched with a hand wand.

Sitting in the spectator section of the courtroom, for every second of every day of the trial, were Rose Grande and Leslie Gonzalez, sister of Vivian Irizarry. Also frequently in attendance were Dorothy Hickman and Melanie Armstrong, the mother and sister of Moraine Armstrong.

The jury consisted of eleven men and one woman. Also seated were four alternates—one female, three male. The panel ranged in age from thirties to sixties. The foreman was a man with white hair, about fifty years old.

At the call of "All rise," some of the spectators who had attended the preliminary hearings were surprised to see that Judge Marks was not entering the courtroom. Because of a busy schedule, and to avoid delays that might jeopardize convictions, Judge Marks had been reassigned and replaced for this case by a visiting judge from out of town.

He was acting supreme court justice Stephen R. Sirkin, who had a reputation for being no-nonsense and a stickler for a tight schedule. Sirkin was a Wayne County judge but had for many years been semiregularly "borrowed" by the Monroe County Court Administration to clean up a backlog. One of the first things Judge Sirkin did was order that the records for Robert Spahalski's impersonation case be unsealed.

Judge Sirkin would later recall that the thing that made the Spahalski case unique was not that four murders were being tried together. Trials for multiple murders occurred regularly. It was the time span involved.

"I know of no other murder trials in which the first and last murders were separated by fifteen years," Judge Sirkin later commented.

Sirkin sat hawklike behind his bench, looking down

on the proceedings. He could be gruff, even rude, and moved the proceedings along at a swift—some might say breakneck—pace.

Always in a hurry, he wasn't going to let anyone get away with anything, especially if it meant slowing things down. The "rush, rush, rush" attitude wasn't to everyone's liking, and there was grumbling on both sides about the pace. One of his steadfast rules was that no court session could go beyond 3:00 P.M. Sometimes the judge would call it a day as early as two-thirty. There were other ground rules, too. Spectators, whether they be friend or foe, were to address the defendant under no circumstances.

Spahalski, in turn, was forbidden to turn around and look at a spectator. If he were to do so, he would sacrifice his right to attend his own trial and would watch the rest of the proceedings on a TV monitor in a holding cell.

Spectators were not allowed to have contact of any kind with the jury. Whenever there was a break or a recess, spectators had to stay in their seats until all of the jurors had left the room. If a spectator saw a juror outside the courtroom—they sometimes encountered one another in the restroom—they were not allowed to talk to or even acknowledge them.

Judge Sirkin and defense attorney Joseph Damelio had been in court together before. In early March 2005, Sirkin ruled that defendant Louis Avino, a contractor convicted of fraud, had failed to meet his burden of establishing ineffective assistance of counsel (a charge he was making against Damelio), and as a result, the defendant's motion to vacate his conviction was denied. It had been Avino's contention that Damelio failed to call several witnesses on his behalf that could have offered exculpatory testimony leading to a different result. Judge Sirkin reviewed the facts of the case and the affidavits submitted by the defendant before denying the motion.

* * *

At the Robert Bruce Spahalski trial, during his opening statement to the jury on the morning of November 2, Ken Hyland told the jury that the prosecution planned to call forty witnesses. More than two hundred items would be entered into evidence.

Because of the large number of witnesses and exhibits, it would be impossible for the prosecution to present its case in strictly chronological order. So it was going to be up to the jury to rearrange the information along a time-line in their minds.

Hyland told the jury they should think of the evidence as pieces of a puzzle, a jigsaw puzzle. Each witness would provide a piece, and the jury would have to put all of the pieces together to form a complete picture of the defendant's guilt.

"By the end, you'll have a pretty good picture of what happened," Hyland said confidently. Pretty good, as in *exact*.

A key piece of evidence in this case was supplied by the defendant himself, he said. The confession—and it was perfectly good. Any objections to the validity of the confession lacked merit.

"It's our position that the defendant was advised of his rights, he waived his right, he was provided food and drinks, and was given breaks," he said. One of the reasons he knew that Spahalski's confession was real was—as the evidence would show—that his claims matched the crime scenes.

"We know he did what he said he did," Hyland said.

Hyland offered jurors his own timeline of events, start-ing with the morning Spahalski turned himself in, and working backward.

"Vivian Irizarry. She was the last of Spahalski's murders, but the first to which he confessed," Hyland said. Spahal-ski had not just confessed to recent murders, but to cold cases as well, even a case police weren't sure was a murder until he admitted to doing the killing. The cases were so cold that some of the witnesses had passed away. Some of the evidence, available a decade earlier, had been lost. "Considering the *age* of the cases," he said, "we've done a good job of putting it together the best we can."

There was no remorse during Spahalski's confession. When he was shown grisly photographs of the crime scenes, the defendant was intrigued rather than repulsed, and coolly commented, "That is the way they look when they go out. That is the way they look when they get strangled."

Hyland related Spahalski's story of how he killed Charles Grande over money. Twenty bucks. He smashed Grande's head with a hammer, stole $1,000, stole Grande's car, and fled. Before Grande's body was discovered, the defendant had been pulled over while driving Grande's Volaré. The killer picked up a suspected prostitute and went cruising for drugs. She was in the front seat with him. Spahalski evaded capture at that point by flashing Grande's driver's license.

Hyland even told the jury the story of how police were unable to charge Spahalski with Grande's murder—these being the days before DNA technology—but had brought charges of criminal impersonation, a case that prosecutors lost because the officer who'd pulled Spahalski over had written a description of Spahalski that didn't match Spahalski's actual appearance, an error that caused a jury to acquit Spahalski.

In the spectator section, Rose Grande clenched her fists and ground her teeth at the memory.

Hyland's timeline continued to retreat into the past, to the murder of Adrian Berger on Emerson Street, a murder that took place during a brutal heat wave. The medical examiner had not been able to say for sure that Berger was murdered because of the advanced state of decomposition when her remains were found, and the case was not officially categorized as a homicide until the defendant confessed. Hyland told the jury that Spahalski's first murder had been of Moraine Armstrong, a down-on-her-luck prostitute who lived across the street from him on Lake Avenue. Someimes she worked the street. Spahalski would come out his building's front door, and there she was.

Hyland said, "Spahalski was a career criminal even before he started killing people."

He told the jury that the defendant had spent only a year or so of his adult life working a legitimate job. Most of the time, he made money by pimping, hustling, or stealing. This had been the pattern even before he came to Rochester. As a teenager and a young adult in Elmira, where he grew up, he'd been a chronic thief. "The defendant has done prison time, four times on felony burglary charges," Hyland said. He finished by asking the jury to listen carefully to the evidence, to carefully consider the facts, and to bring back the only reasonable verdict: guilty on all counts.

After a brief recess, it was the defense's turn. In his opening statement, Damelio told the jurors that all stories had two sides, and he urged them to listen to both sides of this one. "Could it be as simple as what we hear?" Damelio said. "It never is." To understand Spahalski, they needed to look at his actions through the eyes of an addict hooked on crack cocaine. "Robert said that he bludgeoned a woman to death because he'd seen her turn into a demon. Ladies and gentlemen of the jury, I think it's safe to say that doesn't happen every day," Damelio pointed out. And it wasn't just crack cocaine that was clouding up Spahalski's ability to tell right from wrong, the lawyer said. There were other drugs as well. Drugs for mental illness. Drugs for HIV. Handsful of pills. All taken daily.

Robert's defense would focus on his mental problems, his extreme drug use, and inadmissibility of his all-day confession. Damelio wondered aloud just how voluntary

Spahalski's confession was. Sure, he had come into the police station on his own volition, but after that, the voluntary nature of Spahalski's statements could be called into question. "They searched his house with a warrant and found medication that he needed to take four times a day to keep him comfortable and keep the process going. Yet, they didn't offer him any of the medication. And they certainly didn't offer him any crack cocaine, that he must have been craving. Under those conditions, were his statements truly voluntary?"

Damelio did not mention that the police had eventually given Spahalski his prescription medications, but not until he asked for them. According to the police timeline, cops had not confiscated Spahalski's medications until he requested them. Damelio threw into question the order of events.

Damelio said that Spahalski was not unknown to Rochester police at the time of his confession, that Glenn Weather had recognized him immediately when he walked into the PSB on Election Day, 2005. "My client was a blip on the RPD radar screen," Damelio said. "Ladies and gentlemen of the jury, you will learn that fancy detective work didn't have anything to do with the defendant's arrest. He was under arrest because he voluntarily turned himself in and confessed. He told police that he had killed his good friend Vivian Irizarry because he'd had a hallucination and saw her transform into a demon. Hallucination. Demon, That should have been a clue right there that my client was *not* capable of making important decisions regarding his civil rights—rights that police claimed he waived before he told them his story.

"Was it purely voluntary? No," Damelio continued. "There are other factors that need to be considered. What was his frame of mind? Was he coming off drugs? Was he high on drugs?"

Robert told police up front that it had only been a day or two since he'd attempted suicide. Surely, that must have been a sign that Robert was in no condition to make life-altering decisions.

Damelio maintained that the police were not about to give Spahalski a fair shake when he turned himself in. For the RPD, the confession, Damelio said, was like "winning the lottery." Damelio said that the police became slightly giddy at their good fortune, and that their judgment was clouded.

"We're not saying that they deliberately withheld his meds. We are not saying that at all. What we are saying is that the medicine was not made available to him, and it was not offered to him," Damelio added.

Throughout the trial, Judge Sirkin would see to it that evidence was presented in a lightning-quick fashion. When the opening statements were completed, the prosecution called its first witnesses, who took the stand, gave the evidence they had to give, and got off. In addition to both opening statements, *ten* witnesses testified on the first day.

The trial's first witness was Carlos Rodriguez, son of Vivian Irizarry. He testified that Spahalski lived in the building on Spencer Street where he dropped his mother off on the day she died.

Maria Graves and Lourdes Baez were the first police officers Spahalski spoke to after entering the lobby of the PSB on the day of his confession. One by one, Graves and Baez testified that the defendant entered the police station voluntarily. He said he walked there from his home on Spencer Street and asked to talk to a homicide detective, saying he had just killed a friend of his.

Officer Stephen Boily testified that he was the first cop to respond to the Spencer Street scene. Also on the scene were firemen, axes at the ready, prepared to break in through the basement door, a plan that became unnecessary when the landlord showed up with a key. Boily testified that he entered the basement and discovered the body of a middle-aged female.

Kevin Turner, the defendant's last landlord, corroborated Officer Boily's testimony, saying he used his key to let police and firemen into the basement, where Vivian's body was found. With the scent of death in the air, Turner was not allowed to enter the building.

The prosecution's case then jumped from Vivian Irizarry's murder scene to Charles Grande's in Webster. Alan Streeter, one of Chuck Grande's employees, told the jury that it was he who originally called the Webster police when Chuck didn't answer his door.

Carlos Rivera, Vivian Irizarry's father, took the stand. He was followed by Investigator James May and Officers Richard Martin and Dave Williams, who collected evidence from the Irizarry murder scene.

They testified that they not only found blood forming drag marks from the defendant's pantry to the spot in the basement where Irizarry's body was found, but also on Spahalski's clothes that had been shoved into a bathroom hamper.

Williams was on the stand when Judge Sirkin recessed court for the day, so he was the last witness of day one, and the first of day two.

On the second day, the rapid pace of testimony did not subside. Ten more took the oath. After Officer Williams concluded his testimony, Dorothy Hickman, Moraine Armstrong's mother, was called. She was followed by fingerprint evidence technician Theresa Tasso, evidence technician Tom Walton, and autopsy assistant Bernard Holland.

At this point, the prosecution, in order to establish the discovery of Chuck Grande's body, had originally planned on putting Grande's older brother, Carmen, on the stand. Carmen was the first to completely enter the Webster house and discover his brother's body. But Carmen—understandably, given the stressful situation—was uncontrollably angry. Asking him to face Robert Spahalski in the courtroom was inviting trouble.

So, instead, they called Chuck's best friend, Mike Johnson. Johnson brought his wife and his brother to court with him. He told the jury about the horrible night in October 1991 when he had accompanied members of Chuck's family to Webster to see if Chuck was okay.

"You were concerned about Chuck's welfare?"

"Yes, sir."

"Why was that?"

"His employees said he was always there, and he wasn't answering the door or his phone."

"Were there other reasons for concern?"

"Yes. Chuck's geese were running around free and they hadn't been fed."

At the scene, Johnson testified, they checked all the doors and found them locked. They decided to enter through the bedroom window. The air conditioner was removed. Johnson said that because of his size he got the job of crawling into the house. Carmen was thicker and didn't think he'd fit. Johnson was only halfway inside the house, his legs still sticking out, when he saw his friend's body lying on the floor, a dark pool under his head. He was so frightened by the sight that he pushed himself back out the window urgently, recklessly, tearing his shirt and cutting himself.

Johnson's story was backed up by the next witness, Officer Ernest Paviour, of the Webster Police Department (WPD), who had accompanied Chuck Grande's friends and family to the house on Phillips Road on October 4, 1991, the evening Grande's body was discovered. Paviour related the story of Carmen entering the house by kicking in the door and screaming that his brother was dead. The cop subsequently became the first member of law enforcement to enter the crime scene, which he promptly secured.

* * *

The prosecution now presented evidence regarding the murder of Adrian Berger. The witnesses were Shire Brown, a tenant in the house Berger lived in, and David Huslander, who lived nearby on Emerson Street. Brown testified that it was she who had corralled a policeman, Officer Smith, who was on the block on other business, and told him that there were flies covering a bedroom window, and there was a foul odor coming from the front apartment on Emerson. Huslander testified that on Friday night, July 19, 1991, he'd overheard Adrian Berger having a loud argument with a man he presumed to be her boyfriend. Later, at about two in the morning on July 20, he saw a man leaving the house and departing the scene in Adrian's car. Later, when asked to identify that man, Huslander said he picked an image of Robert Bruce Spahalski out of an array of photos.

Then it was back to the Webster case with retired Webster police officer Robert Barton. He explained to the court that he twice answered calls regarding Charles Grande. He first responded to Alan Streeter's October 2 call complaining that his employer was not answering his door, and he'd just seen a stranger driving Grande's car. Officer Barton had also been one of the responding officers collecting evidence two days later after Grande's body was discovered.

That concluded day two.

Day three, November 6, began with the testimony of Neal Dellasanti, a sheriff's deputy who worked at the county jail and processed the defendant after he confessed to four murders.

Although Hyland took Dellasanti through the booking process, step by step, the key part of his testimony was his reiteration that Spahalski was there voluntarily, had been treated well, had been allowed to take his medication, and was not asking for a lawyer.

Investigator Guy Storrs, of the WPD, testified that it was he who transported the defendant from the county jail to the Webster Courthouse on the night of the confession, so that, just after midnight, Spahalski could be arraigned for murdering Chuck Grande.

Officer John Penkitis took the stand. In the entire world—with the exception of the victims' families—there was perhaps no one who wanted to see Spahalski behind bars more than Penkitis. He was the patrol officer who, on the night of October 2, 1991, stopped a 1980 Volaré on suspicion that the occupants were attempting to buy drugs; who failed to notice that the car's driver was at least five inches taller than the height listed on the driver's license he supplied; the poor soul who wrote down in his report of the incident that the man driving the car was only five-foot-eight; the man who, during Spahalski's criminal impersonation trial, had pointed to the defendant and said, "Him. That's the man who was driving Charles Grande's car that night." And he was the man whose head hung lowest when the six-person jury acquitted Spahalski of criminal impersonation, returning him to the streets so he could kill again.

It was with great gusto that Penkitis repeated his identification at Spahalski's murder trial.

"Do you see that man in court today?" Hyland asked.

"I do," Penkitis said. "It was the defendant." And he firmly pointed at the man sitting next to Damelio at the counsel table.

The prosecution's case shifted back to the Adrian Berger murder. Gerald Smith, who had been promoted to lieutenant during the years that passed, said that after pulling up in front of the house next door on another matter, he discovered Berger's body in the house on Emerson Street, back in 1991 when he was an officer.

Medical examiner investigator Andy Treitler testified regarding Berger's autopsy. He said the death was considered highly suspicious, the postmortem failed to pinpoint a cause of death and the medical examiner was, therefore, unable to declare the case a homicide.

Investigator Kevin Webbering testified about his duties as an evidence technician on the Adrian Berger case.

Spahalski had confessed that he took Adrian's car so it would be less strange that she wasn't answering her door. Investigator Gary J. Schultz testified that during his confession, Spahalski had admitted to stealing Berger's car after killing her. The defendant must have been telling the truth when he said he parked it on Ravine Avenue. The car was found in front of the house on Ravine. There was no way for Spahalski to know where Berger's car was found, unless he had ditched it there.

Retired homicide investigator William "Billy" Barnes testified that he had interviewed Spahalski repeatedly, both at Spahalski's apartment and at the police station, and that Spahalski had lied about his whereabouts around the time of Adrian Berger's murder.

Sherrie Picchie, who was a deputy sheriff in 1991, told the jury that she had processed fingerprints at the scene of Berger's murder. Some of those fingerprints belonged to the defendant. On his cross-examination, Damelio induced Picchie to concede that since Spahalski was the victim's boyfriend, one would naturally expect to find the defendant's fingerprints in Adrian's apartment.

Going out of order again, Officer Ronald Baker related his experiences and observations after reporting to the Moraine Armstrong crime scene. Sticking with the Armstrong murder, Henry Pope testified about discovering the body. Officer Robert Burris described his experiences as an evidence technician. Day three concluded with the testimony of Dr. Jeanne Beno, who had performed toxicology tests for the medical examiner on Armstrong's remains. Moraine had a lot of cocaine in her system when she died.

This was a time of extraordinary stress for Rose Grande. Not only was she spending her days in the same room with the monster who had killed her brother, but her mother was very ill. Dying. Rose said, "Chuck had been her baby boy. Now she was clinging to life, waiting for justice. 'I'm so glad your father wasn't here to see this,' my mother said, 'because it would have killed him.'"

The trial was tough. Rose's mind would be partially on the proceedings, partially on the hospital. And there was one day that was worse than all the others. That was November 8, Wednesday, day four, when members of the Monroe County Medical Examiner's Office testified in vivid detail for the prosecution.

Photos of the victims were shown on a large screen in the courtroom. ME Thomas Smith testified that it was he who had performed the autopsies on Armstrong and Irizarry. He was followed by ME Jacqueline Martin, who testified regarding the postmortem on Grande and Berger.

"Luckily for me," Rose recalled, "I wear glasses. I'm extremely nearsighted. Instead of having to bow my head so I couldn't see the screen, I just took my glasses off when I knew something unpleasant was coming up. I would quietly take a Kleenex out of my pocket and clean my lenses. I tried not to make any noise. In the courtroom, you're not allowed to. You just have to sit there. Vivian Irizarry's family, who was there, actually looked at the pictures. Her cousin later said he regretted it, that it was a mistake to look at the pictures of her. I asked her how bad were the pictures of Chuck, and she said, 'You wouldn't have wanted to see.'"

* * *

Following the testimony of the medical examiners, retired police technician Peter Butler testified regarding the Armstrong case, and fingerprint technician Dennis Murphy, a former RPD employee, testified regarding Grande, Berger, and Armstrong.

RPD investigator Tony Campione took the stand. He was asked if he and the defendant had a history, and Campione said indeed they had. Asked if he remembered the first time he'd spoken to Spahalski, Campione said he did. That occurred soon after the murder of Moraine Armstrong. He'd seen Spahalski nosing around the police tape in front of the crime scene building, a building directly across the street from the one in which Robert Spahalski lived. While canvassing the neighbors to see if anyone had seen or heard anything unusual, Spahalski had asked, "What's going on?" He was nervous and curious, a combination that investigators were trained to look for in the vicinity of a crime scene.

"Was that your final contact with the defendant?"

"No, not at all," Campione said. "Seven months later, I encountered him again."

"What were the circumstances?"

"This time it was in connection with another death, that of Adrian Berger." Campione explained that he was interviewing the parents of the dead woman and asked if she had any boyfriends the police should know about. They said, yeah, Spahalski. That made Campione's "Spidey" sense go off like a fire alarm, he said, but there wasn't much he could do. Evidence was weak. "Spahalski denied being a killer, so that was that," Campione explained.

After his testimony, outside the courtroom, Campione said it was "kind of strange" entering the courtroom and seeing Spahalski again. He hadn't seen him in years. "It was good to see someone got charged with the crimes I investigated so many years ago," Campione said. He explained that he had been glad, but not at all surprised, to find out Robert Spahalski was responsible for Armstrong and Grande. Those were the two that Campione was closest to. He always knew Spahalski was the guy.

Following Campione, Investigator Tom Cassidy testified that he had been with the defendant for many hours on the day that Spahalski turned himself in, and that the defendant was not mistreated, was not intoxicated, and had confessed willingly.

After court Damelio was asked by the lone reporter still covering the trial if Spahalski was going to testify in his own defense. The defense attorney could have said no, and no one would have blinked. After all, what could Robert Bruce Spahalski possibly say in his own defense? Instead, Damelio said he didn't know, that the decision would be made at the last-possible instant.

Day five began with minor drama. One of the jury alternates, a man, was a no-show. Judge Sirkin wasn't about to wait around in case the man was running late. Instead, the missing panelist was kicked off, and testimony started more or less on time.

Detective Glenn Weather testified all morning, telling the jury about Spahalski's confession to four murders. Randy Benjamin did not testify at the trial, as he had during preliminary hearings. With Weather covering that ground, Hyland decided Benjamin's testimony would have been largely redundant.

"Usually, police will have two interrogators when a suspect is confessing," Hyland later explained. "In most cases, I'll call one of them and have them give extensive testimony, going over the details of the confession and how the confession came about. Then I'll call the other investigator and just hit the high points, to corroborate the first investigator's testimony. But in this case, I didn't do that. Weather's testimony alone, I figured, was enough."

In the afternoon, a pair of DNA forensic pathologists took the stand. They were Ellyn Colquon and Laura Raye. Hyland had to fight to get the second DNA expert to testify. It was the day before Veterans Day. The holiday fell on a Saturday that year so court was closed on Friday, creating a three-day weekend. Judge Sirkin was itching to get away. It was 2:20 P.M. and the judge wanted to adjourn.

"Your Honor, she has been sitting here all day," Hyland said.

Judge Sirkin relented, but insisted that the expert take the oath while walking up the aisle toward the witness stand.

The trial was taking place in Monroe County's largest courtroom and the witness entered from the back. As she approached, Judge Sirkin said, "Doyousweartotellthetruth-thewholetruthandnothingbutthetruthsohelpyouGod?" The jury laughed, but not everyone was amused.

Along with matching Spahalski's DNA to Vivian Irizarry's remains, the prosecution's DNA experts stated that everyone's DNA is unique—except for the DNA of identical twins. Robert Spahalski was, of course, a twin, but since Stephen was incarcerated during all the murders, the DNA evidence pointed to the defendant, and to the defendant alone.

DNA also positively ID'd blood found in the defendant's Spencer Street apartment—on clothes found in the hamper, in the pantry, and on the bedding—as that of Vivian Irizarry's.

The prosecution rested its case.

"Defense?" Judge Sirkin said.

"Defense rests," Damelio said.

That was a surprise. There would be no character witnesses. There would be no psychiatric evidence, supporting the defense's claim that Robert didn't know what he was doing when he committed his murders because he was too wired on crack. Nothing. Damelio was hoping that his summation alone would sway at least one juror to Spahalski's side.

Judge Sirkin ordered everyone back the following Monday for closing arguments and adjourned court for the long weekend.

With the media, Spahalski's trial stayed under the radar. There were a few stories in the *Democrat and Chronicle* at the start and the end of the trial, but the body of the trial, when the prosecution presented its forty witnesses, received no coverage.

One reason was that cameras were not allowed in the courtroom. Monroe County had learned its lesson after Shawcross, and no longer allowed its trials to become a local obsession. Another reason was that no courtroom drama was anticipated, and none occurred. No "Perry Mason moments."

Ken Hyland's job was simple. He had to convince the jury that when Robert Spahalski confessed to killing Armstrong, Berger, Grande, and Irizarry, he was telling the truth.

"When a guy walks into a police station and says, 'I just killed someone, she's in the basement to my house,' and we go and find her there, that's a pretty solid case. We weren't worried at all about Irizarry. It was the other three that concerned us," Ken Hyland later said. "They were more problematical. We were most concerned with the Adrian Berger case because the medical examiner had failed to conclude that the case was a homicide."

Would Spahalski have been arrested for Berger's murder if the medical examiner had immediately called it a homicide? After all, there was an eyewitness that said he saw Spahalski leaving Berger's home at about the time of her death.

"I don't know," Hyland said. "It wasn't like someone

heard screams and shots and then saw a man running out of the house." Berger's body had been in an advanced state of decomposition when it was discovered, and the time of death could only be determined with a wide margin of error. It would have been up to the jury to determine what "about the time of the murder" meant.

"Even if the medical examiner had called the death a murder, the case against Spahalski would have been very much circumstantial," Hyland added.

As to the question of why Spahalski surrendered when he did, Hyland agreed that feeling remorse because Spahalski cared for Irizarry had nothing to do with Robert's decision to walk into the Public Safety Building.

"The big difference between the Irizarry murder and the others," Hyland said, "is that he killed Irizarry in his own house. With the other murders, he left the victim right at the spot where they were killed and walked away. Then there wasn't enough to connect him. The last one he kills in his own house, so he's kind of stuck with it. He hides the body and buys himself some time by putting it in a cool spot, and then he realizes, 'Hey, I'm not going to be able to get away with it.'"

How did he feel about the theory that Spahalski turned himself in because he had AIDS and thought prison bought him a form of medical insurance? He might have thought he would get better medical treatment inside than outside.

"I don't know. In another case, yes, but not this one," Hyland said. "I had a case once where a guy caught AIDS in prison, and when he got out, he killed someone so he could go back in. He said he thought the state owed him the medical treatment.

"Robert was getting medical care, you know. He was taking a whole list of prescription medications for his various medical and mental problems. Why he would think his medical care would be better in prison, I don't know."

Regarding the low-profile nature of the trial, Rose

Grande was feeling a little paranoid. She believed that the *Democrat and Chronicle* was purposefully not covering the trial because she and other members of the victims' families had not given their reporters interviews. Whether it be drugs, prostitution, or homosexuality, all of the victims had lifestyles that might embarrass their families, and family members had understandably not been completely forthcoming when asked probing questions.

But, according to Ken Hyland, the Spahalski trial's lack of press coverage had nothing to do with a vendetta against uncooperative families. It had to do with economics. Like many daily newspapers in the computer age, the *Democrat and Chronicle* was having financial troubles. It was understaffed and its reporters were overworked. There was only one reporter, Mike Zeigler, assigned to cover the crime news, which included both police and court activity. And the latter category included city, county, and federal courts. He simply couldn't be in court every day for Spahalski's trial, as he was reporting on other matters.

Another factor in the lack of coverage might have been political—a matter of public relations. The *Democrat and Chronicle* sometimes went on a kick where they deemphasized city crime because it made Rochester look bad. Puffy feel-good stories were published, instead.

Sadly, it was during the murder trial of Robert Bruce Spahalski that the Monroe County Public Defender's Office received news that public defender Jeffrey A. Jacobs, Robert Bruce Spahalski's first lawyer after he turned himself in, had passed away after a long bout with cancer.

The *Public Defense Backup Center Report*, November-December 2006 edition, quoted Judge Richard Wesley, who knew Jacobs from his time as a state judge: "He always had an insightful or original view of his case. He was what is right about our profession," Judge Wesley said.

23

Summation

At nine on Monday morning, following the three-day weekend, everyone was back in their place in the large courtroom. Everyone, except the jury. For an hour, court business was tended to with the jury out of the room. That completed, the jury filed in and the defense's final argument began just after ten o'clock in the morning.

To enhance his closing statement to the jury, Joseph Damelio used a visual prop. Juries loved props. They gave the jury something to look at in case they didn't want to make eye contact. He held in his hand two small saline envelopes of crack cocaine and walked right up to the rail in front of the jury so the panel could get a good look at them.

"When Robert confessed to beating and strangling Vivian Irizarry last year, he told police he killed her because he thought she was a demon. The demon is here," Damelio said, gesturing at the bags of crack, "and it affected his mind.

"He was agitated and talkative and was manipulated by investigators," Damelio continued. "They knew who he was. He had been a suspect in two 1990s killings, but police had not been able to prove it.

"When all is said and done, you have one great big mess. When you listen to the prosecution in this case, to the police who investigated this case, what you have is the life of Robert Spahalski as told by the people who have been after him for fifteen years."

Damelio told the jury that there was no evidence that without crack cocaine, Robert Bruce Spahalski was any more dangerous than you or I.

"Cure Spahalski of his crack addiction, and the killer within him dies," Joseph Damelio said.

The defense attorney spoke for about an hour.

Kenneth Hyland began his statement, just after 11:30 A.M., and spoke for approximately forty-five minutes. Hyland told the jury that the evidence against the defendant was overwhelming. The defense's argument that Spahalski was out of his mind on drugs at the time of all the murders was a crock.

"Voluntary intoxication is not an exculpatory defense if the person chose to take drugs while aware of such possible outcomes," Hyland said. Maybe, just maybe, it might be a defense for a person who killed only once, or for a person's first kill. But for a repeat killer. the argument held no water whatsoever. Robert Spahalski knew that he sometimes committed murder when he smoked crack, and yet he smoked crack, anyway. The defense could not successfully argue that Robert didn't know the difference between right and wrong, because he had taken pains to cover up, following each crime, making obvious moves to deceive investigators and mask his identity as the killer. "I ask you to find the defendant guilty of the December 1990 strangulation of Moraine Armstrong, twenty-four, in Rochester, the July 1991 strangulation of Adrian Berger, thirty-five, in Rochester, the October 1991 bludgeoning death of Charles Grande, forty, in Webster, and the November 2005 bludgeoning and strangulation death of Vivian Irizarry, fifty-four, in Rochester."

Ken Hyland asked the jury to see to it that Robert Bruce Spahalski never set foot in society again. He had proven himself unfit to be among us.

Judge Sirkin gave the jury their instructions, from 12:40 to 1:20 P.M.

The jury began deliberations at 1:30 P.M., and their return to the courtroom was stunningly swift, about as fast as a jury could do it, assuming they were responsible and concerned with dotting the *i*'s and crossing the *t*'s. They announced that they had come to a verdict at 4:30 P.M.

A few minutes later, after the parties were given a chance to report to the courtroom, the jury found Robert Spahalski guilty of intentional second-degree murder for Irizarry, one count of second-degree murder and one count of felony robbery associated with murder for Grande, and one count each of intentional second-degree murder for Armstrong and Berger.

Spahalski showed no emotion when the verdict was read. The only outward indication of his anxiety came in the form of a plastic cup of water, from which he took frequent sips.

Hyland's first comment on hearing the news was that he was going to ask for the maximum prison sentence of one hundred years to life in prison. "I think these crimes call for that," the veteran prosecutor said. "Frankly, I think Mr. Spahalski should never see the light of day again." He complimented Damelio, who'd done a good job under *Mission: Impossible* conditions. "When somebody comes into a police station and says, 'I want to tell you about somebody I killed. She's in my basement,' there's not much the defense can do," Hyland said.

"Were you completely satisfied that Spahalski's confession was voluntary?" Hyland was asked by a reporter.

"Oh yes," Hyland replied. "None of the interrogating officers said he appeared high or in withdrawal or disoriented and in the need of medication. Could it be any clearer that the statements were voluntary? The defendant goes down to the police station to confess, and that is what he does."

Damelio was also answering questions—at least some of the questions—outside the courtroom.

"Will you appeal, and if so, on what grounds?" he was asked.

"Yes, on several grounds, but foremost on the grounds that my client should not have been tried for all four murders at the same time," Damelio said.

"With the evidence that Spahalski suffered from mental illness, why didn't you use an insanity defense?"

"No comment."

Among the relatives of the victims who attended the reading of the verdict, there was a new face among the regulars. He was Harry Irizarry Jr., Vivian's son, thirty-six years old, who had traveled from his hometown of San Antonio, Texas, to be there.

"Regardless of how much punishment he gets, it is never going to be enough," Harry said. "I view my mom as a hero. Had she not treated him well, he wouldn't have felt the guilt and turned himself in. And I feel for the families of the other three victims," he concluded.

Nineteen hours after the verdict, Charles Grande's mother, with justice for her baby boy having been served at last, quietly passed away.

"It's because Chuck came and got her," Rose said. "She hung on long enough, and the night before she died, the story came on about the conviction on the five o'clock news. She came out of it for a second and she said, 'Oh, my baby boy,' and then she fell back asleep. She died the next morning. I was there when she died. I brought the morning paper with me and I put it in her hands, and I told her that Chuck's killer had been convicted and her baby boy finally had his justice. She was already starting to pass over, but she moved her lips and tried to speak, and then she was gone. There was such a feeling in that room. It was amazing. I think Chuck came and got her. I believe he said, 'Ma, it's okay, you can go now.'"

24

Sentencing

On December 12, Robert and Stephen Spahalski's fifty-second birthday, Robert's sentencing hearing was held. At the hearing, Ken Hyland asked Judge Sirkin to impose the maximum sentence on Robert Spahalski. He noted the cruelty and brutality of the murders. "These were not quick, painless deaths," Hyland said. Nor were they fair fights. "None of the victims posed a physical threat to the killer."

It was at the sentencing hearing that friends and relatives of the victims had an opportunity to tell the court how much the victim was loved and the killer loathed.

Carrie Peterson was Moraine Armstrong's aunt. She said that the conviction of Robert Spahalski for her niece's murder was a load off their family's mind. "This New Year's Eve, it will be so much better. We won't have to wonder who killed her. We already know," Aunt Carrie explained, referring to the anniversary of her niece's murder. Peterson spoke directly to Spahalski: "You took her for no reason. I hope you see their faces every night and every day. Don't you ever forget her."

The relatives who spoke showed enormous courage, and inner strength.

Rose said, "Charles Grande was my big brother. We grew up together, and he was the most familiar and, in many ways, the most influential person in my life. No one knew him better than I did.

"What stood out most about Chuck was his gentle nature and his lifelong, unwavering commitment to non-violence. There wasn't a shred of evil, or maliciousness, or abusiveness, or threat to anyone *ever*, in that man's entire life. Though there was much to love, that was what I loved most about him. It was the thing that made my brother a most rare and special human being.

"So when Chuck died the way he did, to me it was the triumph of evil over good. The *way* he died was the complete opposite of the way he lived. It was the opposite of what he stood for above everything else. The *way* he died shattered my beliefs. It broke my heart. It violated my soul. It ripped out my roots. It destroyed my mother, and it ruined my wonderful family.

"For fifteen years, I have been haunted by the way one of the most beautiful and harmless human beings I have ever met was stolen from us, and by how senseless it was. You don't ever recover from that sort of desecration. You just go on and do the best you can with what you have left.

"And so, Your Honor, I am asking you to give the maximum sentence to the man who murdered my brother and all those other people. He is what he is. Eventually he would do it again, and that must not be allowed to happen. Thank you."

* * *

Each victim was allowed one representative to give a statement. Speaking for Vivian Irizarry was Leslie Gonzalez, her sister, who said, "Although I realize my sister made some bad choices, she will never have the chance to make better ones. Her grandchildren will never have the opportunity to witness her great sense of humor, her extremely kind heart, and her magnetic personality. As her sister and her friend, I continue to miss her and all that she was to me. We do not seek revenge. We seek justice."

When the relatives' statements were complete, Robert Bruce Spahalski was given a chance to make a final statement, last words before Judge Sirkin told him his punishment. Spahalski said, "I would like to say to the families, 'I apologize. I'm deeply sorry.'"

Damelio then told the judge that "any sentence you impose will amount to a death sentence." Damelio noted that Spahalski was fifty-two years old and HIV positive. "He does not have long for this world. Everyone wants him to explain his actions, but he can't explain his actions. He has suffered for years from mental illness and voluntary intoxication from drugs and alcohol."

Judge Sirkin turned to the defendant and said, "You knew that there would be consequences for your actions when you turned yourself in. You knew, at some level, you would be here today and would be going to prison."

The judge sentenced Robert Spahalski to one hundred years in prison. Court was adjourned, and Spahalski was led away to spend the rest of his life behind state penitentiary bars.

Attending that day was Moraine Armstrong's father, Moses Armstrong, who up until that point had avoided the public eye. Outside the courtroom, a reporter asked Moses how he felt about Spahalski's attempt to apologize for his deeds.

The man wanted to hear none of it. "You lose your daughter, twenty-four years old, and it's very painful," he said. "But justice was served, and hopefully, he will die in prison."

It was only after the trial was over that Rose broke her moratorium on the media. She spoke first to a woman reporter she knew. As Rose remembered it, "I said to her, 'I couldn't talk to you guys. It was just too tough—and it didn't seem like you were playing fair.' And the reporter said, 'Well, you know, we have to do our job.' I should have said, 'Your job was *not* to make my brother look like the perpetrator, instead of the victim.'"

After the conviction, authorities were still not certain that all of Robert's killings had been accounted for. Damita Gibson's mother swore that Spahalski had been visiting her daughter repeatedly during the days and weeks before she was murdered.

Vicki Jobson disappeared from her apartment on Lake Avenue, a building in which Spahalski had lived.

Then there was the murder of Hortense Greatheart, on January 3, 2003. She lived in another building that Spahalski had called home, and the thermostat had been turned all the way up, just as it had in the killing of Charles Grande.

Rose Grande often thought about Spahalski's other victims, both the ones he had confessed to killing and those that he only *maybe* killed. When it came to the "possibles," there sure were a lot of coincidences.

Not that coincidences didn't happen. Rose knew they did. Her brother Chuck had been a friend of a woman named June. As it turned out, one serial killer (Shawcross) had murdered her, and another had murdered him. What were the odds of that happening? When Chuck learned that his friend June was dead, he told his sister what a beautiful person June had been—that she was a little bit lost, but that she was not a prostitute. But history was all too often painted with a broad brush, and June would go down as "one of the prostitutes" that Shawcross murdered.

The Lyell Avenue world was so small that Robert Bruce Spahalski and Arthur Shawcross crossed paths on a number of occasions.

"He was a big bastard and he looked strong," Robert recalled. "I always saw him in his cars with hookers buying cocaine. For some reason, he always reminded me of the fatherly type. That turned out to be a dead wrong assumption."

As for the murder victims with whom he reportedly had proximity, Robert answered all queries with a big shrug.

"I've no idea if I know Damita Jo, Vicki, or Hortense. I was sometimes on King Street (where Damita lived) associating with hookers and drug addicts who were on a mission like me. I've no doubt I probably lived in the same building [with Vicki and Hortense]. In any case, I don't remember. There were so many killings during the fifteen years I ran the streets of northwest Rochester. I lived in social chaos and loved every heartbeat of it. I was like a social alley cat in the midst of chaotic adventure. I didn't murder those people. Of course, the police don't believe that."

Robert thought his trial was a joke. "The court showed no mercy. It was a sham," he said. "No consideration was given for me turning myself in. They acted like they tracked me down and captured me, which was not the case at all."

Robert wanted the readers of this book to know he thought he deserved another chance. "I loved Vivian and meant no harm," he said. "I accept full responsibility for my actions, even though I was temporarily insane at the time. I'm not proud. I am very embarrassed over my transgressions. I hope your readers will learn something about having psychological problems and smoking crack. You see what can happen when you mix the two.

"I was a paranoid schizophrenic with a crack problem when I killed those people. I was temporarily insane."

25

Nature or Nurture?

Perhaps the most fascinating aspect of the story of Robert and Stephen Spahalski is, if we are to believe what we've been told, these identical twins developed independently into killers. As adolescents they played a game of criminal one-upmanship.

In a way, the game never ended. Maybe it will never end—not until death separates Robert and Stephen—two halves of a lethal whole.

Stephen had been winning that noxious game for many years. He committed his murder in 1971, almost twenty years before his twin first killed. Then, with Moraine Armstrong in 1990, Robert evened the score. With the others, he left Stephen in the dust.

From a scientific standpoint, the question becomes: What caused this behavior? Was it genetics or environment? Nature or nurture?

There have been studies done on the hereditary aspects

of both aggressive and violent behavior in families and in twins. Scientists believed that tendencies toward violence could be inherited, and that identical twins were far more likely to share violent tendencies than nonidentical twins or siblings who weren't twins.

Judging the hereditary nature of antisocial behavior was difficult, since children usually grew up in the same home as their parents and had ample opportunity to learn violent behavior, regardless of whether they were predisposed toward it.

Studies of the brain have shown that violence is almost always part of a developmental process, that each experience we have affects our potential for violence. A child who grows up exposed to acts of violence, therefore, is far more apt to choose violence as a viable option, given a certain set of circumstances.

Perhaps it is telling that, according to a now-retired member of the Chemung County Sheriff's Office, Robert and Stephen Spahalski were still adolescents when they began shaking down male sex partners. Exploiting the vulnerability of closet gays became, in a sense, their first job.

"I wish I had gone deeper into the twins' background when I had the chance," said Pat Patterson, who investigated the Ronald Ripley case in Elmira Heights.

Patterson lives today in Texas with his family, including his elderly mother. San Antonio was the site of his last FBI assignment before retirement, and he stayed. But he still received the Elmira newspaper, the *Star-Gazette,* for his mother.

"It's for her, but I also like to keep track of local happenings," Patterson said.

He recalled vividly the day in 2005 when he got the paper, looked at a photo on the front page, and said, "That looks like Spahalski."

He hadn't seen a Spahalski in thirty years, but the guy had one of those mugs on him that you weren't quick to forget. For Patterson, recognition was immediate.

As he read the story of Robert's arrest, he mused about how different this story would be if DNA identification technology had been available to law enforcement twenty years earlier.

"Back then, the best we could hope for was fingerprints and maybe blood type from the semen, if we were lucky," he said. "That, and confessions were the way that we handled homicides at the time."

Like everyone else, Patterson had a couple of theories regarding why Robert turned himself in after the murder of Vivian Irizarry. One was that he'd grown weary of freedom and sought to be institutionalized again.

Another was that he saw his arrest as inevitable, so he would save the police the trouble of coming to him. Every criminal knew that turning himself in was always quieter, gentler, and safer than being apprehended.

One theory Patterson rejected out of hand was that Robert turned himself in out of remorse. Patterson strongly believed Robert to be a psychopath and a sociopath, incapable of feeling guilt, incapable of any feelings of any kind for other people.

Patterson theorized that Robert Bruce Spahalski's friends and lovers were not people he liked or loved, but rather people who served a convenient purpose in his life. He was a liar with a parasitic lifestyle, incapable of emotional connectivity.

"I know remorse wasn't the reason he turned himself in, because he could feel no remorse. He wasn't capable of that emotion," Patterson said.

He noted that by the time the twins first came to the attention of law enforcement as teenagers, they were already exhibiting signs of being well-developed sociopaths.

Were they born that way, or did their environment make them that way? Patterson didn't know, but—admittedly,

sight unseen—he was inclined to think the missing father
had something to do with it. The twins became predators
at a *very* early age.

"I wondered about the father, who was out of the picture. I never even learned his name. I wondered if they
were adopted," Patterson said.

He noted that the mother seemed stable. The twins
were neither impoverished nor orphaned. It was hard to
say what made them so wild, so fast.

Patterson felt that both twins at this point had been so
strongly institutionalized that they were as comfortable
inside the joint as outside. More so, maybe.

The yardstick most commonly used by investigators to
determine if a criminal is a sociopath is Hare's Checklist,
a listing of traits compiled by Dr. Robert D. Hare.

According to Hare, a sociopath's aggressive narcissism
often demonstrates itself in glibness and superficial
charm, a grandiose sense of self-worth, pathological
lying, cunning and manipulative behavior, a lack of remorse or guilt, shallowness, callousness and lack of empathy, failure to accept responsibility for one's own
actions, and promiscuous sexual behavior.

Their socially deviant lifestyle can include a need for
constant stimulation and a proneness to boredom, a parasitic lifestyle, poor behavior control, a lack of realistic
long-term goals, impulsivity, irresponsibility, juvenile
delinquency, and other early behavioral problems.

Sociopaths, Hare said, made versatile criminals, who
as adults tended to have several short-term marriages.

"If you were to trace their lives, I think you'd find that
neither of the Spahalski twins have ever had emotional connectivity with another human being," Patterson said. "Not
their mother, not their father, not a wife, not a girlfriend."

Patterson said that the twins might have had relationships with those people—Stephen had a wife once, and

Robert had a long-term girlfriend—but their interaction was based completely on one or more completely selfish needs.

"Anyone hanging around with a Spahalski twin was serving a purpose in his life—a purpose that had nothing to do with emotion," Patterson said.

That might have been news to Christine Gonzalez. On the other hand, she might have recognized the truth in the statement better than anyone.

Former head of the FBI's Behavioral Science Unit at the FBI's National Academy in Quantico, Virginia, Dr. Stephen Band was asked about psychopaths, sociopaths, and what makes cold-blooded killers tick.

"Sociopaths are, in effect, psychopaths who operate in and are affected—empowered—by criminal group or gang environments and activities. Psychopaths are individuals with a grave organic personality disorder for which there is no cure," Dr. Band said.

He pointed out that sociopaths and psychopaths can never be declared criminally insane, even if their way of thinking strikes the average person as crazy. That's because to be criminally insane, at least in New York State, a person has to be unaware of the difference between right and wrong.

But it is an element of the sociopathic personality that they *do* know right from wrong—they know the difference just as well as the rest of us. They know. They just don't care.

They know when they have to do something in private and when they can do something in public, but they do not feel the accompanying shame and guilt that the rest of us feel when we commit bad acts.

"They go about their business satiating their personal—often violent and sexual—needs, whims and desires—without any remorse or feelings of guilt," Dr. Band said.

It made no difference how extreme the physical and emotional pain they would bring to their primary and secondary victims. Their sadism was insatiable. They savored the suffering.

"Psychopaths are often intelligent," Dr. Band said. "They don't want to be caught, and get better at what they do over time. More often than not, they are cowards if cornered. They don't like personal pain," he said.

Dr. Band said that the extent and depth of psychopathy might be influenced by social and family developmental factors. It was possible that the twins' personality disorders were aggravated by experiences in the home and/or at school during their early developmental years.

Looking at the timeline, their basic pattern of bad behavior—competitive domain expansion, with violent reactions when things did not go as planned—was already in place during Robert and Stephen's adolescence. Perhaps that pattern of activity was learned. Most children, from broken homes or not, did not voluntarily decide during their teen years on a vice-ridden criminal career. If it had been a matter of survival, that was one thing. They probably needed to be exposed to criminal culture in order to assume that lifestyle so wholeheartedly. The twins committed escalating crimes in and around Elmira because they were bored.

"Hypothetically, when a psychopathic child grows up in a home surrounded by abuse, and criminal activity, drugs and violence, their propensity for criminal activity and violence increases," Dr. Band said.

On the other hand, if a sociopath grew up in a home surrounded by caring, nurturing, intelligent parents, they might grow up to be cutthroat attorneys, con artists, or shrewd used-car salespeople. The lack of conscience would be unchanged, but how it manifested itself might be completely different.

Experts agreed that the twins suffered from one or more types of antisocial personality disorders, including being a sociopath and a psychopath. Both psychos and socios have a complete disregard for the feelings of others, they feel no remorse or guilt, but there are distinguishing factors. A sociopath is disorganized, easily stimulated and has difficulty assimilating with society. A psycho can be organized, secretive and manipulative. He is capable of charm.

"Those who've dated a psychopath remember the experience," Dr. Band said. These relationships tend to follow the same pattern, and they are pretty much the same for men and women. "They were charmed, manipulated, used and abused, possibly left wanting more, a bug to a flame. All the while, their psychopathic lover appeared to take some strange pleasure in stringing them along and out—emotionally, financially, and otherwise—as he or she moved on to their next lover-victim."

As this was written, Stephen J. Spahalski was scheduled to be released from the Elmira Correctional Facility on July 22, 2009. His failure to take the antiviolence course will no longer be a factor.

According to prison official Linda Foglia, "With a very minimal amount of room for an exception (i.e. civil confinement), the law requires the New York State Department of Correctional Services to release an inmate to the community once he or she reach their maximum expiration date." Stephen's max date was July 22, 2009. On that date, it no longer mattered what programs he did complete or didn't complete during his incarceration. He became a free man.

Obviously, Stephen never got time off for good behavior. In fact, he has accumulated a multipage list of misbehaviors during his near lifetime in prison. More than fifty separate incidents are on record. A large number of those incidents were clustered during the short stretch when he and his twin were inside at the same time, impersonation charges based on the twins trying to switch places. Many of the others were harassment complaints.

Like his twin, Stephen was quick to threaten violence on anyone who wasn't with his program.

Even his twin, Robert, didn't sound optimistic about Stephen's chances on the outside after all these years.

"He's scheduled for release, and the poor dude has no clue what he's socially and economically up against. I do not know how he will cope with it," Robert said. "He is a paranoid schizophrenic, and I'm sure he has his issues. I cannot tell if he will be a random bullet out there, ready to explode with exasperation from not having enough experience in the world. I don't know what his plans and goals are. Only time can resolve this issue.

"He is highly educated in Eastern and Western philosophy, but he's acquired only outdated job skills, nothing to suit today's employment market.

"I do know he's a black belt and can be dangerous to others if he can't cope with the oncoming social pressures. I don't know how he'll adapt to the stress levels."

Pat Patterson believed that both Spahalski twins were potentially dangerous to anyone who spoke against them, shortchanged them, or irritated them in any way. Sex and robbery comprised their business, Patterson said, and had since they were teenagers. In their perpetual state of depraved indifference, maybe dead bodies were merely the residue of a firmly run operation.

Epilogue

With four years passed since the day Robert Bruce Spahalski turned himself in, Rochester did not cease to be a dangerous place. Huge portions of the city, including Edgerton Park, Dutchtown, and much of the city's west side, remained on the "don't go there" list. Even more of the sagging houses were boarded up. Even more of the boarded houses were torn down. Prostitution remained a fiercely dangerous profession, but on Lyell and Lake Avenues, the ladies were more apt to die from drugs or disease than at the hands of a john. The Crescent was inhabited by too many people who had no choice but to live there, people who either never had a chance or squandered their last chance in the crackling of a glass pipe.

On November 13, 2008, that other surviving Rochester serial killer, Arthur Shawcross, died. He'd been serving a 250-years-to-life sentence, and life won. Although few grieved, the historic nature of his crimes did render his death noteworthy.

Just weeks before his death, Shawcross was transported from the Sullivan Correctional Facility to the Albany Medical Center for an undisclosed illness.

A grown son of one of his victims said he felt sad at the news, because now Shawcross was facing an eternity of burning in Hell, and he wouldn't want to wish that fate upon anyone.

Another relative who would never forget her lost loved one was Kelly Gangemi, sister of Vicki Jobson. Vicki was the party girl turned prostitute whose body had been found stabbed multiple times, in December 1992, not far from the New York Central railroad tracks, a block north of Lyell Avenue.

Gangemi lived in the town of Greece, a suburb of Rochester that butted up against the city's northwestern-most section. Seventeen years had passed since her sister's murder, and still she and the rest of her family had no closure.

For years after Vicki's murder, she assumed that her sister was one of the victims of John White, the suspected serial killer who had never been arrested. Then, when White died, she learned that Vicki had not been on the list of murders that police believed White had committed.

Arthur Shawcross was already in prison by the time Vicki disappeared, so it couldn't have been him. Of the known serial killers working in that area at that time, that left Robert Bruce Spahalski, who lived in Vicki's building.

Kelly Gangemi's life since her sister's death had not been easy. She had a daughter and grandchildren to look after, a niece in prison, an aging father and friend who needed care, and yet she couldn't stop thinking about Vicki.

"I'm going crazy. I'm falling apart," she had said upon the sixteenth anniversary of the discovery of Vicki's body.

After all that time, Kelly still commemorated her sister's birthday. Each year on Veterans Day, Vicki's birthday, Kelly drove to the corner of Rutter and Haloid Streets to see "the spot," the place where her sister's body had been found.

"I do it because it keeps my energy fresh. I do it because

it makes me angry," Kelly said. After visiting the spot, she sometimes visited Vicki's grave site. She could feel her sister's spirit at both locations. It was tough on Kelly, tough especially in October, the month of Vicki's death. Nobody was even sure what the anniversary of her death was.

Kelly was determined to have Vicki's killer caught, even in 2009 after all those years had passed. She sought answers, and tried to always focus her energy on finding the creep or creeps who did it.

Every once in a while, there was a *Democrat and Chronicle* headline—a murderer had been caught. Kelly's heart always leapt. Every time. She still had faith.

"I'm not vindictive. I know that catching her killer won't bring Vicki back," Kelly said. "I have this big cloud hanging over my head."

But she couldn't surrender, either. She couldn't back up, which was weird if she stopped to think about it. There wasn't that much Kelly could do. She wasn't an investigator. All she could do was pester the hell out of the cop assigned to Vicki's case.

She didn't want to interfere. She just wanted to make sure they were all on their toes, the actual investigators. Vicki's murder was now a cold case, and cold cases didn't get priority. She understood that, but she also wanted to make sure Vicki wasn't forgotten altogether by the RPD.

She thought about being an activist. Maybe she would hold a protest, maybe a march. Sometimes she thought about planting a tree in Vicki's memory, or starting a charity that gave coats to the prostitutes on the street in winter.

"Just something," she said.

She had a dream. One day it would be Vicki whose murder was solved on the front page of the newspaper, and it would be Kelly on TV talking about how great the investigators were.

Since it happened, Kelly kept a scrapbook that was filled with memories of Vicki's life and death. There are family photos dating back to the 1960s, Vicki's school picture, and the many letters and cards of condolence she received after the murder.

Kelly patiently pasted the Xeroxes of the newspaper stories on Vicki in the scrapbook. Kelly left the last page of the scrapbook blank. That space was reserved for the solution to the mystery.

There were items in there that were unexpected. Kelly refused to be queasy. There were photos of "the spot." There was a photo of the medical examiner's staff loading Vicki's remains into their vehicle.

But there were also things in the scrapbook that couldn't have been more sentimental, exactly the sort of items that you'd expect, items that broke Kelly's heart, like a copy of a Mother's Day card that Jobson's daughter, Keisha Washington, made as a second grader.

"You can never fill the hole from Vicki's dying. But you can close it a little bit," Kelly said.

Besides the sadness she felt when thinking about the sister she lost, Kelly was disturbed by Vicki's murder in other ways as well. Like so many before her, she couldn't fathom the workings of a guilt-free mind.

"I'll always wonder, was he a veteran? Is he somebody she knew? Did he see me on the news? Will he read this book? Can someone carry this secret for so long? I can't imagine how someone can walk around knowing that he killed someone's sister. There's not a minute I don't think about it. I will not give up."

One might think that a murder case as old as Vicki Jobson's would be ice cold, but multiple sources said this was not true. RPD investigator Randy Benjamin said, "We are following a few leads, and this is a case where I really think we are on the right track."

Retired sergeant Mark Mariano, who had been on the scene after Moraine Armstrong was killed, had also been the first officer on the scene when Vicki's body was found. Years later, as a homicide detective, he had been present when Robert came into police headquarters to give himself up, and had been among those to discover Vivian Irizarry's body.

During his last years on the force, and even after retirement, Mariano fought to keep Vicki's case active. He felt the fact that she and Spahalski had once lived in the same building was just a coincidence.

Normally, in a civilized city, the chances of a woman living in the same building with a serial killer, but being killed by someone else, would be astronomical. But the Edgerton neighborhood during that time was anything but normal. Murder was so rampant that coincidences like Vicki and Robert Spahalski's proximity were absolutely believable.

Because of Mariano's efforts, there was a forensic excavation, and many people were reinterviewed. Regarding Vicki's murder, Mariano agreed with Benjamin that there were positive leads and the investigation was not stalled.

"I don't believe Spahalski did it," Mariano said flat out in 2009. "I'm certain that he didn't, and I know who the suspects are." *Note the plural.*

Mariano did not believe that Robert Spahalski was organized enough to kill someone in one place and dump the body in another. With the exception of Vivian Irizarry, who had been dragged from the upstairs to the downstairs of the same building, Spahalski's known murders all involved a crime scene in which the body lay precisely where it had been killed. With Vicki, though, she had been killed in one place and then—*months later*—had been moved to the place where her remains were found.

"I don't think Spahalski woke up in the morning and said, 'I think I'm going to kill someone today,'" Mariano said. "And in that sense, he is not the prototypical serial killer. He was a guy who repeatedly snapped. He would be in a situation and something would go wrong, something that triggered an uncontrollable urge to kill in his brain, and that was when he committed his murders. He didn't have the type of mind for the kill site to be different from the dump site."

Was it possible that Spahalski had two methods of operation, one when he was a pedestrian and one when he had a car? He'd been a car thief in Elmira. He drove a pickup truck and a station wagon in Rochester. He'd had a driver's license until 1991. He stole Adrian Berger's and Chuck Grande's cars—so sometimes he had a vehicle, even if it wasn't his.

"Spahalski is not sophisticated. I don't think he thought ahead," Mariano said. "He stole the car in Webster because he'd just killed the guy who'd driven him out there. The car fulfilled a simple and immediate need. He had to get back to Rochester."

What was Mariano's theory?

"I worked hands-on, on Vicki's case, for many, many months. I think her murder was a prostitution deal gone bad," Mariano said—the Moraine Armstrong story all over again. "She was a feisty little girl. They were doing a lot of cocaine. She felt like she should get paid after the sex. The johns said, 'We been giving you a lot of cocaine. We ain't paying you shit.' She got pissed-off. There was a physical fight. It turned very ugly and she lost. These two dummies then bury her. For some reason, someone is suspicious of the burial site, maybe a family member, so they get her out of there and dump her along the railroad tracks. That's how I see it." Yes, he did have definite suspects in mind.

During a 2009 interview, Kelly said that, sadly, she had more time than ever to pester the detectives working on her sister's case. She had been taking care of a man named Walt Lake, who suffered from Parkinson's disease. He died the day after Christmas 2008, and Kelly was between jobs. She suddenly found herself with a lot of time on her hands—being forty-five but feeling twenty-five—and not sure what she was going to do.

"I'm going to be a pain in the ass to the homicide investigators," she promised.

Kelly had her own entry into the "small world" department. When Robert murdered Vivian Irizarry on Spencer Street, Kelly Gangemi was only a few hundred yards away, working as a waitress at Roncone's on Lyell Avenue. "We had a dishwasher named Lovey back then, and at the end of the day, he used to give the leftover buns to a guy who lived down the street, and that guy turned out to be Spahalski."

Kelly knew a lot of the "girls in the area" from trying to find out who had killed Vicki. She knew how hard it was on them, especially during Rochester's harsh winters, so she gave them "clothes and stuff."

Kelly was very sympathetic to their plight. She admittedly had been on "both sides of the fence." She had once been on drugs, but against all odds, she had managed to kick her habit and get her life back together. She knew how hard it was.

On the day that Robert turned himself in, and the body of Vivian Irizarry was found on Spencer Street, someone came running into Roncone's and said, "Hey, did you hear they found a girl?"

"I went running down there," Kelly said. "I see the homicide investigators and I said, 'Who'd they find? Who is it?' Right away I thought that this was the work of Vicki's killer.

"The investigators tell me that they have a pretty good idea who killed Vicki, and that it wasn't John White. My mother always thought it was John White. Turns out, at the time Vicki's body was dumped, John White was under surveillance."

Interestingly, John White lived only three streets away from Kelly's mom in Gates.

"I was freakin' obsessed with that guy, because back then, I thought he killed my sister. I used to drive by his house off of Long Pond Road and he'd be outside and I'd look at him in his eyes."

Kelly Gangemi was grateful for all the hard work the police had already put in over the years. She especially appreciated Mariano's efforts. She feared that time was running short for any of it to matter. Her mother had passed away. Her sister and her father were sick. The answers had to come before it was too late.

Ethel Dix, the mother of murder victim Damita Gibson, hoped that this book might stir up some interest in her daughter's case.

She said, "The homicide investigators did not investigate Robert Bruce Spahalski thoroughly enough to see if he did murder my child. Her murder is still unsolved, and I hope that you can help me get any answers in her death. It has been eighteen years, and my daughter, just as well as me and her children that were left behind, would like to have this solved so that she can rest."

How were Damita's three children? Joseph, the baby, was long since recovered from the gunshot he'd suffered years before. Tamaija was doing well, attending college at Geneseo.

William, the oldest, was a father himself by this time, making Ethel a great-grandmother. He had gone over to his girlfriend's house and had gotten into some trouble there. He'd been caught by police carrying a gun and was probably going to end up doing some time. Ethel figured it might be a blessing in disguise. He'd had the gun on him, but he hadn't committed a crime with it. He'd been caught and was off the streets. Maybe he would learn his lesson before he had a chance to hurt anyone, or get hurt himself.

"I still have a lot to thank God for," Ethel said. "The boy has had his problems, his challenges. As a child, he was on Ritalin. He was filled with anger, losing his mother the way he did at such a young age."

Ethel found her participation in the creation of this book cathartic. Her husband, Mason, is a bus driver, and when she rode with him along the #9 line, which went down Jay Street, and passed the spot where Damita's body was found, she always had to look the other way. Sometimes she didn't ride along at all, because she didn't want to go through that area. But while this book was being written, Ethel agreed to accompany photographer Jerry Warren to the spot. While there, she felt her fear dissipate, a pressure lift from her chest, and the area was purified of its stigma.

Even though almost twenty years had passed since the young woman whose friends called her D.J. had lost her life, her mother still thought about her all the time. Sometimes the memories came rushing back in strange and powerful ways. Just recently Ethel was going through some stuff and found a note Damita had written, just a shopping list, really, but it brought with it a flood of memories and feelings.

Sadly, on October 5, 2009, Ethel Dix passed away without ever solving the mystery of her daughter's murder.

Rochester police investigator William "Billy" Barnes died of cancer on October 20, 2008. Barnes had worked the Damita Gibson case, as well as the cases of Moraine Armstrong and Adrian Berger. He had been the recipient of Richard Marchese's letter, written following Charles Grande's murder, telling law enforcement not to question Robert Bruce Spahalski about any murders before his criminal impersonation trial.

Joseph Damelio, Robert Spahalski's defense attorney, is in private practice with his office in downtown Rochester. His practice specializes in personal-injury cases.

* * *

Vivian Irizarry's employer had been the Center for Disability Rights. CDR's motto was "Helping People Help Themselves." Their emblem is Lady Liberty's torch thrust out of a triangle, around which was written, *Civil Rights. Integration. Independence.* Their mission was to create an environment that was free of physical barriers for people with all sorts of disabilities, a world in which no one who was wheelchair-bound would be prevented from participating in an activity because a facility lacked a ramp or an elevator. They provided a variety of services, but the most common was what was called "Independent Living Services," helping everyone from those with mental handicaps to blind and deaf people. They ran their recreation for the handicapped program out of facilities in Edgerton Park, the actual park. Between 2005 and 2008, the organization lost several members to murder.

As this was written, the most recent was Shawndale Walters, killed during the summer of 2008 as he was taking care of his disabled brother. This was something he did every day and every night, when he was shot on St. Paul Street, just outside his brother's house.

When Pat Patterson was an investigator for the Chemung County Sheriff's Office in 1971, and he found himself in the cellar of Your Saladmaster Kitchen in Elmira Heights, he had no idea that he was merely at the dawn of what would become a long and distinguished career in law enforcement.

He worked for eleven years with the sheriff's office, and for four more years as an investigator in the Chemung County District Attorney's Office. Going to school the whole time, he earned an M.S. degree in education at Elmira College. In 1975, while a county cop, he attended the FBI's National Academy for a law enforcement–training

program. He was the elected sheriff of Chemung County for two years—and then the FBI recruited him.

He became an FBI special agent in 1983 and worked for the Buffalo, Pittsburgh, and Baltimore divisions. He was in and out of headquarters in Washington, DC, a few times. For three years after the Berlin Wall came down, he was in international operations, training in Russia, Ukraine, and Belarus. His specialties were drugs and organized crime.

After a couple of hairy gigs in South America, Patterson returned stateside. He went to Los Angeles as an assistant special agent in charge of the violent crime program. He wasn't there for long when he was again called out of the country to investigate the *USS Cole* bombing in Yemen.

"I was there for several months and I got out alive," Patterson recalled. "I used up all my nine lives on that one."

While he worked in Southern California, the most disturbing crime he investigated involved the murder of coeds in a small California town. The young women attended Cuesta College in San Luis Obispo. One was already missing when Patterson first arrived in Southern California. She was never found. Then, soon after he arrived, two more coeds disappeared in quick succession, about a month apart. The key clue was a Magic Eight Ball key ring that could be turned upside down to answer a question about one's future. The victim had it in her purse when last seen, and it ended up with other souvenirs in the killer's home, along with a starter pistol. The guy's name was Rex Krebs, and it was his parole officer who saw the Magic Eight Ball and made the connection.

Patterson recalled Krebs's creepiness: "This guy would go out and dig a grave, six feet deep, out in the woods or someplace—it was a rural area. He would put hard wire down in there so animals couldn't dig it up. After he had all of these preparations made, he would go out and start stalking someone. One victim, Aundria Crawford, was a young coed who he stalked for a long time. One day, when she was home alone in her apartment, he knocked on the door. When she answered, he grabbed her and dragged her into his car. He kept her for three or four days, sexually assaulting her. Then he put her in the grave," Patterson recalled. "Like the Spahalskis, this Krebs guy was an absolute predator."

In 2001, Patterson was transferred back from Los Angeles to Virginia headquarters. "That was fun," he said. "I was there about seventeen months." During that time, he used slides of the Ronald Ripley crime scene in Elmira Heights as part of his lecture.

He was transferred from Virginia to San Antonio, Texas, where he was promoted to special agent in charge of that division, and that was the position he held when he retired.

In 2009, Elmira victim Ronald Ripley's sons David and Ronjay were rapidly approaching retirement after more than twenty years with the New York State Corrections Department.

Of course, neither David nor Ronjay had ever been allowed to work in the same facility that held one of the Spahalski twins. The Ripleys reported the circumstances regarding the twins when they first began to work for the Department of Corrections (DOC). The Ripleys would have been transferred rather than have a conflict of interest like that.

David told this author that he wants the world to think more about crime victims. By that, he means not just those who are murdered, but the families of those poor unfortunate souls who have to live with the reality of their loved ones' murders for the rest of their lives.

As for the murderers of the world, he thought they were coddled. Based on his decades inside prisons, he said, "These guys get treated pretty well. They are taken care of. You'd have to be in there to know. They have more rights behind the walls than we do on the outside."

Ronald Ripley's daughter, Priscilla, has moved to another part of the country, but the brothers still gather around the piano and sing whenever they get together, just as they did when they were little and their father was teaching them how to harmonize.

Bruce Crew was a graduate of Colgate University and Albany Law. He served as the Chemung County DA from 1973 to 1983, and during that time, he put both Spahalski twins behind bars.

Since 1982, he'd been a judge.

During the late autumn of 2008, the man who had prosecuted Robert Bruce Spahalski successfully, First ADA Kenneth C. Hyland, retired at the age of fifty-seven after serving for thirty years in the Monroe County DA's Office. For much of those three decades, he'd been second in command.

Though the Spahalski prosecution was one of his most gratifying, it wasn't his most disturbing. That dubious honor went to a Rochester man who shot his wife and his three-year-old son before turning the gun on himself.

"I couldn't believe a man could do something like that, kill a child, just to get back at his wife," Hyland said.

In addition to Spahalski, Hyland also successfully prosecuted Robert Hartle, who killed his girlfriend and an elderly couple in 2006 and 2007; Jerold and Keya Ponder, who killed Jerold's pregnant girlfriend in 2002; and Jose J. Santiago, who killed two children and attempted to kill their mothers and another relative in 1999.

Though retired from the DA's office, he wasn't retiring from the law, not even from courtroom action—but he *was* switching sides. He joined the Pittsford, New York, law firm of Sercu & Sercu, which practiced criminal defense law.

Cedric Alexander—Dr. Cedric Alexander—who was the acting Rochester police chief at the time of Robert

Spahalski's arrest, moved on to become the deputy director of the New York State Division of Criminal Justice Services in Albany. He was the recipient of the 2008 Black Heritage Pioneer award.

He left the police force soon after Robert Spahalski's conviction and became the federal security director for Dallas/Fort Worth International Airport.

An interview with Stephen when he was still in Attica showed a man struggling with reality. He said that there was stuff in prison that still reminded him of Ronald Ripley, the man he killed in Elmira more than three decades before. For example, all the EXIT signs in his prison were maroon. That was because Ripley was wearing a maroon vest on the night he died. It was all tied together on the cosmic plane.

Of course, crime scene photos revealed that Ripley wasn't wearing a vest at all at the time of his death, but rather a blue-and-black sweater, but that was neither here nor there. The cosmic plane, obviously, was color-blind.

Stephen—who had taken to wearing homemade eye makeup, fingernail polish, and feminine attire in prison—was asked if an unwanted sexual advance had *really* been his motive for murdering Ronald Ripley.

Stephen became coy: "I don't talk on it. If I kill someone, I kill them for a reason. That's all I know."

He claimed to have been in communication with Ripley, having found a link to the spirit world—an open line to the dead—on a prison computer.

There was a rueful Stephen: "If it hadn't been for the murder, I would have been all set," Stephen said.

Referring to Ronald Ripley, he offered this more frightening addendum: "He's deceased, but I did business afterward with him through a computer. His papers are in order with me. He don't owe me nothing.

"He's still going to try to get me, Ronald Ripley, but I

already did business with him. I'm real pissed at that man sometimes. He never saw me hit him from behind. He died. I made sure he died.

"But he never saw me kill him."

According to Robert Bruce Spahalski, his mother, Anita, who would be in her eighties by now, was still alive and living somewhere in the Elmira area.

He recalled the profound effect his mother had on him, a positive effect that continued to serve him even as he sat in his prison cell. "She was a socially shy woman with a strong spiritual belief, and she taught me much of God's consciousness while drinking our traditional cup of coffee together in the morning. Because of her, I'm very spiritual and have God in my prison cell for company every day. My mother could not understand my criminal behavior, and she only coped with it because it's a mother's duty."

His father, Bernard, was long gone. After leaving New York State, he lived in Tampa, Florida, for years. According to Robert's youngest brother, Ben, their dad died in Tennessee, riddled with cancer, paying the big price for smoking two packs of Camels every day since Robert could remember.

Robert has stuck by his statement that he was never angry at his father. But that didn't mean there wasn't hurt. It wasn't anger. . . . It was more like disappointment.

"I was always disappointed with him because he never found the time to give us social guidance. He was always too involved running his dairy business. But I still love him and miss him."

As for his own health, Robert was in his fourteenth year of being HIV positive, a condition that was closely monitored and well-maintained by the doctors in the Great Meadow prison.

The HIV wasn't a problem in prison, but stress was.

"It has taken its toll on me," Robert said. "I've lost weight. I have headaches, aches and pains."

The stress started when he thought about the reason he was incarcerated, the flaw in his brain that made him lose control of himself and kill people.

"Clarity of mind helps," he said, and described being interviewed for this book, taking "a trip down memory lane," as being very helpful in his never-ending pursuit of relaxation.

Sometimes he paced in his cell like a wildcat in a cage. But he got to watch cable TV, listen to the rock stations on the radio—and when he paced, he paced with style.

"I do a moving yoga," Robert said. Seeing himself as a spiritual man, he combined martial arts with "diaphragmatic breathing."

He was spiritual, but not religious. He believed in God, who only sometimes grabbed him by the ear and pointed him in the right direction.

Now, in prison, his demons had been released. "I feel peace and forgiveness inside myself. We'll leave it at that," he said.

If they made a movie out of *Killer Twins*, who would he want to play him? "Charles Bronson," Robert joked. "Too bad he's dead. Anybody who can play the character of a paranoid psychotic and hard-core crack addict gets my vote."

Now that he'd had plenty of time to ponder the matter, did he now think he was a serial killer?

"Maybe I was," he answered. "I think I was the victim of circumstances, and people close to me got killed in my insanity."

Maybe, in his old age, Robert *was* embracing the "serial/psycho killer" tag. It brought him attention. There *was* something his victims had in common, something he could call his signature.

"They all died naked," he said, perhaps finding romance in the notion. And, of course, Robert was wired to the gills and in need of more drugs for each murder, too, but that wasn't nearly as romantic.

What was the greatest irony of his criminal career?

The bizarre fact that he, a lifelong druggie, had never been arrested for a drug crime. The list of crimes he had been arrested for was long—so long it went all the way up his arm—but not one of those counts had anything to do with drugs.

"I have no criminal history for drug usage. I knew how to manipulate police and drug dealers to my advantage," he boasted.

It saddened Robert that he and his twin had been separate for most of their lives. His strongest and fondest memories of Stephen all involved being a kid. Steve was a private guy who even kept things from Robert at times. He loved Sue Cunningham, gymnastics, and good weed. By the time Stephen got in serious trouble, he and Robert had already drifted apart, cultivating their own friendships and hanging with different crowds. So, pretty early on, Robert developed his sense of individuality. And, of course, after age eighteen, he only saw his twin when they were in the same prison.

Some positive things had happened to Robert in prison since his murder conviction. He once met David Berkowitz, the Son of Sam. That was cool. That made two serial killers he'd seen: Berkowitz and Shawcross. Members of the serial killer *elite*.

Plus, Robert had been living without a full set of teeth since the day he was jumped coming out of a dope house in Rochester and had his face kicked in by three gang members. Even though those thugs kicked eight teeth out of his head, they still never found his stash of drugs. He'd been wearing two pairs of pants, and the crack was hidden in a secret pocket behind the knee of the inside pants. He was out eight teeth, but he still had his ten bags of crack. One had to look at the positives. Police and robbers never looked behind the knee. Robert went to the dentist the next day, but it wasn't until April 2009 in prison that he had his final fitting for a new pair of choppers. So things were looking up.

"Only ninety-six more years to go," Robert Bruce Spahalsi quipped.

Hollow humor from a doomed man—a man who had no dreams, only nightmares of rotting away in his cell.

As scheduled, as the law demanded, Stephen was released from Attica on July 22, 2009. He had maxed out his sentence and there was no holding him anymore. No one came to pick him up. According to an Elmira reporter, Stephen was given forty dollars and dropped off at a bus station.

Soon thereafter a dispatch from the New York State Intelligence Center warned state police to be on the lookout for Stephen, who was presumed to be dangerous and possibly armed. The reason for the dispatch was Stephen's behavior on his way out of Attica.

According to the dispach, Stephen said he was going to kill his mother when he got out. Slaughter her. Bludgeon her with a hammer. Then, the dispatch claimed, he was going to go after two retired members of law enforcement. He called them a couple of "Chemung County lieutenants."

These men, though unnamed in the dispatch, were presumed to be Pat Patterson and Eddie Wilkins, the guys who put him away. Wilkins was already deceased and Patterson was far away.

Contacted regarding Stephen's parting words at Attica, Patterson—speaking from his home in the suburbs of San Antonio—said he was hopeful that Stephen would come and try to kill him.

"He might come to Texas," Patterson said. "But he's never going to leave."

A week or so later, an old friend saw Stephen walking the streets of Elmira. Stephen said he was aware of "the rumors" about him being a dangerous man. But that was all it was: a rumor. He had no intention of hurting anyone ever again, he said.